10. Janv.

5/-

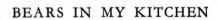

BEARS IN MY KITCHEN

Margaret Merrill

BEARS IN

MY KITCHEN

HUTCHINSON OF LONDON

HUTCHINSON & CO. (*Publishers*) LTD
178–202 Great Portland Street, London, W.1

London Melbourne Sydney
Auckland Bombay Toronto
Johannesburg New York

First published 1957

*Set in eleven point Garamond, one point
leaded, and printed in Great Britain
by The Anchor Press, Ltd.,
Tiptree, Essex*

To the

United States National Park Service Rangers

and Their Courageous Wives

I wish to acknowledge the generous

and invaluable help given me by

W. Jensen Bowers

in the preparation of this book

One

IN the little white courthouse at Mariposa, California, we were married, Bill and I, after he had ridden horseback twenty-eight miles over a rugged mountain pass to meet me in Yosemite Valley. The preacher Bill had engaged, trying to make it more of an occasion for us, had prepared for the wedding by solemnly exchanging his frayed and weather-beaten jeans for an equally sagging pair of shiny blue-serge trousers. It was not his costume, however, but his words following the ceremony that gave me a thrilling sense of fulfilment, which is with me to this day.

'Ranger and Mrs. Merrill,' he said quietly, 'it's happy I am to be first to congratulate you as man and wife!'

It was hot that October day in 1930, but the heat was in no way responsible for my lack of breath. I was so busy thinking of myself as 'Mrs.' that breathing seemed a pure waste of time. Not every girl has the golden opportunity to capture a handsome young ranger like Bill, and I don't mean merely one of the usual trim guardians you see protecting our national parks. Bill is one ranger, the only one I have ever known, to whom things just naturally happen. Things that could never happen to any other person, from stark, hair-raising drama to wild, hilarious comedy. With Bill around I am sure the tamer bears in the vicinity must have scrambled wildly over the highest mountain-tops in search of a bit of peace and solitude in the Back Country. I didn't know it then, but from our wedding day on I would have just cause to savour every naturally drawn breath that Providence might grant me.

Our first seven years were spent at Yosemite National Park in central California; from 1937 to 1938 we were in the Boulder Dam area in Nevada; California's General Grant National Park saw us until 1942; then we were back at Yosemite from 1942 to 1949, when we went up to Olympic National Park in northern Washington. In all these wonderful places, we lived well, found a lasting happiness, worked hard, laughed at others and at ourselves, and on some occasions came perilously near to paying for it all with our lives. It was well worth it, but I'm glad now that at the outset I had no idea what lay ahead.

Surely no other couple ever started their wedded life quite the way Bill and I did. It could happen to no one but a ranger years-wise in the mysteries of the deep forest and a none-too-courageous young bride too many miles from her city home and the conviviality of the family circle. Within the hour after the ceremony we were on our way to Tuolumne Meadows in Yosemite National Park, California, 117 miles away, where Bill had been stationed throughout the summer season.

'You'll love it up there,' he said proudly. 'It's heaven.'

'Just what is it like?' I asked breathlessly.

'Oh,' he said, spreading his arms expansively, 'animals, trees, birds—everything.'

I think I experienced my first twinge of misgiving when Bill wheeled the car off the main highway we had been following and started up Big Oak Flat control road. It was rough, narrow, and bumpy, with occasional rocks as large as footballs scattered along the way, where they had lodged after tumbling down the steep side of a mountain. I also got my first lesson in mountain driving: Bill never failed to stop and remove any obstruction in the road that was large enough to be a hazard.

Rounding a sharp curve, we came upon a cabin so concealed behind overhanging pines that I wouldn't have seen it at all if Bill hadn't stopped. A young ranger, Carl Danner, and his wife, Lisa, were standing in the front yard as if expecting us. I am sure they heard us steaming up the grade for miles. We received a hearty handshake from the man, good wishes from his wife, and a jar of home-canned pickles from them both—our first wedding present.

The road got progressively worse as we climbed. Surely I had never taken any approach to the park that could remotely compare to this. Today this same road is a smooth, high-speed ribbon of asphalt that winds gracefully across the mountain, but when I first saw it, it had no paving except gravel, there were no banked turns, and it was barely wide enough for one car to travel alone. However, Bill was happy as a lark, not a care in the world. I couldn't help marvelling at his lack of concern. Of course this was nothing new to him; he had been a ranger in the mountains for years. Still . . .

'Here's a good place,' he said, suddenly squeezing off to one side of the road.

I peered over the edge. 'Good for what?'

'You take the wheel, Marge,' he said, grinning. 'Want you to get the hang of it. Never know when you'll have to do it alone.'

I would have died right then, without a struggle, if I had known how soon his prophecy was to come true.

I got under the wheel, looked at the mountain reaching far up on one side, and down into the depthless valley on the other. I was simply petrified at the thought of driving up here, but I was determined that my ranger would never know my inward quaking. Bill got in on the other side and closed the car door.

'Keep it in second gear,' he directed. 'Always remember, honey, when you climb a grade in second gear, go down the other side the same way.' With that sage advice he lit his pipe and settled comfortably back in his seat to enjoy the scenery.

We started.

I had done a good deal of driving in my time, but this was an experience for which no human being could be prepared. Where the road had been rough, it now became decidedly rougher, and as the grade got steeper by the minute and harder to climb, the sharp curves gradually gave way to terrifying switchbacks and hairpin turns that zigzagged crazily across the face of the mountain. There was no stretch of straight road to give you a chance to catch your breath. You simply cranked the wheel to the right as far as it would go, then reversed it to the left. Then . . .

I felt myself becoming dizzy, and it wasn't from the altitude. Then a horrible thought suddenly penetrated my reeling senses, though at the time I was so occupied with trying not to take off into space that I didn't immediately recognize its importance. When the full impact registered, I almost stopped the car. The roadbed had been blasted out of solid rock and wasn't an inch wider than was necessary. It was so narrow, in fact, that even by hugging the inside of the turns, you had but a scant few inches of surface left beyond the wheels on the outside.

'Where do we go?' I panted. 'W-where do we go if we meet another car?'

Bill leaned forward and carefully dumped his pipe in the ash tray. Then he said: 'When you see a car coming, stop. Fellow up there will see you first—he's coming downgrade.'

I was busy spinning the wheel. 'Then what happens?'

'Someone has to back up,' he said, matter-of-factly. 'That's the reason they made the turnoffs, where the road is wide enough to pass another car.'

I swallowed hard. 'Who backs up?'

'Up-going car always has the right of way.' Bill relit his pipe and settled back in the seat.

I probably turned green. Nobody could back a car up such a grade as this, I was sure. Lucky if one could even stop while coming down. I tried to keep one eye on the hairpin turns and the other on the lookout for the first sign of a speeding car approaching from above. Luck was with us; we had the road to ourselves.

When at last we reached the top and came to a stop, I was so dizzy from the whirligig we had been performing that I felt faint. The scenery was still revolving in a tight circle before my eyes when Bill put his hand on my shoulder and silently nodded his head. His gesture was wonderful, as if he had said 'You'll do,' and I was proud.

Tuolumne Meadows lay before us deep in the purple shadows of twilight. We didn't utter a sound, just stood gazing, fascinated. It was so overwhelmingly beautiful. I can close my eyes now and see the wind-swept trees gently swaying and nodding their welcome, the immense granite domes pushing up so high from the earth, holding the sky in place. Somewhere in the distance came the rippling of water as it flowed rhythmically down an unseen stream towards the misty valley far below. A moon that was slowly climbing to the mountain-top suddenly appeared, bathing everything in silver and blue. I couldn't help feeling that we were intruding. This was something sacred, not intended for mere humans to witness—God was performing His wonders.

But when my gaze finally returned to Bill, I immediately knew I was wrong. For years, since he was eighteen, he had lived in the deep forests, working among the towering mountains of our great national parks, yet he was as fascinated, as infinitely humble, as I. Bill was no intruder; he belonged here and, someday, I prayed, I too would become a part of it.

Our little cabin came into view as we strode across the meadow. It was built of peeled logs with rough shakes for a roof, and a stubby chimney at the far end completed the picture. It wasn't in any sense grand and it certainly wasn't imposing, but it was so much in harmony with its surroundings that it too seemed to belong. At the door Bill picked me up and carried me across the threshold.

'Welcome home,' he said proudly.

When he lighted the Coleman lantern I found we were standing in the kitchen. It was a square room with windows looking out from two walls. One corner was occupied by a large cabinet for dishes and another by a freshly varnished table and four chairs. Hunched low, as if straining to hold in place the heavy chimney balanced above it, was a rather strange-looking cookstove.

The next room was larger than the kitchen, but one could see at a glance that it was the only other room in the house. Against one wall stood a ranger's single cot with a mattress; two chairs were drawn up at either side of a potbellied heating stove, and that was it. There was no door leading into a colourful little bedroom, as I had dreamed there would be, and as for the bathroom—there simply wasn't any.

'Might seem a little primitive at first,' Bill said brightly. 'But you'll love it once you get used to it.' He was kindling a wood fire in the heating stove, and I was thankful that just then he couldn't see my face.

His eyes simply glowed with the love of his wild world as we stood warming our hands over the stove that was already turning a bright red. There were so many advantages to living in the mountains, he pointed out. This was our own little world, nobody to intrude except an occasional park visitor passing through on his way down into Yosemite Valley. No neighbours yelling to me over the back fence every time I stepped outside. In fact, the nearest one was thirty-eight miles down the road. Our neighbour up the road was a little farther—seventy-five miles. Of course we had no electric light, gas, or inside plumbing. But we did have a good lantern and plenty of free wood for the stove, and the stream nearby was brimful of pure, cold water from the glaciers farther up. As for the plumbing, that simply solved itself: hadn't I noticed the little plank house back in the trees, with the crescent cut in the door? Well, it was a little detached from the house, but adequate.

Something was scratching at the kitchen door, and when Bill opened it a great furry thing rushed inside and leaped straight at him. I was sure it was a wolf, though I wouldn't have been surprised if it proved to be a ring-tailed tiger, but it was only Bill's bear dog, George, greeting him after their separation of a day. When things quieted down a bit Bill properly introduced us, but George seemed to take a dim, if not a suspicious, view of me, and I'm afraid that just then the feeling was mutual.

When Bill went to remove our provisions from the car, I tried my hand at building a fire in the kitchen range. I couldn't merely turn on the gas or snap an electric switch; so I stowed the thing full with lengths of wood and held lighted matches against them until I burned my fingers, but nothing happened. I huffed and puffed, rapidly losing my temper. When finally a tiny spark appeared I desperately seized my wedding hat and fanned it wildly, but the ember slowly faded out and died. I had smoke in my eyes

14

and soot on my nose and was practically out of breath by the time Bill returned with a handful of dry twigs. He started the fire almost immediately and soon had a hot meal on the table, too. So simple when you know how.

Sleeping accommodations, I had noticed, seemed to be a bit lacking in comfort. Ever since we arrived I had wondered just how two grown people could possibly sleep on a single iron cot scarcely wide enough for one. But Bill took care of that, too. From somewhere outside he brought another cot, lashed the two together with a rope, and piled on four mattresses, cordwood style, while he directed me to the store of heavy blankets in the cupboard. I peeled off six or seven from the top of the stack, for the fire had almost burned itself out and the room was getting shiveringly cold. My sheer silk nightgown was fast losing its attraction for me.

I slipped into our improvised double bed while Bill went across the room to turn off the lantern. Slowly George rose from his place beside the stove and stalked across the room towards me. I raised my head to watch, but he completely ignored me as he marched serenely on and disappeared beneath the bed.

'For heaven's sake!' I exclaimed. 'Why did he do that?'

Bill sent a casual look my way. 'Always does,' he said. 'He sleeps under the bed.'

'But why?' I asked, not a little perplexed.

'He likes it there,' he said with a grin, as if that settled everything.

He had just reached over to turn off the light when it happened —a clattering crash just outside the kitchen door that sounded, in the stillness of the night, like a major explosion.

'What was that?' I shrieked.

Bill and George took off at the same instant. Bill had a broom in his hand and George was growling savagely in his throat.

'Stay where you are,' Bill warned me, struggling with the door.

'What is it?' I cried.

'Bears!' he shouted, as he and George pounded out into the night.

My first impulse probably was to cover my head and bawl, but

I managed to get out of bed and over to the door. It was a bear, all right, and he was feeding from our garbage can, still had his big snout buried in the overturned container. I was just in time to see Bill take aim with his broom and swat the huge thing a mighty blow across the tail. With a roar the bear lunged forward, wedging his shaggy head tightly inside the can.

'Get back and shut the door!' Bill yelled at me. But I was too numb to move.

George was yelping and taking his toll on one hind leg while Bill took aim with his broom and fired again. The can shot off the bear's head like a catapult, and he made off for the woods, but only for a short distance. Suddenly he turned and started back, growling hoarsely, his wicked teeth bared.

Bill looked at his broom and decided against it. 'Come on, George,' he called, and came trotting back towards the door.

'Look out!' I screamed. The bear had lunged ahead and almost had him in his huge paws. Bill sprang, darting a quick glance over his shoulder, and ran head on into a tree directly in front of him. Sure of his prey, the bear reared on his hind legs and lashed out with one powerful paw, but at the same instant let loose a terrific bellow of pain as George again seized a hind leg. It all happened in a split second, but it gave Bill time to stagger into the house and slam the door shut behind us.

'You should've stayed in bed,' he panted, rubbing his bruised chin and surveying my silk nightgown. 'Catch your death of cold dressed like that up here.'

His left eye was already turning a greenish purple from the impact of the tree, and his pyjamas were torn to shreds across the shoulders where the long claws had ripped down entirely too close.

'You should have taken your gun with you,' I said wisely, 'and used it, too! That bear could have killed you.'

Bill shook his head. 'This is a wild-game sanctuary, Marge. Don't kill anything here, except in an emergency.'

'Emergency!' I blinked my eyes for a better look at my ranger. 'He tried to kill you, didn't he? And what about George? He's probably being murdered this very instant!'

Bill walked over and opened the door. 'Listen.'

Far off across the mountainside we could hear them plunging wildly on through the underbrush. An occasional bellow from the bear told plainly that George was still interested in that choice hind leg.

'Having the time of his life,' Bill said, gently rubbing his swollen eye. 'Lots of fun!'

Long after we had gone to bed, George scratched at the door and Bill got up and let him in. George was still panting a little, and there was a certain gleam in his eye. But what held my attention was the positively regal manner in which he strode grandly across the room to his favourite spot beneath our bed. He had been about his business and it was good. I could have sworn I heard him chuckling in his dreams, a few minutes later, but it was probably only his lusty snoring that finally lulled me to a sound sleep on our wedding night.

B.I.M.K.—B

Two

IT was not many weeks later in the little cabin at Tuolumne Meadows Ranger Station that we realized the season was getting late. It was mid-November. In the mountainous country of California you have only two climatic seasons—open and closed. During the open, or summer, season the mountains enjoy the same fairyland climate that the lowlands bask in the year round, while the closed, or winter, season brings snow and ice that is almost unbelievable to the uninitiated.

Each day seemed to get a little colder, and at night we were rapidly developing a fervent passion for the company of our old potbellied stove. The tourist season for park visitors in the high country was practically at an end, but Bill, as district ranger, had been ordered to stay on until the Tioga Pass Road, at an elevation of 9,941 feet, became impassable. The seasonal rangers at Merced Lake and Benson Lake, as well as the four at Tuolumne Meadows, had left in September. We were waiting word to move down into

Yosemite Valley, where we were to spend the winter at park headquarters.

Bill's birthday was due in a few days and I was making plans to celebrate the occasion. I could hardly wait to extend invitations to my friends in the valley, and to Bill's friends—he knew everybody. The first few calls I made didn't distress me too much; there are always times when one is bound by other duties. But when I received the same polite refusal to every call I made I couldn't believe my ears.

'Snow,' Bill explained, when he came in that evening. 'People don't like being snowbound up here.'

'But there isn't any snow,' I argued.

He nodded. 'Any day now. They know how fast it comes this time of year. Remember, we're living at an elevation of eighty-six hundred feet.'

That didn't stop me; I was determined that Bill's birthday would not pass unobserved. I would think of something. My dinner was all planned, some of it already prepared. But two people simply could not do the honours.

Next morning I remembered the road crew; we weren't entirely alone up here yet. Bill had said that the crew men were due to leave for the winter, but I had heard the clanking of shovels only the day before. I found the crew, or rather, what was left of it—one man—busily stowing gear in a heavy plank chest by the side of the road.

I said: 'Hello. I'm giving a birthday party tonight for my husband. Would you like to come?'

The man straightened up, took off a wide-brimmed hat, and grinned. What he said probably was very proper. I never knew. He was a Mexican who looked like an Indian and who spoke Spanish with his hands like a Frenchman. I was embarrassed, as I always am on such occasions, but although no English came out, I understood him perfectly. The shrug of his shoulders, the language of his hands—it was elegant. He accepted gracefully, I was sure.

It snowed a little as I was making my way home. I mean, it snowed for a short time. Never had I seen anything like this. For a few minutes I lost sight of the meadows; even the cabin disappeared behind the falling white wall. I could imagine a person smothering in the swirling mass. It was a little frightening. But it stopped as suddenly as it had begun, and I hurried on.

Back at the cabin I could scarcely wait to get the cake into the oven. For weeks I had been dreaming of it, and when everything was in readiness I opened the door and popped in the first pan. I was a little concerned about baking in a wood-heated oven as this was my first attempt and, of course, there was no regulator to determine the proper heat. One would have to judge by instinct. When I couldn't wait a minute longer to see my handiwork, I took a quick peep. It was wonderful—the cake had risen so high it was practically airborne. A few minutes later, when I was sure it had finished baking, I again opened the door. The cake was as flat as a tired waffle.

I was completely stunned. What could possibly be wrong? I checked the recipe and I had followed it to the letter. It must be the heat. Piling in all the wood the firebox would hold, I tried with the second pan. The result was the same.

Bill was as pleased as Punch when he returned home, just after dark. The house was aglow with candles, dyed paper streamers hung from the ceiling rafters, and the table was a sea of shimmering white. The tablecloth was only a carefully folded bed sheet, but in the mellow candlelight it looked as beautiful as rare old Irish linen.

When a tapping sounded at the door, Bill answered it, and there was my Mexican friend of the road crew, grinning and bowing, hat in hand. Introductions were a little awkward as our guest was a stranger to us both, but he pointed to himself and said 'Enfracio', and that helped. Whether it was his family name or one given him by his Aunt Lucy we never knew. But he had come and he was heartily welcome.

The dinner was a grand success. Bill paid me extravagant compliments and assured me he meant every word; Enfracio nodded agreement and displayed his pearly teeth. When we had finished the main course, I brought in the candle-decked cake. Enfracio saw it first and jumped to his feet. I was hardly prepared for the rich baritone voice he added to mine as we sang the

'Happy Birthday' song. His Spanish words didn't blend too well with my English, and one of us was slightly off key, but no one could say the spirit was lacking.

'I'll do the carving,' Bill said eagerly and reached for the cake.

'But, Bill,' I said. 'This is——'

With an elaborate gesture he placed the cake in front of him, blew out all the candles with one breath, and raised his knife.

'Bill!' I spluttered. 'You can't——'

'I have the honour.' He bowed low. 'Who else but me would cut my birthday cake?' The knife bit into the top layer and stopped. He paused and looked strangely up at me.

'I—I tried to tell you,' I managed to say.

With the knife point he scraped back some of the beautiful pink icing and glanced quizzically at me again.

I tried to explain. 'It fell flat. I can't imagine what happened, but it——'

Bill suddenly laughed, reached over and kissed me. 'High altitude,' he said. 'You baked it too quick. Next time use more flour, less baking powder and sugar. Works that way.'

I was thankful for his wonderful sense of humour, for I'll admit the two upended baking tins with a thin layer of cake on top, and another sandwiched between, didn't look any too appetizing after the icing was removed. Enfracio was plainly disappointed. 'It was only to look at,' I explained. 'You can't have a birthday without a cake!'

Enfracio laughed heartily with us, but I'm sure his heart wasn't in it.

All evening, after Enfracio departed, Bill appeared ill at ease. His laughter died too quickly, and several times I noticed him staring worriedly into space. Just before we went to bed, I learned what was bothering him.

'Got to get you out of here,' he said out loud. 'No time to lose, either.'

I waited.

'Snow,' he went on. 'Any day now. Tons of it. I called headquarters today.'

Early next morning, on advice from headquarters, we started for the valley. It was a hurried trip for the purpose of getting the

21

horses out of the mountains while there was still time. Bill took George, the bear dog, and the pack and saddle animals and went cross country by the short cut; I travelled by road in the car, and that is one nightmare I would gladly put out of mind, for ever and a day.

I had been scared limp while driving part of the way up on our wedding day, with Bill at my side, and the thought of going down that steep grade all alone simply left me paralysed. I stopped the car at the beginning of the grade and tried not to peer down along the zigzagging narrow road that seemed to plunge straight down clear out to the horizon at the other end of the world. I tried to screw up my courage with every argument I could bring to mind, with no success. I even tried laughing at myself, but only brought up a weak gurgle. Finally I took myself in hand and, coiled on the edge of the seat with a strangling grip on the wheel, closed my eye to the drop-off and started down. It was horrible, and I died a thousand gasping deaths before finally getting down into the valley where Bill was waiting for me at headquarters.

Before daylight the following morning we were on our way back to Tuolumne Meadows in a government pick-up truck, with Bill at the wheel. He had insisted on going alone as he was to stay only until the closing of the road, but I had managed to out-talk him.

I can't truthfully say that I greatly enjoyed myself after arriving back at the cabin. It was already far into November, and Bill was becoming a little tense. He was too good a ranger to overlook the ominous signs that were so obvious to him. Except that it was rapidly becoming colder each day, I thought very little about the weather. What worried me most was bears.

During the summer, droves of them would come in from the forest and feed at tourist-camp garbage pits. When the tourists left for the season, the beasts moved on to where the road crew disposed of their refuse. Now that there was no one up here but Bill and me they descended on us in full force. It was most disconcerting to me to see ten or fifteen of the big brutes waiting in the back yard for a handout. It finally got so bad that Bill had to stand guard with an automatic shotgun while I put the wash on the line. Another thing, I never entirely overcame my self-consciousness about bathing. It wasn't sitting in the tin bathtub placed on the kitchen floor that bothered me; it was the realization that before I could possibly finish there would be several pairs of huge staring eyes ogling me from the window—it seldom failed. Bears are such curious animals.

For several days the skies had been leaden, threatening, the air so still that the snapping of a twig in the forest sounded like a pistol shot. Bill was constantly on the alert. Then during the night the weather suddenly turned warm, and about noon the following day it started to rain. A few hours later the rain turned to sleet, and the landscape soon became a solid sheet of ice. Before Bill could get home from the park boundary at Tioga Pass, it was snowing hard. He rushed in and told me to prepare to get away immediately. Then he got headquarters on the telephone.

'Tioga Pass is snowed in,' I heard him say. 'We're getting ready to leave at once.' He paused a moment, then: 'But nobody can possibly get through the pass by morning. The road's closed. . . . All right. Call me later.' He replaced the receiver.

I waited.

'Headquarters has a report that a car loaded with hunters from outside the park is headed this way.' He turned and looked steadily at me. 'I've got to make sure they aren't caught in the pass.'

'Can't they go back?'

'Not a chance if they're already up there. I'll have to get to them and bring them out with us. Last spring I found what was left of one. Been there all winter.'

I tried to occupy myself doing things that didn't need doing, but my mind simply wasn't on my work. What if Bill got stuck up there in the pass? At over nine thousand feet it gets bitterly cold. If something untoward happened, how long would he last? What if he broke a leg? Why did people have to go hunting this time of year when notice to stay out of the high mountains had been posted for days?

Bill came back from inspecting the car, stomping snow from his shoes.

'It isn't right!' I couldn't remain silent a second longer. 'Why should you risk your neck to save anyone foolish enough to go up there after being warned to stay out? Why should you?'

23

He didn't look up as he said, 'I'm a ranger, honey.' His fingers were deftly arranging the equipment of his rescue pack—an extra set of skid chains, a shovel, food, and a tow chain, along with blankets and a first-aid kit.

'That's of my part job,' he added. 'Most people that get marooned don't know what to do. Lucky if they'd last through the night.'

I wondered if I would ever become a ranger's wife, if I could ever accept his strange point of view. Here we were, standing idly by, with every passing minute lessening our chance of escaping. Already there was more than a foot of snow on level ground and more coming down by the tubful.

An hour later, and after another six inches of snow, I nearly jumped out of my skin when the telephone jangled our number. Bill was there in an instant. 'Ranger Merrill speaking.' His face was grim, impassive, while he listened. Then: 'Yes, sir. I'll start at once.'

'Where?' I was barely able to control my voice.

'Hunters reported back okay,' he said evenly. 'Now we're getting out of here quick!'

I have never seen Bill really excited. He just isn't made that way. In an emergency he may work so swiftly as to appear ruthless, but underneath he is calm and leaves little room for error. He wasn't excited now, but I could tell from his actions that every moment counted. All perishable foods were disposed of, staple groceries were quickly stacked on kitchen shelves, and with everything in shipshape order we were ready to make a dash for it.

It was snowing so hard by now that Bill could see but a few feet in front of the car as we started. It didn't matter too much, as the axles were dragging like a sled in the deep snow and he was unable to make much time. Our chances looked pretty slim to me, but Bill pointed out that as soon as we were across the meadows and started downgrade the snow would grow less and less as we approached the warmer level of the valley.

What he was worrying about right now was keeping the car on the road, which takes a lot of manœuvring when you can't see any indication of a road. It was laid out in a manner which would least mar the natural beauty of the meadows, curving around trees and boulders, skirting the gullies, keeping to high ground. The snow had now completely obliterated everything; what lay before us was a perfectly smooth white blanket.

We were almost out of the meadows when the car started slowly sliding to one side. Bill stepped on the gas in an effort to get back on the road, but the chains had little effect on the slick ice beneath the snow. With a sickening lurch we came to a sudden stop.

'Rocks,' Bill said. 'We're off the road, hung up on a boulder.' He jumped out, took a shovel from the back of the truck, and began burrowing under the rear end. 'It's a boulder, all right,' he said after a moment. 'Big as a cub bear.'

'What will we do?'

'Jack it up. Axle's balanced right on top of the rock.' He chipped away the ice and placed the jack in position. 'Left wheel is still on the ground,' he said. Then he straightened and looked carefully at me. 'Now when I raise it, you pull ahead—but not till I tell you. And sit still in the car; I've got the other wheel blocked but don't want it to slide downhill.'

I nodded and carefully moved to the driver's side, got my foot on the accelerator, and waited. The rear end of the truck began to rise and I sat tense, waiting for him to tell me when to move the car ahead. Inch by inch it came up, and then stopped. I knew he was underneath, scooping away the snow to see if he had raised the truck high enough to clear the boulder. Then, without warning, the rear end slid to one side and dropped with a sickening thud.

For a staggering second I was frozen in my seat, then I sprang out and rushed around to the rear. I could see Bill's feet sticking out, but his body was caught beneath the truck. He was so still I was sure he was dead.

'Bill,' I gasped. 'Oh, Bill!'

Then, after an eternity, 'Dropped on my back,' his muffled voice came from underneath. 'Get the jack and try to raise it again.'

His calmness had an immediate effect on me. I had never before used a car jack, but everything seemed to fall into place almost as if by magic.

'Easy,' he directed. 'Just a little at a time. Don't want the car to slip again.'

Carefully I worked the lever. The right wheel began rising from the hole where it had dropped; then gradually, while I didn't dare breathe, the long axle lifted from his back. I hesitated.

'Now see if you can pull me out,' he said. 'But don't touch the car.'

Grasping a foot in either hand I pulled with all my strength and, at last, when I was sure I never would make it, he slid out into the open. I could have collapsed with relief, but there was no time for hysterics. Bill was giving more instructions.

'Take those small stones and fill the hole under the right wheel.'

'But, Bill,' I wailed, 'you're hurt!' He was still lying, face down, perfectly quiet in the snow.

'See about that later,' he said. 'Get the jack out, too.'

I obeyed, automatically, then dropped down beside him.

'Oh, Bill——'

'Thanks for getting me out.' He grinned. 'Know something, Marge? For a little squirt you're strong as a truck horse.'

I knew he was talking to calm my shattered nerves—and it worked.

'Help me get into the truck,' he went on, reaching up his hand. 'We'll head back for the cabin. Snow's so deep now we'd never make it to the valley in the truck. You'll have to drive . . .'

I put my hands under his shoulders and tried to raise him. But pain was already twisting his face. 'I'm doing nothing of the sort until you tell me how badly you're hurt.'

'Don't know yet,' he said through his teeth. 'My legs are numb. Can't seem to use 'em. But we've got to get back to the cabin before it gets dark—or we might never find it.'

I got him into the truck—I don't know how—and settled myself under the steering wheel. But I was immediately forced to get out and unburden the windscreen, which was heaped high with swirling snow. The snow was coming down so hard and the howling wind was driving it so furiously that the wipers simply couldn't keep the glass free.

'Run down the window,' Bill advised. 'You'll have to watch from there.'

26

I did, and the frigid blast that raged into the cab all but took away our breath. For a moment the engine coughed, sputtered feebly, then gave forth with a full-throated roar as we fought our way back onto the roadway.

I headed back, trying to follow our tracks, which had practically disappeared, not daring to think of what could happen if we didn't find the cabin. From the set of Bill's jaw I knew his mind was as troubled as mine, but he made reference to nothing but the job at hand. With all landmarks erased except the drooping trees, with each looking exactly like the next, I was soon hopelessly confused and finally completely lost.

Bill lowered his window and was intently studying the landscape as he directed me where to drive. For once I wondered if his amazing sense of direction could have deserted him. But he never wavered. Beneath that mound of snow over there would be, he pointed out, the big boulder where he had killed a rattler last summer—the road passes on this side of it. That tree up ahead, the one with the single branch jutting out below the rest, that's where we had our picnic lunch a few weeks ago. Remember? The road curves to the left just after you pass it. . . .

We were wallowing through the deeper drifts like a miniature snow-plough. Bill told me to keep the engine in first gear in order to utilize its full power, but even so, I thought every drift would be our last. The snowfall lessened a little, but the howling gale was piling it in drifts higher than our heads. Finally we did stall, and after that we were forced to make several runs at the larger drifts in order to force our way through. Then the engine stopped entirely, and nothing I could do would make it start.

'Condenser burned out,' Bill surmised.

'What will we do?'

'Can't stay here,' he said grimly. 'We'd freeze stiff before morning.'

'The cabin. How much farther is it?'

'About half a mile.'

'We'll have to make it on foot.' I climbed out and opened the door on Bill's side of the cab. 'Can you walk at all?'

Wordlessly he slid out of the seat and immediately collapsed in a heap on the snow, his legs folding crazily beneath him. I

27

turned my head; I didn't dare look at him just then or I would have cried. He grumbled under his breath, then reached up and seized the door-handle, pulling until the cords stood out on his neck. He couldn't support himself.

'Bill!' I tried to control my voice. 'What will we do?'

'See that fir tree just ahead?' He pointed a steady finger. 'If you go in that direction, and keep going straight, you will find the cabin. But before you reach the first tree, pick out another one you can see farther ahead that is in a straight line with the first one. That way you won't be going in circles.'

'But what about you?' I cried. 'I'm not leaving you here like this.'

'Get a fire started in the cabin as soon as you can,' he went on, ignoring my protest. 'I'll need it by the time I get there.'

I shook my head. No. Not even a ranger could possibly drag himself half a mile through snow as deep as this. I knew that he would try it and that if anyone could make it he would, but there must be a better, a surer way. I couldn't help feeling a little panicky as I looked at Bill sitting there in the snow, his face contorted in pain. I couldn't possibly carry him. He is a big man, all bone and muscle. I weigh 113 pounds. Our plight was getting more serious by the minute. We had to get to shelter without delay. Already the light was rapidly beginning to fade, and in the mountains darkness comes down swiftly. After nightfall, with the blinding blizzard still raging, I knew we could very well miss the cabin by a few feet and never be aware of its nearness. As usual, though, Bill had a plan worked out, and we put it into action at once.

The first attempt—locking his arms around my shoulders—was not too successful, but this way I was able to help support him while we forged ahead for a short distance. The next effort was more tiring but covered a greater distance: I simply grasped a foot in each hand and dragged him across the snow like a sack of meal. Bill kept our straight course lined up with the trees while I tugged and pulled, resting when I had to halt for breath.

It grew dark with the utter blackness of a blizzard-swept mountain night. No longer were trees visible by which Bill could steer our course, and several times 1 bumped into them without knowing they were in my path. It was cold, terribly cold, and I was worried about Bill. Without being able to move, he couldn't perspire, as I could, and I was afraid he was becoming numb. When I was sure I could never pull another ounce or move ahead one more foot, I paused again to rest.

'You made it,' he said.

His voice came to me almost as a shock. For what had seemed hours no word had passed between us. There was no time to talk and no breath to waste. I had unwittingly been enveloped in a sort of mental fog that left me alone in the storm.

'What?' I panted. 'What did you say?'

'The stable,' he said. 'I smell it. It's close by.'

It was. I could almost reach out my hand and touch it. A few minutes later we were safely inside the cabin.

With a roaring fire turning the potbellied stove a cherry red and candlelight filling the room, our cabin was soon cosy and comfortable. Bill's back, where the truck had fallen on him, was horribly bruised and lacerated, but whether or not it was broken we couldn't tell. His legs remained numb and useless, and I could see from watching his face that he was suffering excruciating pain. But his immediate concern was getting in touch with headquarters in Yosemite Valley, and I helped him onto the table where he could reach the telephone.

'Hello,' he said, after cranking the handle. 'Ranger Merrill speaking.'

'Where in the world are you?' I could hear the voice even from where I stood.

'Back at Tuolumne Meadows Station,' Bill answered. 'Can't make it out now—burned up the condenser pulling through the snow.'

'What about food?'

He turned to me.

'A little,' I said. 'Not much.'

'We have enough for a few days,' he said into the transmitter. 'But the snow is getting deep—six-foot drifts by morning, and it's still coming down.'

'There'll be plenty more,' said the voice at the other end. 'Weather Bureau says we're in for the worst storm in years.'

29

'Any orders?' Bill asked.

'Yes. Stay right where you are. We'll start men up on snow-shoes in the morning.'

'I can't come out on snowshoes,' Bill said quickly. 'Hurt my back and my legs are paralysed.'

'You what?'

He repeated, and the line was silent for several moments. Then: 'All right, Bill. Sit tight. We'll call you in the morning.'

That left us just about where we had been before starting out. Since early afternoon we had slaved like Trojans, put the car out of commission, and injured Bill's back, and now I was so exhausted I could have dropped to sleep standing on my hands. We certainly hadn't accomplished anything of consequence, and what might happen in the morning I didn't even want to think about. One thing I was sure of, though: if I could reach that carload of hunters who had prolonged our getaway until too late, I certainly wouldn't go tongue-tied telling them what was curdling in my mind.

From the kitchen shelves I found enough canned food to satisfy our hunger, then I got Bill stretched out on the bed and began applying hot and cold packs to his back. He didn't utter a word, but I could tell from the tenseness of his muscles that he was in agony. How long this treatment continued I have no recollection; neither would I have known when he finally fell asleep but for his deeper breathing. I, too, must have dozed off shortly after that, for it was broad daylight when his movement on the bed aroused me.

'Look,' he said, pointing to his feet.

I sat up straight in my chair and looked. 'Thank heaven!' I exclaimed. He was actually moving the toes of both feet.

I asked, 'You're going to be all right?' I was so relieved I could scarcely speak.

'Of course.' He grinned at me. 'Like I always say, there's good stuff in old leather.'

Swinging his legs over the edge of the bed, he quickly got to his feet and just as suddenly sank back onto the bed, his face drawn with pain. His legs would support him, all right, but when he attempted to take a step, his back became 'unhinged', as he put it.

'You get right back in bed,' I said. 'You're in no condition——'

He interrupted. 'Got to call headquarters.'

'I can do that for you. You've got to stay in bed.'

'No,' he said flatly. 'Get me that broom over there, will you, Marge?'

I looked at him, incredulous. I was just beginning to know my ranger husband. He wasn't above asking for aid when needed, but though he sincerely appreciated any offer of help, something inside him simply refused any assistance unless it was desperately necessary. I hadn't yet discovered that a man in the Back Country, days away from civilization and any possible help, learns to rely entirely on himself. His very life depends on it. It's a lesson he learns well, and it's often a costly one. It becomes a sort of religion. Self-reliance is a quality not uncommon among rangers. I handed him the broom.

Using it as a prop, he hobbled painfully across the room and cranked the telephone. 'Ranger Merrill speaking. Yes . . . What? . . . Hello? Hello?' Slowly Bill replaced the receiver.

'What is it?'

'Line went dead,' he said. 'Just as he started to tell me what they were going to do.'

'Maybe they'll call later.'

He shook his head. 'The phone is gone, tree probably fell across the wires. We'll just have to wait and see what happens.'

We waited, all day and all night, the next day and the next after that. Four long anxious days passed, days and nights that gave birth to a mounting fear in me that could not be thrown off. What had headquarters meant to tell Bill when the phone went out? How could rescuing rangers ever hope to make the steep climb up the mountains choked with snow as deep as this? How much longer would our limited supply of food last? For the past two days now Bill had put us on rations. Could the rangers possibly make it before it was too late? For the first time I was beginning to realize the emotions of other marooned people as they helplessly wait for rangers to rescue them.

The weather had given us hope. For three days it was clear and cold, but this morning the sky suddenly darkened, and now it seemed to be snowing harder than ever. Drifts that had climbed above our windows now swept entirely across the roof, almost blotting us from sight. But the forced rest was a lifesaver for Bill; the numbness was gradually passing from his legs, and twice he managed to drag himself up and shovel the chimney free when snow choked off the draft.

It was the fifth day and almost dark when we heard them coming. I dashed outside, wildly waving and jumping up and down while Bill hobbled after me. I tried to call out to them, but my throat was strangely constricted. My eyes, too, were giving me a bit of trouble. They were barely visible in the gathering darkness, these two floundering rangers, and they resembled nothing so much as weary snowmen weaving drunkenly towards us on steaming white horses that were barely able to drag one exhausted foot after the other. Bill was as grateful as I, but his greeting gave voice to none of the tremendous admiration I felt for these two men. For five days Bill had steadfastly promised me they would come, and here they were—as simple as that. Just another job for the rangers and it had been done as he had expected it to be done.

The men were so completely exhausted that we had to help them from their saddles. Bill led the four horses and two pack mules to the stable while the men staggered into our warm cabin. I couldn't be sure who our rescuers were until the snow and ice had melted from their faces. They proved to be old friends, district rangers Carl Danner and Jerry Mernin. I heated some canned tomato juice for them while they got out of their clothes, which had frozen stiff from the condensation of steam from their labouring horses. In a few minutes they were tucked in our bed, fast asleep. Bill and I occupied an extra mattress on the floor beside the stove.

Early the next morning we got ready to start the trip out. We didn't dare wait any longer to rest the men or the horses because our food supply had come to an end. From the last can we had, I made as many sandwiches as possible, put them in paper bags, and tied them to the saddles. The men were dressed as warmly as possible, and I was so loaded down—three pairs of Bill's pants, sweaters, and coats, plus a scarf and mittens—that I could scarcely walk. It wasn't yet daylight when we closed the cabin and got under way.

From the very beginning the going was much harder than I had imagined. We rode single file, with each following horse stepping in the tracks left by the one in front. Carl Danner rode the lead horse, with Jerry Mernin second. Bill was behind him, leading the pack mules behind his horse, and I brought up the rear. Bill had set our goal for the day at the Tenaya Lake ranger cabin, nine miles away, but we hadn't got out of Tuolumne Meadows before I was sure we would never make it at all. Although it had stopped snowing, the fall had been so heavy that the horses' bellies were dragging. No attempt was made to follow the road, which was impassable, and when Carl could find no way around drifts and had to go through, his horse simply plunged ahead, backed up, and continued plunging until it finally wallowed a path to the other side.

Every few minutes the lead horse had to be changed and allowed to rest while another took its place. An hour later, when daylight finally came, we were still within sight of the chimney of our cabin. Time wore on and the horses wore out. At last they became so exhausted that we were forced to whip them into continuing, and at ever shortening intervals had to halt to allow them time to rest and cool off. I didn't realize what a toll our rationing had taken on us until I saw Bill unwrapping his sandwich. Then I became so ravenously hungry that my hands trembled as I reached for my sack. When he calmly returned his to the paper bag untouched, I was sure he had lost his reason, but mine soon received the same treatment. The sandwich was frozen solid.

It was late afternoon when Jerry's mount, which was lead horse at the time, halted and simply refused to take another step, even the whip had no effect on him. It was a desperate situation, and even I knew it. Bill got off his horse and, followed by Carl, made his way up to where Jerry was waiting.

'We'll never make it this way,' Jerry said. 'The horses are done for.'

Carl nodded agreement. 'We'll have to shoot them—they'd soon starve up here. Then we'll try to make it out on foot.'

'No,' Bill said grimly. 'I couldn't walk fifty yards with my

B.I.M.K.—C

legs the way they are. We'll give the horses a little rest and have another try at it. If we can reach Tenaya Lake cabin, we might find a pair of snowshoes there, maybe some food, too, and one of us can go on out for help.'

That ended the parley, of which I knew nothing until much later, and the men soon remounted. It was now almost dark and with the dusk came more snow, which the wind drove into our faces like infinitesimal particles of ice. The horses were desperately tired, and it required alternate coaxing and whipping to force them on. But at last, after fighting nine hours to gain nine miles, we finally reached Tenaya Lake ranger cabin.

There were no showshoes inside the cabin—I didn't ask, it wasn't necessary; it was plainly written on the disappointed but still determined faces of the men as they hurriedly built a fire and fed the horses and pack animals. The only food in the place was in a metal box, safe from the bears—two cans of frozen apricots. Jerry thawed them out along with the sandwiches I had made, while we stood dripping in front of the flames. Our clothing was so stiff with ice that we felt as if we were encased in suits of armour; our faces were almost hidden in frost and particles of ice —even our eyelashes were beaded and partly frozen together. We ate the sandwiches, and the cans of warmed juice passed from mouth to mouth as we drained them to the last drop. It was delicious.

'Got to go on,' Bill said shortly. 'Can't move at all if the snow gets much deeper.'

They turned to look at me. Nothing was said, but the question in their eyes was unmistakable. I pulled on my heavy mittens and we all trooped outside.

For a short way the horses seemed to have gained strength from their brief respite in the stable, but they soon settled back into the weary, straining struggle that once more had them winded and trembling with exhaustion. Each time we stopped, the animals wanted to rest longer, and the distance between stops was growing so short that it seemed we were scarcely making any headway at all. My feet and hands again grew numb, and my face was soon stiff with cold. The blizzard was getting worse by the minute, piling snow to unbelievable heights; everywhere was a bleak Siberian landscape that looked utterly impenetrable. It was like being entirely alone in another world, deserted and forgotten. What we didn't know, of course, was that most of the country had been alerted to our plight by newspaper and radio broadcasts.

When Carl's horse, blinded by snow, walked off an embankment and landed fifteen feet below, it seemed fantastically unreal; it was almost as if we were seeing it on a screen in slow motion. Cushioned by the deep snow, neither was harmed in the least, and Carl didn't even look surprised as he grinned up at us. But a second later he was furiously pawing in the snow and prodding his horse to one side. I was so dazed with cold that it didn't immediately occur to me what was about to happen. Then I suddenly realized that my horse, which had been following in the tracks left by Carl's mount, was going to continue right on over the cliff.

'What will I do?' I cried.

Bill said, 'Let him go!'

I tried to pull back on the reins, but my arms were so deadened that I had no effect whatever on the horse, and over we went. I was still in the saddle when we landed, and Carl had to pull me out before getting the animal to its feet. It was a long circuitous route we had to follow before getting back to the others. Bill and Jerry were waiting beside their horses when we arrived.

'Have to walk now,' Bill said.

Carl nodded. 'They're too tired to carry us any farther.'

I started to dismount, but the men decided it was safer for me to stay in the saddle. I thought they were being very considerate of me and let it go at that. There was no way of my knowing that we had reached the most dangerous passage in our long trip out. Before us lay Mount Watkins, a sullen mass of solid granite polished smooth by elements of the centuries. At its base was Yosemite Valley, safety, the end of the trail. Everything was obscured with swirling snow, but somewhere close at hand was the trail, if only we could find it. It had been blasted out of solid rock on the side of the mountain and was just wide enough for a single pack animal. Actually it was more of a toe-path than a trail, but it descended in a series of steep switchbacks for four miles, zigzagging almost straight down into the valley nearly a mile below.

When we finally got on the trail, our progress was hardly a snail's pace. Jerry was leading the caravan and advancing a step at a time, testing the footing as he went. Actually I was nervous for the first time; the bird's-eye view I commanded from the top of my horse made me long desperately to plant my feet on the solid trail, narrow and icy as it was. For a time Jerry would be out of sight, hidden somewhere ahead in the blinding storm, then he would appear again, a dim figure moving cautiously, step by step.

My heart almost stopped when the heavy-laden mule in front of me suddenly skidded sideways and dropped to one knee in an effort to save himself from the sheer drop. Slowly he regained his feet and went on, but I could see that the pack animals were getting restless, hugging the inside of the trail until the bundles on their backs scraped the rocky ledge. My horse was surprisingly calm, or too tired or too blinded to be aware of the danger; with each stop we made his head was sinking lower until his flaring nostrils were almost buried in the snow.

Everything seemed to come to an end when we reached North Dome. The pass was so completely filled in with snow that not a trace of the trail could be seen. With night coming on fast we were still far up on the mountain. Something had to be done quickly, and Jerry did it. Dropping to his knees, he began frantically scooping snow with his hands and kicking it out of the trail with his feet, hurling it over the side. Burrowing in up to his elbows, he would search until his fingers found the trail, then move ahead a few feet and scoop again. One false step beyond where the trail reversed on the switchbacks and he would go plunging down the icy mountain.

It was slow, torturous work, and Jerry had to do it alone. No one could relieve him as it was impossible for the men to pass their horses on the narrow ledge to reach him. Bill's face was a mask of agony that he could no longer conceal. I noticed he was constantly shifting his weight from one foot to the other while we waited. He never complained, didn't even mention it, but I knew he was suffering terribly with his injured back.

Once we got inside the timber line, the air became warmer as we descended. By the time night was upon us the snow was a wet slush that caused our exhausted horses to slip dangerously close to the edge on the sharp turns. Then, without warning, the pack mule ahead of Bill suddenly squealed hoarsely, reared on his hind legs, spun around, and came down on the trail facing me. Before Bill realized what was happening, he was knocked down as the mule bolted over him and came lunging towards me.

'Are you hurt?' I cried.

'No,' he yelled. 'Stop that mule!'

There was no way the animal could get past me, and he was forced to stop when he reached my horse. Bill got painfully to his feet and managed to get a grip on the trailing halter rope and pulled hard. When the mule saw that he was going to be forced sideways off the trail, he again reared and came down headed once more towards the valley.

The last pale rays of daylight disappeared beyond the horizon, and the blackness of the night was almost suffocating. It was the kind of darkness you can touch with your hand; even the mule directly in front of me was lost to sight. The snow was turning to rain as we got nearer to the valley, and soon the trail was a cascade of frothing water streaming down the mountainside.

'Hold it!' It was Jerry's voice from up ahead.

Carl asked, 'What's wrong?'

'The trail's washed out. I almost fell into it.'

'How bad is it?' Bill called.

'I can't see anything, but I tossed a rock across and it sounds like five or six feet of trail is gone.'

Bill asked, 'Can we span it with logs?'

'I think so.'

'Ought to be lots of them 'round here,' Carl said. 'We're just about where that big blowdown was a couple of years ago. I'll take a look.'

We could hear him sliding over the edge of the trail, and it didn't take much imagination to picture him exploring in the dark with one hand while his other clutched a convenient sapling or some firmly embedded rock for support. Presently we heard the clunk of wood striking the edge of the trail.

37

'Try this one for length.'

There was a scraping of wood on stone and then the sound of a small timber falling into place. Several more followed, and finally the washout was bridged. Jerry went first, slowly, leading his horse behind him, Carl followed, and Bill was next in line. But the pack mules stood their ground and refused to be budged. With each passing horse the caravan would move ahead a few feet and I knew the lead mule must be at the bridge. Bill pleaded, coaxed, and finally swore voluminously, but it was to no avail. Then he simply looped the halter rope around his saddle horn and practically dragged the mules across.

'Mules!' I heard him grumble. 'Sometimes they've got more sense than we have.'

When my horse crossed the logs I breathed a little easier, but not for long. While mules are always aware of their danger, our horses were now so completely exhausted that their labour was entirely automatic. Neither looking where the trail led nor caring, they were in danger of stepping off into space at the end of every switchback. But the path was getting wider now, and the men stationed themselves at every turn and flailed the air with their hats to turn the weary animals around the bends.

'Look!' Jerry shouted. 'I see lights down there!'

Sure enough there were lights down there. Through the heavy rain we gradually came to see what looked like scores of fireflies flitting about below. It was an astounding sight to me. I kept telling myself it must be people waiting there to welcome us back, but at first thought it was simply too overwhelming to grasp, to realize that there could be other beings in the deserted world in which we had been trapped.

When our horses finally stumbled into the valley floor at Mirror Lake, I was so overcome with weariness that the sea of faces for a minute swam crazily before my eyes. People were shouting, laughing, calling to us. George, Bill's bear dog, leaped out of Chief Townsley's patrol car and all but bowled us over with a wild greeting as he barked and licked Bill's face; he even grinned up at me. Reporters from city newspapers were bombarding us with a barrage of questions, flash bulbs exploded in our faces, and news-reel cameras were grinding away from the top of their trucks. Then strong hands lifted me from my horse, and once more I felt solid earth beneath my feet.

At the edge of the crowd an ambulance was waiting, but Bill insisted on accompanying me by car to the modern, electrically equipped apartment at headquarters that had been assigned to us for the winter, shower and all! A quick examination by the doctor proved that Bill had suffered two cracked vertebrae in his back, but he refused to be hospitalized until the following day.

'Right now I'm climbing into that bed,' he declared. 'And Lord help anyone that wakens me before noon tomorrow.'

The door had scarcely closed on the last of our friends when we fell into the new bed Bill had given me as a wedding present. We not only fell into, but through it, to the floor. Sheepishly, Bill admitted that he didn't know too much about assembling a bed and it was entirely possible that he had discarded with the rest of the crating the supporting slats that held the innerspring mattress in place. I couldn't lift the springs and mattress and Bill didn't dare try.

He said: 'Let it lay. Right now I could curl up in a boiler factory. I'm going to sleep.'

I said, 'Me too.'

We did.

A morning newspaper carried the report:

RANGER, BRIDE RESCUE
FETED AT YOSEMITE

In the Yosemite, surrounded by snowdrifts seven feet deep, rangers celebrated the rescue of W. K. Merrill, one of their fellows, and his bride, Margaret.

Three

NEVER will I forget the vacation Bill and I spent together the first year after our marriage. We were stationed at Deer Camp which, in those days, was just about the most primitive spot in all the outlying regions of Yosemite. I was working desperately hard trying to become a ranger's wife, but there were so many things in the woods for a city girl to learn that at times I was close to despair. Then Bill told me about the few days' leave he had coming, and the whole picture changed completely; even our bare little cabin took on a rosy hue.

For months we had been isolated in the Back Country wilderness, and now my old familiar world was about to reopen for me —I could scarcely contain myself. Wonderful visions crowded about me: the skimpy little curtains hanging at our cabin windows became flowing plush drapes, the trees and mountains beyond were an elegant canvas created by the brush of a master, the pot-bellied stove all but disappeared as the old pine boards I stood on began to gleam with the polish of a dance floor. I knew I was dreaming, but it was such great fun recalling the world I had left behind. Knowing that rangers and their wives are often invited to formal affairs at headquarters and in the nearby cities, I had brought an evening gown along with me to the cabin, and that evening I was pressing it, with my non-electric flat iron, when Bill rushed through the doorway.

'I got it!' he shouted. 'Three days off, starting tomorrow!'

I almost swooned with joy.

'Know where I'm going to take you?'

I nodded, happy beyond words.

'Good girl!' His eyes were gleaming with excitement. 'We'll go so far back in the forest we'll have to teach the owls to say "Who". At last we're going to get away from civilization.'

'What——!'

'We'll make camp right beside a mountain lake and then . . .'

For a moment I couldn't believe my ears. Go deeper into the forest? Get away from civilization! Weren't we already hanging on to the last outflung fringe? How much farther could one go? I was thunderstruck, but Bill's face was glowing with such wondrous delight that I simply could not bring myself to put my thoughts into words. While I watched, the rich, billowing drapes once again became sleazy little window curtains, the lye-scrubbed pine-boards slowly appeared through the polish of the dance floor, and even the potbellied stove with the Coleman lantern hanging overhead was again back in focus.

'Gee! Think of it, honey.' Bill could barely control his enthusiasm. 'I've been planning this for a mighty long time. Sort of takes your breath away, doesn't it?'

I agreed, completely. After he left the cabin I folded my gown back into the trunk and sat down and bawled. There was nothing ladylike in the way I did it, either. I howled, squawked, and bellowed to the top of my lungs, even took a few swings at a table leg with the toe of my shoe. But I eventually calmed down and then suddenly sat bolt upright in my chair. Was I being quite fair, I wondered. Had it ever occurred to him that I might prefer going elsewhere? Bill is a true woodsman, and his entire world revolves around the mountains and the solitude of the deep forest. Slowly it came to me why he was taking me there: I was

41

at last to become a real wife to a ranger, as familiar with his world as he was, and he was offering to become my instructor.

Long before daylight the next morning we were busily preparing for the trip. Systematic as usual, Bill divided the work between us. While he was loading the camping equipment, I was packing the two boxes he provided. Only the bare necessities, he had said, and I tried to follow orders. Into one container went the pots, skillets, pans, and percolator; the other was carefully packed with a slab of bacon, eggs, butter, beans, frying fat, pancake flour, dishes, coffee, and, as an unexpected treat, a beautiful three-layer cake I had baked the night before.

The sun hadn't yet put in its appearance when we took off for the hinterland. Bill was in the highest of spirits and soon was singing at the top of his voice. It was then I discovered for the first time that little-boy look in his face that always reminds me of a man in short pants who has traded his hoe for a fishing pole. I soon joined in the song. We were climbing a steep grade when a loosened boulder suddenly came hurtling down the mountainside. Bill tried to avoid it but the left rear wheel struck it squarely enough to rattle the dishes resting on the back seat. We halted a moment to inspect the tyre, which fortunately was undamaged, and, of course, Bill rolled the rock from the highway before continuing.

As we topped a high crest, the sun came up in all its golden glory—it was as beautiful as only a sunrise in the mountains can be. Bill slowed the car to a snail's pace and finally came to a complete stop on the shoulder of the road. We sat, breathless, drinking in the beauty of the scene before us. Everything was coloured in the brightest hues of green and gold; the trees were swaying and sparkling as the sun reached the dewdrops teetering on the edge of their leaves, and the open sky beyond formed a backdrop that simply left us entranced with its radiant splendour. Bill looked at me and smiled. I couldn't speak.

It was late afternoon when we reached one of those little story-book lakes you read about, and we quit the slight trail we had been following and jostled off through the trees to the far side before coming to a final halt. I gazed about us. We were at the very edge of the water, with virgin forest reaching out in every direction farther than the eye could see.

'Been wanting to bring you here,' Bill said, 'for a long time.'

'You've been here before?'

He nodded. 'Once. Been saving it for you, honey.'

'You know,' I said thoughtfully, 'I believe we have the whole lake to ourselves.'

He nodded eagerly. 'And the sun, too, and the stars and the whole forest for more miles than you can count. Not another soul to disturb us. It's all ours, Marge. This is really living!'

Selecting a smooth level site for our camp, he immediately fell to unpacking the car. I was happy as a lark as I lifted the box of cooking utensils into my arms and, with head held high, drinking in the exotic scenery, strode blithely off towards the camp site. A moment later I was flat on my face, with the toe of one shoe firmly hooked under an upended root and pots and pans clattering down around my head. Bill dropped his work and ran to my assistance, but I hastily scrambled to my feet unhurt. Although he didn't say a word, I was sure I detected something in the look he tried to hide that made me thankful of the chance to turn away while retrieving my scattered tinware.

I was determined not to give a repeat performance with the food-box as I gently lifted it from the back seat, but before I moved a step I realized that disaster had already struck. When my hand came out from under the box, it was dripping with a sticky yellow substance that could only be well-scrambled eggs. The boulder we struck in the road, I thought grimly to myself, and clawed frantically at the lid in my haste to discover the seriousness of the calamity. Everything I had placed in the box was still there, but no human hand could have accomplished the chaos that leered up at me from within. The bacon slab lay garnished with a mixture of butter and fine-ground coffee; pancake flour was unsparingly blended into a limpid pool of smashed eggs with shells added. And my beautiful three-layer cake, crushed beyond recognition, was breathing its last beneath a protective coating of hard-shelled beans and a generous sprinkling of broken glassware.

I wanted to bawl, or kick the biggest rock I could find—or sneak away and bury my head in a bush. For the first time Bill

43

had trusted me with selecting the food, unattended. No more was I to be treated as a green city girl; I had become a ranger's wife and knew how to meet situations as they arose. We're camping three days, he had said. Take only the bare necessities. I realized that I had enough edibles to feed a crew of hungry loggers for a month. Between the car seats I even had stowed away some canned goods just in case. And the cake—good heavens!

Furtively I glanced towards where he was occupied with the tent. Of one thing I was dead certain: he must never know about the mess I had made of things. Quickly I salvaged the slab of bacon, part of the pancake flour, half a sack of beans, and some coffee. The rest I dumped into a paper sack and, keeping the car between us, placed it, well covered with leaves, behind a convenient tree. I was almost myself again as I marched stoically into camp with my box of depleted groceries.

Genuine outdoor people always fascinate me. Even to this day I've never grown indifferent to their sure, direct manner of accomplishing whatever task is at hand, and with the speed and ease that comes only with a born insight that never can be gained entirely from books. Our little home in the woods was already in apple-pie order. The new arctic tent, which Bill had never before unpacked, was standing proud and erect, awaiting us with open flap, and inside I caught a glimpse of our sleeping-bags smoothly unrolled on the floor. Nearby, on the lee side of a huge boulder, the campfire was already licking around a rock he had placed in the centre of the flames.

'One thing about camping out, it sure does wonderful things to the appetite,' Bill grinned. 'What's for dinner tonight, Marge?'

I gulped and darted a glance at the food-box. 'How about some stew?'

'Stew? Out here! You mean out of a can?'

I nodded hopefully. 'It's getting chilly, and a good hot stew would be fine.'

'Sure.' He peered at me a moment, then started towards the food-box.

'Not there,' I said hastily. 'It's in the car with the other cans. I forgot to bring them over.'

In a minute he was back loaded down with cans which he

44

placed neatly beside the food-box. 'We never leave any food unguarded,' he said, scanning the labels. 'It's never safe. Sometimes
the animals will go right through a car to get at it.'

He found the stew while I was searching for a can-opener, and
deftly slit open the lid with his knife. 'Want to take care of the
car before it gets dark,' he said, striding away. 'Call me when the
coffee's ready.'

'Water,' I said suddenly. 'I've got to have water for the
coff——' I could have bitten off my tongue.

'The lake,' he called back. 'It's full of the stuff!'

I stamped my foot in disgust, thoroughly angry with myself.
Of course I knew there was water in the lake, good, pure water
from the glaciers. The trouble with me was that I spoke too often
without thinking. There was no excuse for it, I told myself. I had
lived long enough now in the forest and mountains to realize that
water could be had from sources other than a kitchen faucet, that
heat wasn't dependent on a furnace, or light from flicking an
electric switch. I marched off towards the lake with a pail in each
hand.

Making coffee immediately posed another problem, though.
Filling the percolator with water and adding coffee was simple
enough, but when I attempted to place it on the rock at the centre
of the fire, that was something else. Flames were leaping up
higher than the rock, and fire seemed to come to my fingers like
steel to a magnet. I considered the risk and approached the problem from every possible angle, but with no success; finally, with
streaming eyes and firmly clenched teeth, I deliberately reached
out and plunked the thing down on the rock, stood glaring at it
a moment, then began inspecting my singed eyebrows and well-
done fingers. By the time I had rubbed the smoke from my eyes,
the wooden percolator handle was blazing merrily and, with a
mighty swing, I kicked the whole mess far out into the
bushes.

If this were a novel, the writer would probably have me
spinning around only to come face to face with my smirking
husband. That's exactly what happened, too, except there was no
smirk on Bill's face, not even the trace of a smile. For a moment
he stood looking sternly at me, then took me in his arms.

'Gee, I'm sorry, Marge,' he said. 'Guess I never showed you how to manage an open fire. Wait.'

He strode off towards the car and appeared a moment later with an old coffee can blackened with smoke from countless campfires. He washed and filled it at the lake and then dumped in a handful of coffee. With the toe of his shoe, he pushed the blazing wood to one side, set the can on the rock, and replaced the embers. In a few minutes the coffee was boiling, and he removed the can from the fire, poured in some cold water to settle the grounds, and grinned up at me.

'Now for the stew,' he said, setting the can on the rock just as he had done with the coffee. 'We'll be ready to eat in a jiffy.'

Darkness crept in over the mountains while we ate our dinner. It was a lot of fun listening to Bill recounting his adventures in the Back Country, and our appetites surely had improved with the high altitude, but I couldn't quite enter into his high holiday spirit or dismiss the eerie feeling of unrest that constantly nibbled at my nerves. It was just that this experience was startlingly strange to me, I kept prompting myself. Never before had I spent a night camping out in the wilds. There wasn't really anything to worry about, of course. But the bobbing shadows crouching around the fire, the occasional flutter of unseen wings, and the sudden mournful cry of some night creature in the dark forest simply didn't inspire me with any great sense of security.

Then I noticed the eyes! How long they might have been there, I didn't know, but when I first saw them they were staring straight at me from behind Bill's left shoulder, and they looked at least the size of cannon balls. I wanted to break in on his yarn, to warn him about it, but I couldn't push a sound beyond my lips. Be calm, I chattered to myself. You're a little nervous to-night, and imagination produces strange bedfellows. With an effort I forced myself to close my eyes, then looked again. The thing was still peering at me, but I now noticed something else: another pair of eyes was glittering over Bill's right shoulder. I smothered a scream and forced myself to look away. But there were eyes there too, and, it seemed to me, we were now completely surrounded by a ring of staring eyes!

It was like a horrible nightmare. I tried to break the spell and get to my feet, but I was held fast to the ground. Although inwardly I shouted and screamed to the high heaven, not a gurgle came out. I was soaked with perspiration and trembling like an aspen leaf when Bill happened to glance my way.

'Anything wrong, Marge?' he asked. 'Don't you feel well?'

I still couldn't utter a word but managed to raise my trembling hand enough to point behind him. He glanced over his shoulder before sliding over beside me.

'Looks like you've seen a ghost,' he said, pressing my hands. 'What is it?'

'Ey-eyes,' I finally stammered. 'Look—look at all the eyes out there! We're surrounded by wild animals!'

'Oh, that.' He seemed relieved as he got to his feet and heaved a few well-directed rocks into the darkness. 'All gone now,' he said, and sat quietly down beside me.

'But—but what is it?' I demanded. 'W-what kind of animals are out there?'

'Oh, probably a doe and her fawns—a bear or two,' he said serenely. 'Came over to look at our fire and see what we're up to.'

He went on to explain that this was the opposite of people going to the zoo to stare at strange animals; here the animals had come to peer at the strange people. He said a lot more, but I'm afraid I didn't profit much by it, for my mind simply wasn't on what he was saying. What peril we might be facing or how far he might go in an effort to calm my nerves, I didn't know, but I was dead certain of one thing—the staring eyes were coming back again. I could see them moving in towards us.

I couldn't make a sound when it happened, and I was far too paralysed to move a muscle. It started with the most horrible growl I had ever heard and grew immediately into such a screeching, snarling roar that my blood immediately turned to ice. Bill leaped to his feet and started running.

I suddenly found my voice. 'Wait for me!'

'Stay by the fire,' he called back, and was instantly swallowed in the darkness.

I heard him yelling and hurling sticks and rocks around for a reeling æon before the turmoil died down to a steady roar. Then, after an interminable spell, while I stood quaking, it became so quiet it was almost unbearable. At last I saw Bill approaching from the shadows. He walked straight towards me but didn't utter a word until he was so close I could see the fire reflected in his eyes.

'You dumped some foodstuff out there.' He waved a hand in the direction from which he had come. 'Bears fight over any food that's left around, and small animals often get killed. If visitors to the national parks made a practice of dumping their refuse behind the nearest tree, it would take just about thirty days to transform the most gorgeous scenery of this country into a first-class garbage dump. If there isn't a container for that purpose nearby, get a shovel and bury your garbage. That's what I just did.'

I told him I was genuinely sorry, that it would never happen again—and meant every word of it. He believed me, the incident was dismissed, and we sat down close to the fire to watch a full moon soaring in the heavens like a bright jewel high above the mountain-tops. Unnoticed, the fire had died to a bed of glowing coals, and the brisk mountain air was beginning to penetrate. Finally Bill stood up and helped me to my feet.

'Lots of fishing to be done tomorrow,' he said eagerly. 'I'll take care of the food, then we'll get in the sack.'

All our edibles went into the waterproof bag I held for him, then, tying it shut with one end of a rope, he tossed the other end over the limb of a tree, pulled the bag well out of reach, and secured it.

I had a sudden impulse to get back in his good graces by displaying my woodmanship. 'Ants,' I said knowingly.

He shook his head. 'Bears.'

I had another impulse, and headed straight for the tent.

Next morning we were wakened by the slow drip of water splashing on our faces. My first conscious thought was that the day's fishing would be ruined by the rain. But how, I wondered, could the tent be leaking when it was brand new? Then I came fully awake as I noticed the early sun shining brightly on the canvas. I sat up in my sleeping-bag and looked at Bill. He was already up, inspecting the soggy nylon and mumbling dangerously beneath his breath.

I said, 'Must have rained during the night.'

'No.' He wagged his head and shook the water from his fingers. 'Condensation. This is an arctic tent, Marge, and it's too airtight for this climate—no ventilation.'

Carrying the bags outside, he spread them in the sunshine. Then he built a fire and we stood close by, shivering, while our clothes steamed on a pole near the flames. To me it seemed a minor calamity. Bill said it was a part of camp life.

'You get the food,' he said brightly, as we finally wriggled into our dried clothes. 'I'll get more wood for the fire. Bacon and flapjacks would taste mighty good right now.'

Lowering the waterproof bag from the tree, I took out the slab of bacon, some coffee and pancake flour, and brought them into camp. While slicing the bacon, I suddenly thought that now, right now before Bill returned, was a splendid time to prepare the coffee—to show him I had profited by my mistakes of the day before. Dropping the bacon on a convenient rock, I seized the old can he had used and hurried off to the lake.

The water was so clear and sparkling that I simply couldn't resist a long cool drink to start the day. On an impulse I dropped the can, reached down with cupped hands, as I had seen Bill do, and raised the water to my lips. It was cold and so good I scooped up another helping. That water must have been more heady than champagne; it did something to me that called for expression. Gazing up at the lofty pines, the unbelievable blue of the lake, I stood watching a hermit thrush settle on a nearby branch and fill the forest with his bell-like song. This, I said to myself, is the way we were intended to live. Free as birds on the wing. Master of all we survey . . .

Bill yelled, and I nearly fell into the lake as I spun around. It wasn't an everyday shout that he let go; it was the sort of wild bellow one might associate with a berserk lion. He was charging straight towards me, and I suddenly felt faint when I glimpsed the wild look in his drawn face. Bitten by a rattlesnake! I gasped to myself. Or gone mad! When he was almost upon me, I grabbed a heavy stick and darted a glance behind him. Visions of pursuing Indians were swimming before my eyes! But Bill dashed right past me and pounded away towards camp while I stood, stick in

49

hand, gaping after him. I knew he was deranged, and it didn't calm my fears any when he suddenly leaped headlong over the fire and rushed wildly on into the forest. While I stood staring, unwilling to believe my senses, I suddenly caught sight of a huge furry thing ahead of Bill bounding off through the trees, and everything suddenly became clear. It was a bear, and in its dripping mouth was our lone slab of bacon.

I reached camp before Bill returned, empty-handed, and was prepared for any imprecation he might bring down on my bowed head. Somehow I had managed to do it again. Never leave food unguarded, I had been told, and while I had stood dewy-eyed, drooling over the wonders of nature, a 500-pound bear had stalked in and raided our larder. I don't know just what I expected Bill to do or say, but it certainly wasn't what he did. Striding off to the lake he retrieved and filled the can I had forgotten, came back, and without a word began stirring up flapjack batter. I was hurt, deep down inside. Why didn't he bawl me out as I well deserved, call me a knucklehead, even say I still was a green city girl! I could have taken anything better than his silence.

After a while he said, 'Marge.' I was sure it was coming at last, and I was glad. 'You make the toast while I get the flapjacks in the skillet, eh?'

'Sure!' I almost shouted. I was so relieved at the amiable tone of his voice that I would gladly have turned handsprings. 'Sure!'

Eagerly I snatched a few slices of bread, and stopped. How could one possibly make toast over a flaming fire? Your fingers would toast before the bread was even warm. I looked at Bill to see if he was fooling, but his back was towards me. I certainly didn't want to bungle this simple chore if he was serious about it, and I tried to imagine just how he would go about doing it himself. Then I noticed that he was pointing.

'Over there,' he said.

'Where?' I hadn't the slightest idea what he meant.

'Under that tree.'

I looked. Beneath the tree were a few assorted boulders and a fallen limb. It's firewood he needs, I thought. At least I can get that. Grasping the sprawling thing, I dragged it over and deposited it, like an eager retriever, at his feet. Expertly he turned the flapjacks, then with his knife cut off a small forked branch, took the slice of bread I still clutched in my hand, and speared it on the branch. I hoped, desperately, that my open-mouthed surprise wasn't showing too much as I seized the end of the stick and pointed the bread over the flames.

Long before breakfast was finished, I decided against fishing for the day, much to Bill's amazement. So far I had been able to make a complete flop of everything expected of me on the trip, and I was silently resolved to make one last bid. I knew just what would accomplish this, too. Beans! Through generations in my family a recipe for preparing boiled beans that would melt in your mouth had come down to me, and Bill could never get his fill.

Soon after he departed with his rod and tackle, I had my redeeming beans on a low fire, and I couldn't help indulging in a private little giggle. This time I was safe; I knew my beans! There still were many things to be desired in my transition from city life to forest living, but beans held no mystery for me; I had practically grown up with them.

The day was delightfully warm and sunny, the air filled with the tangy aroma of pines and growing grass. It was simply impossible to loll around camp all day with nature so unfurled at my feet. This was one temptation I knew I was powerless to resist, but I took elaborate pains to ensure the safety of the camp before starting on my nature walk. When I had hauled the food-bag far up into the tree, I made sure the campfire was safe to leave, covered the beans with sufficient water, then secured the tent fly, and tripped gaily away into the beckoning forest.

Today, when people so often ask what a ranger's wife does out here for entertainment, I like to remember the secluded little retreat I happened on to that day. Subconsciously you might say I was searching for some intangible utopia tucked away in a corner of my memory, and if I was I certainly recognized it the moment my gaze fell upon it. It was a quiet and secluded spot far back from the lake, so deep in the towering forest that only the lacy reflection of a bright sun above managed to filter through. The air, cool and inviting, was laden with rich perfumes from the exotic wild flowers that grew in profusion at my feet.

51

Sinking down in the deep grass, I leaned back against a majestic lodgepole pine to enjoy the scene. At first there was no sound anywhere, save for the splashing of a small waterfall nearby; then, from an adjoining tree, I spied a little chickaree squirrel as he flitted out on a high limb, tested the air with his sensitive nose, and gave his odd little bark. Immediately he was answered from every direction, and soon there were dozens of them chatting back and forth.

Presently I saw the antlers of a gorgeous buck deer appearing over the crest of a sloping hill, and the squirrels were strangely quiet. I sat perfectly still, and the buck didn't seem to recognize my presence. He was joined a moment later by his mate and two small spotted fawns. The big deer stood guard while the mother nibbled some grass and chose a few tender buds from low-hanging branches. All the while the fawns were jumping about stiff-legged, working off excess energy like their human counterparts.

After the deer had gone, the birds took over as if on signal. The forest fairly rang with their song. It was beautiful, inspiring, made one long to join one's voice with theirs. What a Damrosch or a Toscanini could do with such a wilderness choir if only he could marshal it all into one grand symphony.

When the birds suddenly stopped singing, I knew I was due for more visitors. Soon a mother bear and two cubs came ambling through the trees straight towards where I was sitting. I was so frightened I just sat staring, remembering Bill's warning that a female bear is extremely dangerous while rearing her young. But they halted before coming too close, and the little fellows crowded near to her side as she sniffed the air with her huge nose. For a moment I thought she had detected my scent but, lowering her head, she grunted something to the cubs that relieved their tension, and immediately they were romping around, falling over each other, looking for all the world like a couple of woolly teddy bears come to life.

As I watched I was so fascinated that for a moment I almost forgot my alarm. Then the mother gave a peculiar whining grunt that, in bear language, evidently meant take to the trees. Brownie, the light-coloured one, obeyed at once; the red one waddled off in the opposite direction. He didn't go far, however, for with a powerful swipe of her paw Mama brought him up short and sent him scurrying after his brother. After making sure they were lodged safely in the tree, the old bear, with an occasional backward glance, plodded away in the direction from which they had first appeared, probably returning for some food she had noticed.

The big tree made a wonderful playhouse, and the little cubs took immediate advantage of it. While Brownie scrambled to the top of the uppermost branch, Red tested his weight on all the lower ones, climbing out until they were bent at dangerous angles before making a quick retreat. Then he climbed up to his brother, and I could almost hear him whispering in his silken ear, but Brownie would have none of his foolishness. Defiantly Red let himself down through the branches until he was below the bottom limb, where he carefully peered around the forest to see if Mama was in sight. Then he came quickly tumbling to the soft earth.

Once on the ground he proceeded to roll indulgently on the pine needles, sharpened his claws on a fallen tree trunk, even stood on his hind legs and, I'm sure, openly dared Brownie to disobey Mama and be as brave as he. His brother was intensely impressed, but it required quite a lot more gymnastics, or perhaps name calling, before Brownie finally dropped to the ground. I couldn't help chuckling as I watched them playing their little bear games of scratching holes in the ground, chasing each other around the tree, and rolling like oversized kittens in the sweet-smelling pine needles.

I thought it was the mother returning when I first caught sight of the big bear approaching, but something about the way it stopped and riveted its attention on the tiny cubs warned me that it was a full-grown male. Then, slowly, and with surprisingly little noise for such a huge animal, it drew closer, step by step. I wanted to shout, do anything to distract the cubs' attention from their frolic, but I didn't dare as the beast might turn on me.

Many times I had been told how the males often destroy the young, and now it seemed sure to happen while I sat helpless, watching. But Brownie finally sensed danger and stood on hind legs to sniff the air. Red seemed annoyed at the interruption of their game and was about to take a playful swipe at his brother when the immense bear made a sudden dash for them. Brownie, who was nearer the tree, lost no time in scrambling up to safety, but Red was so taken by surprise that the big male was upon him before he could move. One lightning-swift blow of the powerful paw sent him spinning end over end, and the bear leaped for the kill.

Red landed against the trunk of the tree and somehow kept right on going, barely managing to elude the slashing claws as he scurried up out of reach. Gaining the lower limb, he paused to catch his breath and peer slyly down at the killer, who was growling savagely as he slowly circled the tree. For a moment Red blandly ignored the warnings of the big bear as he inspected himself and carefully licked his wounds, then suddenly scrambled for the higher branches as the old male determinedly sunk his long claws into the bark and began inching his way upwards.

Once he had reached the lower limb, the big bear fairly lunged ahead as he climbed higher and higher, ripping off smaller branches that were in his way. Red was climbing in earnest now, as fast as his stubby legs could manage, but the old bear was gaining at every thrust of his powerful body. Then Red glanced back, saw the killer almost upon him, and in desperation scrambled out on to a limb that grew straight out from the tree trunk. I was sure this was a fatal mistake, that he was hopelessly trapped. I held my breath as the old bear slowly eased out after him.

But Red's wild flight didn't end until he was so far out on the tip of the limb that it was dangerously sagging with his weight. There he sat like a little ball of fur, whimpering pitifully as he watched the killer drawing nearer with every step. Then there was a sharp crack, and the limb began sinking under the tremendous weight it was supporting. The big bear paused, and the limb snapped once more. Seeming to realize that he was bested, the old male turned and made it back to the base of the limb and, with a last horrible growl directed at Red, who was still desperately hanging on, slowly descended to the ground and lumbered off through the trees.

I took a deep breath of relief and was about to get to my feet when I saw the mother returning. The cubs also spied her and came tumbling down to earth. I couldn't help wondering if she had somehow known that her little ones were in danger, and if she was comforting them now as they stood for a moment with noses pressed together. What a panorama of life, I marvelled. Comedy, pathos, drama. But it was not play-acting at all, but real breathing life, that had been unveiled before me. The bears had long disappeared over the hill before I finally rose and headed back to camp.

The beans were boiling. I was nearly famished after my tramp in the woods and could scarcely wait to ladle out a giant helping on my plate. Something warned me that all was not well as I dipped a spoon into the pot, and the absence of the customary delicious aroma should have stopped me, but I was too hungry to ponder over such minor things. Without even waiting for the beans to cool I slipped a spoonful into my mouth, and sat bug-eyed as the little white pellets rattled like red-hot castanets against my teeth.

Pressing one between my fingers, I found it was hard as a rock. It couldn't be, but it was, and so was every one I tested. This time I was too amazed to get angry. It was now full noon—they had been boiling for hours. I hadn't the slightest idea what had happened, but, I declared to myself, if it takes more boiling, I'll give them the works. Piling on enough wood to stoke a steam locomotive, I stood staring at the frothing pot, defying the old axiom that a watched pot never boils—mine did!

Hours later—it was almost dark and I was slowly starving—the beans were still boiling. I was sure they were palatable long before now, but I decided not to remove the pot from the fire until Bill returned. Night had blotted out the nearest trees before I heard him approaching, whistling happily as he strode serenely along the moonlit trail.

'Look at this!' he called, holding out a long string of mountain trout. 'I'll be chef tonight, honey—you're going to have pan-fried trout as only the master can fix them.'

'But I have your favourite beans,' I said quickly. 'I thought——'

'Sure,' he grinned. 'Beans fit for a king's taste, too. They'll be our dessert.'

He stopped suddenly, his glance lingering a moment on the campfire. Then, taking a spoon, he dipped into the boiling pot, and I refused to believe my ears as I distinctly heard the stone-hard beans still rattling about the spoon. Without a word he went to the lake and returned with a pail of water.

'You see, Marge,' he said, pouring some cold water into the pot, 'at this high altitude, water boils at a lower temperature so that the beans don't have time to soften before they come to a boil. You should have kept adding cold water to keep them from boiling too soon.'

He popped the trout into the pan, and I sat back to watch. I felt that this was the time for me to remain silent and wait for results. When he served me a heaping plate, I sampled the trout and found it delicious. The beans, although Bill ravenously ate three helpings, I avoided religiously. Beans had for ever lost their attraction for me.

After breakfast next morning we struck camp. While Bill was busy loading the car, I looked around to see if there was something, one single act, I might do to ease the memory of the day before. My gaze finally rested on the campfire which was still alive, and I knew my problem was solved. With the lake but a few yards away anyone could put out a fire—even me. I seized a pail and hurried down the bank.

With the first pailful the fire all but disappeared, but I was determined, this once, to make a thorough job of it. I brought another pail, carefully poured it over the dying embers and added another as a safety measure. Then, hoping he would notice what I had accomplished, I turned and called to Bill.

'Anything I can do to help?'

He straightened from his packing and glanced around. 'Yes. You might put out the fire while you're waiting.'

'I did put out the . . .' My voice trailed off as I turned to point. The fire was beginning to burn as merrily as ever.

I stooped over and looked suspiciously at it. After all the water I had carried, it was a little staggering to see wisps of flames spring up from the dead ashes. I dashed away for more water, threw it on the embers, got more, and still more. Every time I paused to wipe my brow, the flames began popping up again. I carried more water, poured it on with infinite care, carried more, and hurled it defiantly. The flames grew feeble but always came back to leer at me.

Steaming smoke filled my lungs and my eyes were streaming as I started blindly off once more for the lake. But I was brought up short by stumbling over a shovel which Bill had placed by the fire; it wedged painfully between my ankles and sent me sprawling. I jumped to my feet and stood clutching the thing with unsteady hands as I looked wildly about for a good place to hurl it.

'Atta girl!' Bill said, coming up and taking the shovel from my hands. 'Not every girl would know how to put out a fire here in the woods. You're getting to be a real woodsman, honey.' Tossing a few shovelfuls of dirt on the flames, he stirred it around with the shovel, mixing wet dirt with the coals.

The fire was out.

'Have to do this again real soon,' Bill said eagerly, leading the way to the car. 'Nothing like roughing it a bit, eh, Marge?'

I tried to smile and weakly nodded my head.

Four

ONE balmy spring morning not long after our brief vacation idyll I was busily preparing breakfast when I caught a fleeting glimpse of Bill sprinting across the kitchen and out into the front yard. I had long since learned that anything is likely to happen at any time around a ranger station, and I hurried after him. I must have gone through the doorway as if there were no door to open, for when it slammed shut on its spring hinges, it sounded like a pistol shot. Bill spun around.

'Don't come out here!' he called. 'Might be some shooting.'

I stopped, staring. Bill was running towards the checking station, where cars entering Yosemite must register at the park entrance in front of our cabin, and I caught myself holding my breath. He was in his shirt sleeves, minus a hat, his face still flecked with lather—he had been interrupted while shaving. I saw his gun come out of its holster as he edged around the corner of the small building, and I squeezed behind a tree to watch.

Arch Rock entrance, where we were stationed, is the main

gateway from the west into the park, and the usual heavy traffic was now at a standstill. I couldn't see what was happening from where I stood and had just started across the yard when a bundle of flailing arms and legs came tumbling around the corner of the station. I recognized one man as the ranger who was on duty at the checking station; the other was a brawny, heavy-set Indian, who seemed about to annihilate his opponent as they struggled wildly in the dust of the roadway. Then Bill came into view.

'Get up!' he snapped. 'On your feet!'

They had rolled to a stop, and the ranger scrambled to his feet. 'He's drunk,' he said, pointing to the Indian. 'I wouldn't let him in the park, and he took me by surprise.' With that he picked up his hat and hurried back to his job of getting the honking traffic moving.

Bill reached up and shook the young buck by his broad shoulders. He was a copper-coloured giant at least a head taller than Bill, a solid two hundred pounds of rippling muscle. 'You're drunk, Joe,' he said sternly. 'No drunks go inside the park. You know that.'

'Me not bad drunk,' the buck grunted. 'Me good Indian. You know me, Two-gun.'

Bill nodded seriously. The local Indians had mistaken the case in which Bill carried his handcuffs to be another holstered gun. They had shown great respect for a man who could handle two guns, and 'Two-gun', as they always called him, had every reason not to disillusion them.

Right about then, when things seemed under control, I remembered that our breakfast was still on the stove and made a dash for the kitchen. Nothing had gone up in smoke and, after preparing the table, I peered through the window to see if Bill was on his way back. He was nowhere in sight. I was turning back when I saw him, over on the side lawn, locked in the Indian's arms, rolling furiously about in a struggle that had once more halted traffic. Smothering an impulse to scream, I seized a hot skillet from the stove and dashed outside just as the buck shot straight up in the air and landed with a crunch on the back of his neck—a victim of jiu-jitsu, at which Bill is an expert.

'Wanted to play,' Bill grinned up at me. 'Was showing me some Indian wrestling.'

Indian Joe seemed to have suddenly lost interest in his native skill. Bill helped him to his feet and calmly led him to the garage where he handcuffed him to the steering wheel of the patrol car. All during our late breakfast we ate our overcooked cereal to the blatant squawks of the patrol-car horn, which the buck, to his keen delight, had discovered. When he graduated to the shrieking siren and added his own bloodcurdling yells as accompaniment, Bill called the paddy wagon and hurried outside to silence the din and get traffic moving once again.

Our Indians are never predictable. When the paddy wagon arrived, the big buck's playful mood had evaporated, and it required the best efforts of four men to boost him inside. Over at the jail pandemonium really broke loose when they tried to force him into a cell.

After ten minutes and several bloodied noses, one of the rangers, who had just come in, wagered that he could accomplish the trick alone, and he did, too. But Bill swears the man had advance information that certain parts of Indian Joe's anatomy were extremely sensitive. Nothing had been accomplished by grabbing the buck by the scruff of the neck, but as soon as the ranger reached down and seized him by the seat of his pants, Indian Joe let loose a wild whoop that would have done credit to the *Queen Mary's* whistle and shot through the doorway so fast the ranger didn't even have time to disengage his hand and was dragged inside with him.

Bill always says it pays to know your Indian.

It was early in the summer of 1934 when the four temporary rangers reported at Yosemite. They were to work under Bill's supervision and were quartered together in the same duplex station in which we were living. Bill and I always look forward to the season which each year brings us young men from every part of the country to assist the regular rangers during the rush period.

A position as a temporary ranger is looked upon as a rare bit of good fortune, for it affords an exciting paid adventure in the mountains and forest of the sort most young men merely dream about. They come from every walk of life—rich men's sons, poor men's sons, medical students, writers, college professors, lawyers, actors, even an occasional playboy, who lasts a surprisingly short time. Of the four arrivals that summer, Ted's father was a congressman from Texas, Jim was the son of a citrus tycoon, Al hailed from Washington, D.C., where his family name had so long been connected with the political scene, and Clark was sweating out an appointment as midshipman to Annapolis.

One thing the four boys had in common: they all had been reared as Southern Gentlemen, which accounted for their delightful drawl. And, having been well attended by servants all their lives, none had the faintest conception of what the national parks might expect of them. Their drawing-room manners were at first a bit disconcerting to Bill. The enormous amount of necessary training they must undergo in such a short period of time didn't leave much room for etiquette, and I'm sure Bill shuddered inwardly when Jim walked into his office one day with a stable fork in each hand.

'I'm mighty sorry, suh,' he drawled. 'You asked me to clean the horse stalls, but I just don't know which fork to use, suh.'

Bill paled a little and looked at the three- and four-tined forks Jim was displaying. 'Just clean the stalls,' he snapped. 'I don't care what fork you use. You don't have to eat with those things!'

Of course they became top summer rangers before the season was over and, like many of their kind, have written us from all over the world, or later brought their families to visit at our home. But in the beginning they were so helpless that they were pathetic. They were always inducing motherly old ladies, and some not so old, to show them how to prepare food, as part of their job was the cooking of their own meals. All of them were especially fond of ham gravy, but they could never quite understand my theory that it was first necessary to have the ham.

Put down in the middle of the forest, they were the lonesomest group of boys imaginable; even the influx of park visitors didn't seem to have much effect on their morale—they were just plain homesick. That was when Bill began referring to me as 'Aunt Marge', and he gradually became 'Uncle Bill', a homey title which, somehow, has clung to us to this day.

Then a startling transition took place. Bill was working the boys hard from morning to night, as the limited training period demanded. It was necessary that they learn to control heavy traffic, know what to do on rescue missions or other immediate emergencies, understand how to protect themselves while fighting forest fires, become familiar with uncounted miles of park trails, and learn the million other details that even a temporary ranger must know and act on at a moment's notice. But a sudden change had come over the boys, and even a gruelling day on the steep trails could not erase their contented expressions.

'Girls,' Bill said one night. 'It has to be girls.'

'Did they tell you?' I asked.

He shook his head. 'No need to. Nothing else could do it. Even your home-made cake didn't make them act like this. It's girls.'

He was right. It was girls, four college seniors, who were driving over to the park from Bass Lake almost every night. It wasn't the best arrangement in the world for the boys, but they had to accept it since, of course, none of them had brought a car of his own. It was a relief to us both to see them suddenly so energetic and once more fairly oozing with contentment. Then disaster struck without warning.

The boys, turned out in their Sunday best, were waiting one evening on the porch of their quarters. I saw them as I left for a rehearsal of the musical the park was preparing, but I pretended not to notice the colourful neckties and white collars, just as they had refrained from mentioning to us the new interest that had captured their attention. When I returned several hours later, the scene hadn't changed, except that their dejected faces reflected a lost hope that I was sure could never be reclaimed—the girls had failed them for the first time.

The following night they again occupied the front porch, waiting in silence, and there was something in the way they sat staring straight ahead that made it plain they were not merely admiring the beautiful scenery in front of them. Presently Ted marched out to the checking station, and we could see him talking on the phone for some time before returning and going into an excited huddle with the other boys. I recognized the twinkle in Bill's eye just then that warned me he was up to something, but before I could interfere he suddenly got to his feet and shouted for them to come over to our quarters.

'Aunt Marge has a new cake ready to cut,' he called. 'I'll brew some coffee. Come and get it.'

They came, but not in the manner of the thundering herd we were accustomed to dodging. The first servings disappeared as swiftly as usual, but not one of them would accept a second helping, which was beyond belief. There was a nervous tension among them, too, that even Bill could not dispel with tales of his service life, adventures which they had previously clamoured to hear. We tried not to appear surprised when they decided to retire for the night. It was still quite early, but they assured us they desperately needed their rest.

'The girls must be coming,' I said to Bill when we were alone.

'Don't think so.' He grinned mysteriously. 'We'll see.'

When I heard four pairs of shoes thudding to the floor, I decided my deductions were unfounded and said so. Bill said nothing. After his usual inspection tour outside, we prepared for bed, turned out the lights, and waited. When I was sure I couldn't keep my eyes open one second longer, I was brought up with a start. A board had creaked in the boys' quarters, just once, and was followed by the ear-straining silence of a tomb. Bill and I tiptoed to the window and watched as the boys appeared one by one in the moonlight, shoes in hand. Bill motioned for me to be quiet as they slipped on their shoes and hurried off across the front yard.

'They're going to the garage,' I whispered. Then I saw it clearly. The government patrol car was in there, and the key was always left in the switch ready for a quick getaway. 'Bill,' I said under my breath, 'are they—they're going to take the patrol car!'

He nodded, and whispered, 'They'll be back.'

Silently they pushed the big car out on to the roadway and

leaped inside as it coasted off without a sound down the steep grade towards the park boundary.

'Th-they took it!' I sputtered. 'The patrol car is gone. What'll you do?'

'Still got our car if I need it,' Bill said calmly.

'But what are you going to do about it?' I demanded.

'Nothing,' he grinned. 'When they get back I think they will have learned their lesson.'

'What lesson?'

'Let's get to bed,' he said flatly. 'Tomorrow's going to be a mighty long day.'

The first ghostly light of morning was creeping in through the top of the trees when I heard the noise outside. Awakening from a sound sleep, I at first couldn't imagine what it might be. It was a sort of rasping sound, like a shoe being scraped heavily across a hard surface, followed by low guttural groans that came in short gasps that might have been made by a distance runner trying to regain his breath after a four-minute mile. Then I sat straight up in bed as reality came slowly into focus. I noticed that Bill's bed was empty, then I saw him in the dim light near the front window, chuckling to himself.

'What is it?' I asked anxiously.

'Sh-h-h.' He beckoned me to the window.

At first glance I thought it was a stalled car parked in the middle of the roadway. Then I recognized it as Bill's missing patrol car, and it was slowly moving up hill, with no one at the wheel. Cars, I knew, just don't find their way back home, as the old grey mare was reputed to do, and I rubbed my eyes to clear my vision. It didn't help. The car was still crawling inch by inch up the steep incline, steering its own course with no sign of locomotion. When I was ready to pinch myself to see if I was actually awake, Jim appeared from behind the car, grasped the wheel, headed it up the last slope towards the garage, and quickly joined the other steaming temporary rangers at the rear for the final push.

They made it, but I'm sure another ten feet would have been beyond their endurance. Their generally dishevelled appearance gave evidence of a weary night of backbreaking labour. Never have I seen such a bedraggled group of boys as they were, tottering unsteadily off towards their quarters, collars wilted to a soggy band around their necks, and faces dripping.

I couldn't imagine what could have happened during the night that had backfired on the boys. Of course I knew the courting plan they must have had in mind when they coasted silently away towards Bass Lake, but I simply couldn't imagine what had gone awry when they reached the bottom of the long steep grade that had made them toil all night long pushing the dead patrol car back home. The tank was always filled and the car in perfect running condition—the mechanics at the government garage saw to that—and Bill was religiously strict about the key being left in the switch.

We waited until the boys were comfortably settled in their bunks before Bill walked into their quarters. He explained that he was calling them a little early because it was to be a long day they had before them.

'Aunt Marge has a hot breakfast waiting on the table, and you'll need it,' he went on. 'Lots of climbing to do. It will probably be a red-letter day you won't soon forget.'

A few minutes later they trooped into our dining-room, a sorry-looking lot, dead-tired, their eyes red from loss of sleep, and showed a profound lack of interest in the ham, buttered toast, fried eggs, and coffee awaiting them.

During the meal, which they ate grudgingly, their eyes seldom left Bill's face as he outlined the long day's work ahead. Not one word was mentioned about the episode of the night before, but every face showed plainly that it would be a relief to all if Bill would only admit that he knew and they could say they were sorry. They later proved over and over to be one of the best groups Bill had ever trained, but right now they were four very much disturbed young men. When Bill finished his meal and suddenly stood up, they seemed to welcome it with a sort of now-it-comes-and-thanks attitude. Of course, they didn't know Bill's technique in handling young buckaroos.

'You know,' Bill said quietly, reaching for his hat, 'if I had needed the patrol car last night, I could have accused any one of you of having forgotten to leave the key in the switch. But I

65 B.I.M.K.—E

would have been wrong.' He grinned, looked around at them and held out an open hand for all to see. 'Strange tricks our memory can play on us, eh, boys? That key was in my own pocket all the time. Now let's get to work.'

Bill was once an untamed youngster who got into his full share of scrapes, and I sometimes remind him of it when he appears too concerned over the latest whimsy of some young ninety-day wonder he is training as a seasonal ranger. The most effective one at my command, to which Bill will admit, was told me by Fred Funke. At one time Mr. Funke was a district ranger in the Forest Service and Bill was a lad of eighteen doing his training under the veteran's supervision. A government notice came in that ordered the replacing of old comfort stations [toilets] at Twin Peaks, California, with new chemical equipment, and the entire job was laid in Bill's lap.

'You will dig a hole there,' Mr. Funke directed, driving a stake into the earth. 'Make it twelve feet long and ten feet wide.'

Bill grinned and flexed his muscles. 'Is that all, sir?'

'That's all, except for one thing—the hole goes straight down five feet!' Mr. Funke walked away whistling merrily to himself.

The smile on Bill's face disappeared, and he swallowed—hard. Around Twin Peaks the soil is made up chiefly of de-composed granite, and sinking a shovel into it would be equivalent to undermining Gibraltar with your fingernails. But the job had to be done, and it was up to him to do it, somehow.

His first weapon was a heavy-duty flat spade. It lasted ten minutes before the cutting edge curled over like a leaf of wilted lettuce. Then came the shovel, and it soon went the way of the buckled spade. The rest of the day was spent hurling a big sledge-hammer down on the top end of a pointed iron bar which occasionally bit out chunks of decomposed granite as large as a golf ball, but more often the size of No. 2 bird shot.

The next morning, stripped to the waist, Bill again tackled the job with the last untried weapon in the tool-house—a huge pickaxe. It had a curved cutting iron with tapered ends, which was secured to a long hickory handle diabolically designed in the Dark Ages, Bill still insists, as an instrument of torture—especially

66

for the one who wields it. But it worked, after a fashion. It still was a painfully slow process, and when combined with equal parts of broiling heat and shrieking muscles, it sometimes seemed hopeless, but the hole was growing deeper, inch by agonizing inch. Then, on the following day, when he had reached a depth of three feet, the digging became so impossibly unmanageable that Bill finally decided to take drastic action.

'Dynamite!' he muttered dangerously. 'I'll blow it out!'

Securing some of the explosive from the tool-house, he tamped it into the decomposed granite, lit the fuse, and took off. The earth heaved mightily, spewed forth a shower of debris, and once again settled back in position. With fire in his eye Bill leaped into the smoking hole, surveyed his masterpiece, and decided he had won. Rolling in the four septic tanks now seemed like child's play, and he flicked the dirt from his hands with a great flourish as the last big tank dropped into place. But his elation was short-lived, for he noticed that the tops of the tanks were too near the surface of the ground; the hole was still a foot short of the required depth.

For a moment he scratched his head and mumbled dark words beneath his breath. Then a blossoming smile spread across his face as the Great Solution came to him. He hurled a few rocks, defiantly, into the yawning hole and spat after them by way of showing high contempt for all decomposed granite. It was quite simple really: instead of placing the metal collars, that were provided, atop each tank—which would hoist the toilet bowls into the air sixteen inches too high—he'd simply discard them.

As days passed and Bill was still left to his own devices, the little comfort station at Twin Peaks began to take shape. A hand-mixed concrete floor soon covered the top of the septic tanks and afforded a floor on which the two-room redwood building would rest. When the building was finished and the bowls were set and cemented into place, Bill was ready to open for business. He was standing by, smugly admiring his handiwork, when the first customer appeared. The manner in which the man entered the building was normal enough but, a few minutes later, when the door flew open and he dashed out into the open, he was a radically changed man.

67

'Spiders!' he yelled. 'There are spiders in there and one bit me!'

That was when Bill had his first serious doubts concerning the wisdom of the short cut he had chosen. The next customer swore he was breaking out with a rash he had just discovered. Another insisted a hornet had drawn a bead on him. 'Nothing else could be that painful!' And he vigorously massaged his posterior as he leaped away into the woods.

By the following day Bill had enough first-hand evidence to convince even himself that he had made a grave mistake. It now was plainly evident that the metal collars he had discarded—which would have placed the customers sixteen inches higher above the chemically loaded tanks—were a very important item, also one that was now impossible to install. But Ferrell, a druggist friend, advised him that an application of vinegar or a few pats of ammonia water might counteract the chemical burns. It worked, and Bill's flagging spirits rose once more. Perhaps it wasn't yet too late to save the day.

Both rooms were supplied with a can of the soothing lotion, a box of cotton pads, and a neatly typed instruction card which he tacked to the wall in each room. For several days, while Bill scarcely dared to breathe, all remained quiet on the Twin Peaks front. Then came the day when the forest supervisor came by and went inside to inspect the new building. Almost immediately, he reappeared and went directly back to headquarters, where orders were dispatched forthwith for young Billy Merrill to report to his office.

'Young man,' the supervisor said sternly, 'when you get an order, it is to be carried out to the letter—if it takes all summer. About one-fourth the energy you spent trying to camouflage your omission in building the comfort station would have done the job properly in the first place.

'Now the building must be raised high enough to accommodate the metal collars you threw away. The bowls must be chiselled out of the cement, a new cement floor must be laid sixteen inches higher, and additional steps must be added to reach the new floor. You will then have to install more lattice around the entire building and rearrange everything accordingly, to make it appear that the job was properly done the first time. The cost of all additional materials used will be deducted from your salary. You will begin operations this evening, performing all labour after regular hours, in your own time.' He paused and eyed the nervous boy before him. 'If the job is satisfactory, I may not ask you to turn in your badge!'

The job was done as directed. Bill learned his lesson.

Five

IT always amuses Bill to remember the advertisement once carried by a national sporting magazine: 'Be a ranger! Hunt, fish, and trap. Cabin sometimes furnished.' It is true that being a ranger has, for the outdoor man, many advantages not found in other walks of life, but it also demands the combined skills of a wild-animal trainer, horse wrangler, mountain climber, and ski expert. You are called on to make water and snow surveys in the Back Country, days away from civilization; you become a trail blazer of course; you fight roaring forest fires; and, if you're a little slow on the draw, you sometimes find yourself looking into the business end of a killer's gun. But first and always you are a gentleman—even if the other fellow isn't. And although you may smile as you direct old ladies to the nearest comfort station, you are at times forced to be as firm and exacting as the law you represent.

Early one morning the telephone rang, and Bill was out of bed at the first jingle. I opened one eye and peered at the clock. It was 5 a.m. Chief Ranger Townsley was on the wire.

'Two prisoners have escaped from the Salinas jail,' he said quickly. 'We think they're headed this way and should be at your station any minute. They knocked a highway patrolman cold and stole the sheriff's car. Don't take any chances. They're armed to the teeth and plenty dangerous.'

Bill dropped the receiver, dived into his clothes, and rushed out of the room, snatching a forty-five from the stand as he ran. The heavy chain which is used at night to block the Arch Rock entrance to the park was still across the highway, and before Bill could reach it, a car careened around a bend in the road and came to a screeching stop. For a second the driver stared at the chain and at Bill running towards him, while his companion slid down in the seat, nervously fingering an automatic. Then with a clashing of gears the car swung around and roared off down the road.

The patrol car was on the park side of the chain, and there was no time to lose. Swinging up the sharp bank and back down beyond the barricade before the car could overturn, Bill raced after them, siren screaming. A few miles down the road he caught sight of a stalled car, across a wide, sweeping curve, and laid his gun ready in his lap. But before coming to a full stop, he realized that this was not the car he had been tailing. A man and two women looked up from inspecting their crumpled fenders as he drew alongside.

'How far ahead of me is that green Pontiac?' Bill yelled.

'About half a mile,' the man called. 'They sideswiped me coming out of that curve. One had a gun and——'

Bill waited for no more. It was a sharp-curving mountainous road, narrow and tortuous. Although it was dangerous at high speed, he opened the siren full on and pushed the gas pedal to the floor. The Pontiac had a good start on him now, and he would need every bit of luck to overtake it. The car that had been forced into the bank back there proved how desperate the criminals were. Just when he was beginning to despair of ever overtaking them, he caught a fleeting glimpse of the racing car as it passed out of sight around the curve a short way ahead.

A mile and several curves farther down the road he caught up with them. His siren was still wailing and he knew the driver could see him in his rear-view mirror, but they only increased their speed, which already was hurling them over the road practically out of control. Reaching a straight stretch of highway, Bill managed to draw abreast and yelled for them to pull over and stop. For answer the driver suddenly swung his car sharply to the left, but Bill braked hard, dodging the thrust, then spurted ahead and crashed into the side of the fleeing car. It spun once around before leaving the road and crashing with a sickening thud against an overhanging mud bank.

Halting the patrol car as soon as possible, Bill raced back to the scene of the wreck. The car was all but buried in the earthen bank, a total loss, but the occupants were nowhere in sight. Bill darted one searching glance behind him at the deserted open country across the road before springing up the steep bank and rushing into the undergrowth which reached down to the edge of the highway.

Fighting his way back through the dense brush until he was almost winded, Bill paused for breath and listened. Somewhere ahead a man was plunging wildly through the tangle; no evidence of the other one came to his ears. Slowly, and with studied silence, he began parting the tall undergrowth as he moved ahead, placing each foot where no telltale crackling of dead twigs would announce his presence. On and on he crept, watching, listening. Then he stopped so suddenly one foot was still off the ground. Right in front of him, not ten feet away and still breathing heavily, stood a man. He was peering intently into the underbrush beyond him, his back to Bill, listening. Leaning over carefully, Bill picked up a small pebble and tossed it into a bush. When the man wheeled around, he found himself staring down the barrel of Bill's gun.

'Put 'em up high and turn around!'

The man obeyed, sullenly. Bill quickly searched him, then directed him to a nearby pine, made him circle the six-inch trunk with his arms, and secured him by slipping the handcuffs on his wrists.

'I'm going after your partner,' Bill told him. 'I want you to keep quiet while I'm gone. Understand?'

'You goin' to leave me here like this?'

'You won't be going any place,' Bill snapped.

'But—but supposin' somethin' happens to you?' the man

wailed. 'If Fred kills you I'll rot before anybody finds me out here!'

'I'll be back.'

Bill hurried off through the undergrowth, making no effort to conceal his presence until he had covered quite a distance in the general direction taken by the other criminal. When he spied a small clearing just ahead, he paused a moment, surveying the matted clump of growth in the middle of the area. A perfect spot for the criminal to hide, it offered concealment with no chance of being taken by surprise. Padding to the edge of the clearing, Bill crouched behind a big tree and raised his gun.

'Come out of there with your hands up!'

His voice echoed and died in the quiet of the forest.

'Come out right now,' he called sharply, 'or I'll blast you out!'

There was a sudden commotion in the brush, and a denim-clad figure rushed out, hands aloft.

'I'm coming!' he cried. 'Don't shoot!'

Bill cuffed the man's hands behind his back before searching him.

'Where's the gun?' he demanded.

'I—I ain't got no gun.'

'Didn't think you would have,' Bill said. 'Had plenty of time to get rid of it. All right, get going.'

Collecting the other prisoner on the way and cuffing the two together, he marched them back out to the highway.

'Where did you get this car?' Bill demanded.

'It's mine,' replied the former driver. 'I bought it.'

'What's your name?'

'Pfeifer,' he said hesitantly. 'John S. Pfeifer.'

Bill stepped over to the wrecked car and removed the registration card from the crumpled steering column. It was made out to John S. Pfeifer and signed with a bold hand. That settled two things at once: it was not the sheriff's car that had been wrecked, and the men glaring at him were not the two prisoners who had escaped from the jail at Salinas.

Bill turned back to the prisoner. 'So you're John L. Pfeifer?'

'Not John L.,' he growled. 'I said John S. Pfeifer. Ought to know my own name.'

Bill handed the man a pad and pencil. 'Write it on there.'

When the pad was returned to Bill, he glanced at the awkward scrawl.

'You can pronounce Pfeifer, all right,' he said evenly, 'but you can't spell it.' He took a step forward. 'Now, who are you?'

'All right.' The man dropped his head. 'What you want to know?'

'Just one thing,' Bill replied. 'Where did you steal the car?'

'Fresno.'

Back at the station Bill seated the two prisoners on a log where he could keep a careful eye on them while he called the Fresno authorities. Afterwards he brought them into the house, and I prepared sandwiches and coffee. They ate greedily and twice drained the percolator, but they would answer no inquiries or as much as make a sound. While they were eating, Bill removed their handcuffs, and they remained perfectly still, except for their eyes which constantly strayed back to the forty-five in Bill's hand.

They seemed a little surprised when Bill herded them back to the front yard, without replacing their shackles, but his reason soon became evident.

'Now that you've had breakfast,' he said, 'might as well get something done while we're waiting for the sheriff to pick you up.'

They stared at him sullenly.

'You.' He indicated the prisoner nearest him. 'Get that rake over there and start cleaning up the leaves. Your buddy can turn loose on the woodpile.'

'I don't need to work for you,' the second one retorted. 'I ain't splittin' no wood for anybody.'

'You've got it all wrong,' Bill snapped. 'I'm not asking you to do anything for me because I gave you breakfast, understand? This is government property, and you're going to have the pleasure of doing a little work for Uncle Sam. He'll be feeding you for a good long time, and you're going to earn a few beans while we're waiting for the paddy wagon. Get going, and don't get any cute ideas about that axe. I'm watching the both of you.'

The yard was free from leaves when the sheriff's men arrived, and the woodpile had grown considerably. Bill stood idly by, exchanging gossip with the deputies as they loaded the prisoners into the car for the trip to Fresno. Then, all of a sudden, his face became grave, and he jerked his gun from its holster and stood a moment gazing at it in disbelief.

'Must be more careful,' he said to the deputies. 'Last night I was cleaning my guns, and this morning I picked this one up by mistake.' He shook his head. 'Look, the clip is empty, and the chamber doesn't have a shell in it, either.'

One prisoner leaned from the car for a closer inspection, then glared at Bill.

'If I'd know'd that, you'd be dead right now!'

Bill grinned and waved them on their way.

'Sorry, boys,' he said. 'My mistake. Better luck next time.'

It seems our life never quite finds time to fall into a conventional pattern; something unusual is for ever cropping up. Like the time Bill stepped on a rattlesnake in our back yard. When he came back to earth and removed his sock we saw two tiny red dots on his ankle that just couldn't be anything other than marks left by the rattler's fangs. They weren't. They were mosquito bites. Probably inflicted while he was airborne, Bill said. Or take the occasion one evening when I casually stepped into the ranger's club during a mock wedding ceremony. Someone called out for me to be the mock bride for the little ceremony they were having, and a few seconds later I was trying to regain my breath as I gazed into the eyes of Bing Crosby, the mock groom, while he sang a love song to me. Some things we chuckle over for years, others we would rather forget—if we could.

One morning, when we were once again living at the station near headquarters, we were sitting at the breakfast-table, chatting over our coffee-cups and little dreaming what the day held in store. Bright sunshine was slanting down into Yosemite Valley, a delightful cool breeze was toying with the curtains at the open window, the sky was blue, the grass an emerald green—the summer season was upon us in all its glory.

'This is living,' I said to Bill. 'God must have made this a special day.'

'Look.' He pointed to the towering mountains glistening

75

with morning dew. 'Diamonds,' he said. 'Millions of diamonds, and they're all for you.'

I smiled, lost in contentment.

'Tonight will be beautiful,' he went on. 'Suppose we eat at the Wawona Hotel and do something afterwards? What would you like?'

'Let's do something different. How about the movies?'

'Know what's playing?'

I shook my head. 'But I'll find out.'

'No drawing-room romance,' he warned. 'I'm allergic.'

After he had gone I hurried through the housework, slipped into a breezy summer frock, and, snatching a book from the table, headed for the forest just outside the back door. The day was entirely too glorious to waste inside. Following the winding path I had worn between the trees, I soon reached the secluded little spot I considered as my very own—I shared it with no one. Sunlight reached its mossy floor only as a dancing lacy pattern cast by the leafy dome above. It was still and restful there, the muted whispering of the pines barely reaching the ear. This was my private sanctuary where I could read and dream; even a nature-built seat was provided in the crook of a low-hanging limb. Soon I was lost in the pages of my book.

It was nearing midday when I left my retreat. A group of ranger wives were getting together at Lisa Danner's home for lunch and a few hands of bridge afterwards. I was starting early as I preferred walking the mile or so across the valley to where she lived. My route carried me through the heart of Camp Curry, the focal point for all park visitors, but if the absence of the usual throng of sight-seers registered in my mind at all, I was enjoying the hike too much to notice. It wasn't until after I reached my destination—and found the place wide open with no one in sight—that I remembered about it.

I was frankly puzzled; it wasn't at all like Lisa. And what had happened to the other girls? After a few moments' deliberation, which got me nowhere, I started back for home, intending to stop by the movie house on the way to see what was playing. I was nearing the theatre, lost in my private little world, when I suddenly became aware of the empty streets. Hardly a soul could be seen anywhere. Camp Curry, the very centre of the valley community, seemed almost as deserted as a crumbling ghost town. It gave me a weird sort of feeling to walk alone down the quiet street; I was a little frightened, too. Something was wrong, I was sure of it, but what it was I couldn't imagine.

A patrol car came speeding towards me, swung off towards nearby Mirror Lake, and was followed almost immediately by another. I quickened my step and was nearing the turnoff the patrol cars had taken when an ambulance came screaming up from behind and raced off to join them. That was when it came to me, something Bill had mentioned a few days earlier. Two young men had persistently plied him with queries about climbing Half Dome, a huge mountain of solid granite rising almost a mile above the floor of the valley. Bill admitted it had not been scaled and told them it never would be. Professional climbers had all agreed that the sheer wall was so nearly perpendicular and, above a few thousand feet, became so smooth and polished, with no possible toe hold to cling to, that it was impossible to climb. But the boys hadn't seemed entirely convinced, he thought, and he was worried. 'If they ever try to climb Half Dome,' he said to me, 'someone will have to risk his life to rescue them.'

When I came within sight of Mirror Lake, I knew at once why Camp Curry was deserted. An enormous throng of people were crowded into a tight knot at one end of the lake, and my first thought was that there had been a drowning. But I was wrong. When I reached the gaping crowd, a man touched my arm and pointed above.

'Up there, lady,' he said excitedly. 'One is 'bout half-way up, other one's a little higher. Can't hang on much longer, either! See 'em?'

At first I saw nothing but the great expanse of Half Dome, reaching so far up into the sky that the summit was all but lost to sight in drifting white clouds. I looked closer, carefully searching the vertical stone wall as my gaze moved downward. Then I spied a dark spot on the side of the mountain, more than half-way up; another was to the left and slightly below the first. But those tiny specks up there couldn't be men; they were hardly the size of ants.

'Have a look,' my neighbour insisted, proffering his binoculars. 'Looks like he's 'bout ready to fall!'

'No—no, thanks,' I managed. I suddenly felt ill and wondered what had possessed me to come. Then Bill's words again came to my mind, 'Someone will have to risk his life to rescue them.' I grasped the glasses and raised them to my eyes.

One of the dark spots leaped out at me, and it was no ant; it was the figure of a thoroughly frightened young man with his toes wedged precariously in the slit of a shallow crevice, his face and shoulders pressed hard against the surface of the mountain while his bloody fingers clawed frantically at the unyielding rock. I lowered the binoculars, more ill than before.

'Hey! He almost dropped!' The man snatched his glasses from me and clamped them eagerly to his eyes. 'He's tryin' to come down. Foot must of slipped. Thought he was comin' sure.'

A woman rushed up to join our party, and the man quickly brought her up to date on what was going on.

'But why did they go up there in the first place?' she demanded.

'Thought they was mountain climbers, I guess. Started up sometime yesterday, they say. Somebody spotted 'em a while back. Got up that far an' couldn't go no farther. You know, nothin' to hang on to.'

'They can come down, can't they?'

'Don't seem so. One's been tryin' to an' he come close to fallin' off.' Grudgingly he lowered the binoculars.

'You see, lady, it's like this: when you're tryin' to step down behind you an' you can't look around to see where you're puttin' your foot . . .'

I walked away. I wanted desperately to leave the place, put it away from my mind. I couldn't do it. Something about the clinging figures up there held me as securely as if I were chained. They were so pitiable, so utterly frightened that their trembling had passed from them; they were still as if life had already gone—two unburied corpses stuck to the side of the mountain with a spot of glue. Too well I knew what they were suffering. Bill had squeezed out of too many tight situations to leave me a stranger to fear.

78

A murmur rose from the crowd. They were pointing upwards, watching expectedly. I didn't want to look, but I had to. The first figure was still in place, pressed tightly to the wall, motionless. Then it must be the other they were watching, the one higher up. But he was gone, something had happened, nothing was left but the smooth surface of the towering mountain. No—I found him again; he was still there, a tiny dark spot blotted against the grey stone. Something else must have drawn the crowd's attention, something I couldn't see.

I leaned back my head and looked up the barren mountain, on and on, through the mist of a hovering cloud and up to the dizzy heights of the very summit. And there I found the answer. Shading my eyes with both hands, I could barely make out the dim forms moving about up there, and I knew who they were. After a long, circuitous ride up from the back side, the rangers had arrived, and like a faint whisper I seemed to hear Bill's words persisting, 'Someone will have to risk his life . . . '

I waited, and in my mind's eye could see them swiftly arranging their rescue gear, coiling the long slender ropes so they would unwind without a hitch, bringing up stretchers where they would be handy, making a last-second inspection of everything before the long descent could begin. I became increasingly nervous and tense; my mouth was dry, and my eyes ached from strain. Somehow the two helpless climbers were still hanging on, but their strength couldn't last much longer. . . .

'There he comes!'

At the crest of the mountain the barely visible figure of a man was beginning to inch his way out on to an overhanging ledge. He paused and for a moment looked down, then gave a signal to the men handling the rope, and swung out into space. I held my breath—it was like watching a tiny marionette dangling on a string. His descent was painfully slow, or so it seemed from so great a distance, but gradually he was falling away from the ledge above. When a crosscurrent of air swung him like a reeling pendulum far out from the sheer wall, the crowd gasped but held him fast with their eyes.

I lowered my head to rub the cramp from my aching neck—it was plain torture to stand so long staring almost straight up. For the first time I noticed the faces around me, and I wasn't quite prepared for what I saw. It was an anxious crowd, and the strain was beginning to show, but there was something in their faces that reminded me of other crowds I had seen, crowds watching exhibitions of skill that had nothing to do with saving human lives. People were straining forward, unblinking and expectant, even perhaps a little prayerful, like a crowd watching to see if the aerialist plunging across the dome of the Big Top would miss his swing, or if the racing-car driver would make the last roaring circuit of the track before his frayed tyre exploded and sent him crashing into the wall, but fully prepared to enjoy those few choice seconds to the very last juicy morsel if disaster should strike. It made my stomach turn over, and I gave silent thanks that my man was safe in his patrol car somewhere over on the far side of the park.

Again an exclamation burst from the crowd, and I shaded my eyes to look. The wind had clutched the man once more and was swinging him on the long rope far out from the mountain. He seemed to hang motionless a moment while the wind held him, then swung back in a long arc and crashed into the side of the mountain. I watched, breathless, while he hung there limp as a rag. When I was convinced he was rendered unconscious, or worse, he slowly raised a thin hand in signal to the men peering down from above, and his descent began once more.

He was drawing near the trapped man now, the one farthest up, and I could see him straining to spin himself around to face the mountain. He was coming down directly over the climber, who was still clinging to his slender toe-hold, and the man gave no evidence of being aware of the ranger's presence. For an agonizing moment the two figures seemed to merge into one, then they drew apart, and as the rescued man began to rise and the other remained dangling in space, I realized for the first time that an extra rope had been brought into play.

The crowd were silent as death until the rescued man disappeared from view over the ledge at the top of the mountain; then they gave forth with a hoarse cheer that echoed far off through the valley. But my gaze was riveted on the ranger still dangling up there at the end of his slender rope. His task was but half finished, and his wife, if she was unfortunate enough to be in the crowd, still had a reeling eternity of worry to endure.

The rangers above were beginning to lower the marionette on his string again, and he settled downward until he was hanging at about the same level as the man he was trying to reach. But he couldn't manage to make contact with the man, who was several yards to the left of him, clinging motionless to the sheer wall. I groaned inwardly. Was all their nerve-racking effort going for nothing, after all? It wouldn't be humanly possible for the marooned man to cling to his perch until the entire operation was repeated in a manner that would bring his rescuer close enough to reach him.

'A rope!' someone near me shouted. 'They're letting down another rope.'

I peered closely and could see the long line snaking down from above. It came squarely into the ranger's outstretched hand and he appeared to be making it fast to his person. Then the other end of the rope, up above, began moving to the left across the ledge. When it became taut, the ranger, slowly and surely, began swinging towards the trapped man. The taut rope passed close by the nearly exhausted man, and he released one bloody hand long enough to grasp at it, then barely managed to retain his hold on the wall as a small section of rock on which his foot had been wedged suddenly broke loose, came hurtling down the mountain-side, and crashed into the lake.

'What a souvenir that'd make!' someone said. 'Sure like to have it.'

Another patrol car whirled into the area and came to a stop just behind where I was standing. Two rangers leaped out and began directing the pressing crowd back from the roadway. Spying me at the rear of the throng, one of them hurried over.

'You shouldn't be here, Marge,' he said. 'What made you come?'

'I didn't mean to,' I replied truthfully. 'I went over to Lisa's, but there was no one there, so I——'

'I'll take you home,' he broke in. 'Too hot for you to walk, anyway.'

We had just turned to leave when we were brought up short

81

by another gasp from the crowd. I whirled round to look above. The ranger on the rope was being pulled up and away from the trapped man. He appeared to pause a moment, then began a descent which was dropping him directly down on the man below. But again he stopped and hung motionless, except for the slow turning of his body as the tension in the rope swung him round and round.

'What is it?' I asked my companion. 'Something has happened.'

For a moment he didn't reply, his binoculars pressed tightly to his eyes as he peered up the mountain. 'He can't make it,' he said at last, still watching. 'There's a ridge of stone jutting out from the wall above where the man is standing, and it holds the rope too far out. He can't reach him.'

'What can he do?'

'He's signalling to the boys on top. I don't see . . .' He paused a second. 'Wait! He's beginning to move when they pull on the rope that's tied to him. That's it. They're going to try to swing him in where he can reach the fellow.'

The mounting tension of the crowd seemed to close in on me; it was hard to breathe. I shaded my eyes in an effort to see.

'Not a chance,' someone said.

'He'll never make it . . .'

'Lucky if he doesn't fall, himself, before——'

'Come on, Marge.' The ranger put a hand on my arm. 'I'm taking you home.'

I lowered my head to rub my aching eyes.

'He almost got him!' came from the crowd.

'Marge.' The grip on my arm tightened. 'Come on. You don't belong here.'

For a reeling instant I stood staring helplessly at him, and his face suddenly became a churning blur. Was he trying to tell me . . .? No. I know better than that. Still—I reached over and seized his binoculars.

'Marge, I don't think you——'

I trained the glasses up above and once again had the sensation of seeing the tiny figure leap towards me. The man on the rope was swinging in an ever-widening arc that slowly was bringing

82

him nearer and nearer to the trapped man. Something seemed familiar about the suspended figure, although his back was turned my way. It was the uniform, of course, I told myself. All rangers in uniform look pretty much . . . A gust of wind caught him, and he began slowly revolving as he swung back and forth, his momentum now almost strong enough to bring him to the narrow stone rim where the marooned man was still pressed against the wall. As he swung around I could see the ranger's fingers clutching the rope, the muscles standing out on his neck. He had revolved almost completely around now and, for some reason, he leaned to one side and peered below.

'No!' I gasped. 'It can't be!'

I was staring straight into Bill's eyes as he looked down into mine. The world began to spin in a crazy circle, and I sat suddenly down on the solid earth.

'But he was in his patrol car,' I sobbed. 'Safe in his patrol car.'

'I thought you knew.' The ranger put a steady arm around me. 'He'll be all right, Marge. He's done this before.'

I scarcely heard what he said as I struggled to get the glasses back to my eyes, and I was just in time to see the final arc as Bill swung up on to the rim of rock beside the trapped man. He seemed to be speaking to him as he inched his way nearer, and when he was within reach, the man suddenly seized Bill in a freezing grip that almost toppled them both into space. I felt myself growing faint, but I couldn't lower the glasses. Then I saw Bill's fist flash out and the frenzied man crumple in his arms. A moment later the figure of the rescued man was drawn over the top ledge, and Bill followed on the other rope close behind.

When the ranger once more insisted on taking me home, I accepted, gratefully.

Hours later Bill came swinging through our front door, tossed his Stetson on the desk, and swept me into his arms.

'Get slicked up, honey,' he grinned happily. 'There's a western on at the movie tonight. Might be exciting.'

Six

ONE bright June morning the telephone rang just as we were finishing breakfast. Headquarters was calling. A skeleton had just been discovered up at Yosemite Creek station; a road crew had found it while ploughing the road. Bill was to get right up there and see if he could identify the remains.

Bill and a party of rangers left immediately. The Yosemite Creek cabin was located in the only area of the Back Country that had not been scheduled for snow surveys that winter, so it had not been stocked with the usual blankets and food supplies and the rangers had had no occasion to visit it since the preceding fall. When they arrived at the scene, they found the skeleton in the backyard between the cabin and the stable, where it evidently had been dragged by marauding bears. During the many months it had lain there it had practically been picked clean of flesh, but the skeleton was still intact, save for the right arm, which had been pulled off and was now lying a few feet to one side. Bill picked it up and examined the hand—there still was some withered flesh at the tips of the fingers.

84

Back at headquarters, with the aid of the spatula from Bill's finger-print kit and the close co-operation of the local undertaker, a number of surgical operations were performed. When the hand had been soaked in a strong caustic solution, the fingertips expanded almost to their normal size, and prints were made and sent to J. Edgar Hoover at the Federal Bureau of Investigation, Washington, D.C.

The prints were readily identified as those of Karl A. Bentel, alias Otto Miller, etc., an alleged Communist illegally in the U.S.A. Among his effects were his diary and a Red flag bearing the familiar crossed hammer and sickle. From the diary we learned of the strange odyssey that had ultimately led to his death in the Back Country, and it took little imagination to reconstruct his story in detail:

It was well past midnight when Karl left the highway and crept stealthily off through the dark forest. The night had a chill in the air that you would not expect in California, even in the high mountain area in November. A narrow slice of moon rode high in the sky, but its light was too faint to penetrate the leafy canopy of the trees around him. He stumbled and almost fell, then stood still, cursing under his breath, listening. His heart was beating a little faster than he intended. He wasn't excited, not exactly, and he hadn't made enough noise so that he was likely to attract attention, but a man has to be cautious when he's being hunted. Prisons held no fascination for him, and he had work to do, important work. But right now the most important thing for him was to disappear, hide out a few weeks until his face was no longer a familiar sight in the police and FBI bulletins.

The only sound that reached his ears was the sighing of the wind in the towering pines, the flutter of unseen wings as some bird returned to its hidden nest, the occasional call of nocturnal creatures somewhere ahead in the darkness. Karl almost smiled as he made his way ahead, feeling a strange kinship with the night life around him. It certainly paralleled his own undertakings, he thought, doing your job in the hush of the night or, at least, performing so silently that no one was aware of your presence. Something ahead caught his eye, something white, that appeared to be suspended in air. He moved forward, cautiously, and halted. It was a metal sign with green letters painted on its face that read: PARK BOUNDARY—NO HUNTING. Karl nodded to himself and silently moved ahead.

With the first grey shadows of dawn he selected an isolated clump of dense undergrowth and made his way far inside its shelter before halting to inspect his immediate surroundings. Be ever alert to your peril, he said to himself, repeating the orders that had so often been drilled into him. Make sure of yourself and trust nobody at any time. That lesson he had learned well, and he was taking no chances, now that he was so near his goal. The stupid rangers of Yosemite—his face twisted into a sly grin—instead of apprehending him, they actually were playing right into his hands and weren't even aware of it! Dropping to the ground, he removed the little pack from his shoulders, untied the drawstring, and dumped its contents out on the leaves—three potatoes, one bunch of carrots, a small slab of bacon, and a loaf of stale bread. A cooking fire, since it would attract attention, was out of the question, so he ate a raw carrot, chewed on one corner of the bacon for a few minutes, and then filled his stomach with half a loaf of bread. And he smiled as he ate—a few more days and he would be beyond detection, eating from a well-stocked larder. From a concealed fold of his pack he drew forth a frayed, paper-bound notebook and began detailing the events of the day. His journal was his own innovation, one that would never leave him at a loss for explanation in case he was required to give account. Then he lay on the ground and was almost immediately fast asleep.

A few days later he found himself far up in the Back Country of the high Sierra, away from prying eyes, and victory was almost within his grasp. Now he could travel by day, and his eyes were bright as he constantly climbed and searched the mountainside for the cabin. It was all very simple, really, and tailor-made for his purposes. These lonely cabins, he had been instructed, separated by a day's march from each other and located at strategic points throughout the Back Country, had been built for the emergency protection of rangers on snow surveys. They were stocked with blankets and an abundance of food, and food was something that

Karl was intensely interested in at the moment. Ever since his meagre supply had given out the day before, he had been plagued by a gnawing pain in his stomach that constantly prodded his lagging feet to greater efforts.

It was near nightfall when he first saw the cabin. It was nestled beside some stunted lodgepole pines at the base of a majestic reach of mountains, barely visible in the gathering dusk. With the end of his journey in sight Karl quickened his pace, for the cabin still was quite a distance away. Dark, ominous-looking clouds were pushing against the mountain peaks, and a stillness both strange and unreal seemed to hover over the desolate mountainside.

When he reached the little porch, he was nearly exhausted, but he had made it and was supremely happy. Now he could eat his fill and sleep comfortably between warm blankets until it was once more safe to be about his business. Pushing open the unlocked door, he entered the cabin; it was dark as a tomb inside, and the squeaking of the floor underfoot lent an eerie, disquieting sound to the lonely room. But he had no time or patience for these idle thoughts—food was there, and he had a painful craving for food, lots of it. His groping hands met the cold metal of the stove, and he immediately returned for the corded wood he had bumped into on the front porch.

When the fire sprang up in the stove, he stood a moment warming his hands, peering around the room in the dancing light. There was no bed, he noticed; in fact the only furnishings were a pot-bellied stove, a rough table, and a handmade bench at its side. Some barren shelves stared out at him from one wall, and he suddenly turned and walked over to the cupboard built diagonally across the far corner of the room. As he threw open the door, his breath seemed to stick in his throat, then escaped with a rush—the closet, save for an old broom and shovel, was as empty as the barren shelves. He whirled and ran to the cupboard behind the stove. With one hand on the door he hesitated a second, dreading to know the truth if it, too, was empty. Then slowly he pulled it open and stood staring at the shelves—they held only an old stew kettle, one bent spoon, and a blackened coffee-pot. Stumbling back in disbelief he continued to stare. His information had always been correct. 'Blankets and food are provided in all ranger cabins,' his instructions had stated. Then, as he stepped farther back, his eyes caught sight of something in the shadows of the top shelf.

Seizing the table, Karl jerked it over beneath the open cupboard. He was on it in a second, greedily running his fingers over the cans stacked there—two cans of pork and beans, one can of apricots, and another of tomatoes. His eyes lit up, and he rubbed his hands in anticipation. A feast, he told himself. That's what he'd have. With his knife he slit open all the cans, dumped their contents together in the big stew kettle, and placed it on the stove.

With his belly filled to bursting, he sat down at the table, groaned in contentment, and drew from the concealed fold of his pack the frayed little notebook no man but he had ever seen. Karl loved to talk, but he dared trust no one. He could confide only in this one friend, and it had proved a great comfort to a lonely man. 'Arrived at Yosemite Creek ranger station November 25, 1934,' he wrote. 'Cabin not stocked as advised. I will continue on tomorrow and locate one that has plenty of food and blankets . . .'

The weather was turning cold—he could feel the sting from the air blowing through the cracks of the clapboard cabin—and when he finished with the notebook and went to the porch for more wood, he was surprised to find it was snowing. But he didn't give it much thought. Right now he had a full stomach and the red-hot stove kept him warm as toast. Tomorrow he would move on to another cabin where the supply of food and blankets was such that he could live in comfort. But tonight he was here, and there were a number of magazines and old newspapers near the stove just waiting to be read.

Dropping fresh wood on the fire, he spread some of the magazines on the table before him. Unconsciously his left hand slipped in and out of his coat pocket, travelled up to explore the empty breast pockets of his shirt before he was aware of his actions, and his face twisted into a crooked grin. For the first time in more than a year he was feeling the urge for a cigarette—a pleasure he had denied himself for reasons of security. But now he would have enjoyed its tangy taste immeasurably, could almost feel the smoke curling from his lips. It's knowing that I am safe, he told himself. Absolutely safe for the first time. The return of custom and old habits that were almost forgotten was a true indication of his contentment and peace of mind.

Near the bottom of the pile of magazines he came across a few law-enforcement folders, left there by some ranger, and a bulletin from the Federal Bureau of Investigation. These he read to the very last word. Some of the faces shown in the pictures were familiar, but the names of the men were not those by which he had known them. After hours of a solid contentment he hadn't thought himself capable of, he finally filled the stove with wood, pulled the table nearer, stretched out on its top, and closed his eyes. What a huge joke this was, he thought, as he drifted off into sleep. Hiding out in a shelter built by the government, eating food provided for the rangers, lying here beside a roaring fire with no immediate care in the world. . . .

It was daylight when Karl wakened, and the cabin was uncomfortably cold. He sat up, shivering, and peered at his watch. The hands pointed to ten minutes past nine. Shaking the time-piece, he listened to its steady ticking. Strange, he thought, it should be broad daylight at this hour. Walking to the door he threw it open and stood in amazement looking out on a desolate world buried in a swirling blanket of snow. He closed the door and quickly kindled a fire in the stove. Might as well get warm before starting out; it would be a day's walk to the next cabin. His gaze wandered about the bare room; he was hungry and there just might be some food stacked away somewhere. But there was no food except some particles that had clung to the cans he had opened the night before. Scooping one can full of snow he melted it over the fire and poured the water back and forth into the other cans until the last crumb was collected. This he placed on the stove until it was hot, then drained the can to the last drop. It wasn't too appetizing, but better than nothing. Selecting three of the most likely-looking magazines, he stuffed them into his pack for reading that night, shrugged the pack on to his back, and headed for the door.

With the door latch in his hand he hesitated, then strode out on to the porch and stopped. Snow was coming down so thickly that the countryside had all but disappeared. Light was obscured until it seemed almost twilight, and it gave one the feeling of being smothered just to peer into it. The valley was gone, the mountains were hidden behind the white falling curtain; it was impossible to distinguish objects a few feet beyond the edge of the porch. Slowly Karl turned and walked back into the cabin. No use to start out now. You could walk in circles all day and never know it; chance of finding the next cabin was too slim, nobody could be sure of anything in a storm like this. Let it snow, he said, dropping his pack to the floor, and the harder the better. It's just like a rain-storm that turns into a cloudburst—won't last long.

By noon he dismissed the idea of starting out that day. Even if there were a full moon, it would be next to impossible to locate the next cabin if he arrived after nightfall. Adding more fuel to the fire, he went out into the yard to probe around behind the cabin; you never know what can be turned up in odd places. What he turned up was a plank stable where the rangers sometimes quartered their horses and pack animals, and he was almost within reach of it before it loomed up in his path. He walked inside and looked around. Nothing was there but a small pile of hay in one corner, a broken halter hanging from a peg on the wall, and a five-gallon rusty tin container almost at his feet. He was turning to leave when his glance again fell on the container, and he stooped to remove the lid. Inside were a few broken pieces of rock salt and some barley.

Lifting the can in his arms, he waded out into the deep snow and headed for where he thought the cabin should be. When he had covered more than the distance that should have brought him to the back door, he stopped and made a short excursion to the right, then to the left. Smoke from the chimney was heavy in the air, but the building was nowhere in sight. He stood still a moment, collecting his thoughts, then began retracing his steps for a new start—and suddenly found himself sprawled on the cabin's front porch.

It was good to be inside again, and he placed his find on the table while melting more snow in the big kettle. When the water was hot he poured in some barley, added a lump of rock salt and sat back to wait. The situation was becoming more critical with each passing moment, he told the notebook. Already snow was deep enough to make travelling a real burden, but it couldn't snow like this for ever and as soon as it stopped he would be on his way, probably starting in early evening, which should bring him to the next cabin during daylight hours. When the porridge was cooked, he ate his fill and lay down on the long table to catch a nap. He noticed it was still snowing. When he wakened, just before dark, the storm gave no indication of abating. He finished the barley, replenished the stove, and turned in for the night.

It was cold when Karl wakened, bitterly cold, and the wind was driving snow between the wall-boards and depositing it in straight white lines that reached out almost to the middle of the room. The fire was out. He walked stiffly to the front door and pulled it open. An imprint of the rough door was traced into the packed snow that stood up straight before him blocking the way. Standing on the tip of his toes, he was able to peer outside into the dim light of morning. At last it had stopped snowing, but a howling gale was piling the white flakes into huge drifts higher than he had ever seen; the little canyon where the cabin stood between the towering mountains was drifting fantastically deep. He dug out a few sticks of firewood and slammed the door.

For the first time Karl was really concerned. No one could possibly force his way through snow as deep as this; the drifts appeared to be as much as ten feet high, with two or three feet of snow on the level ground. After rekindling the fire, he stood warming his hands, cursing and considering his plight. One thing was certain, he couldn't live here for ever without food, and there should be plenty of food in the next cabin if only he could reach it. Suddenly he strode to the rear door and flung it open. Another wall of snow greeted him. A hard crust was freezing over the drift, but it was not yet solid enough to support his weight. Fetching the shovel from the closet, he probed until he found an old barrel he remembered seeing standing beside the door. He dug it free, carried it into the cabin, and collapsed it on the floor with a sharp blow from the shovel. Selecting two of the strongest staves from the pile, he placed them on the table and stood a minute considering them before once more seizing the shovel and moving to the rear door.

For several hours he laboured, forcing a narrow, shallow tunnel through the deep snow in the direction of the stable. He was weak from hunger and close to exhaustion when he finally reached its doorway and climbed to his feet. Lifting the broken halter from its peg, he paused to loosen a few nails from the rough walls before returning to the doorway. He dropped to his knees before the open tunnel, then halted once more as his gaze rested on a round tin box beside the door that he had somehow overlooked. Opening the lid, he pressed a finger against the waxy content. Axle grease, he said to himself, and took the box with him into the tunnel.

That night he sat down at the table and opened his notebook. 'My snowshoes are ready,' he wrote. 'Made them from barrel staves and straps from a halter. Will try to get away tomorrow. I still can't understand how my information about food could be so wrong. One mistake like this on my part and—p-f-f-f-t!'

Karl was up early next morning and cooked a generous helping of barley to sustain him on the trail. On the bottom of the crude snowshoes he rubbed some of the axle grease, not being sure if he should or not, then filling his pockets with dry barley, in case of emergency, he slung his pack across his back and picked up the snowshoes.

Once outside the cabin it immediately became evident that without snowshoes he would be entirely helpless. After wallowing across the drifted front porch, he sank to his armpits and cursed as he struggled to raise himself to the surface of the snow, but the weight of his body was more than the frozen crust would support. He finally made it, by placing the barrel-stave snowshoes on the surface and resting his weight on them while lifting himself up from the hole he had churned in the snow. It was another battle to get the halter straps wound around his ankles and securely tied. But when they were made fast, he lost no time in shoving off. Coasting a few yards to the bottom of the slope, he managed to walk up the little rise to the long incline leading steeply down towards the valley. It was a difficult manœuvre for an inexperienced man to make, and was made doubly hard by the clumsy staves that would not cling snugly to his feet, but when he finally gained the crest he took a long breath and leaned forward.

He had gone but a few feet when he realized it was impossible to control his glide; every sharp rise in the snow sent him careening wildly off in another direction. Then it happened so suddenly he had no chance to break his fall—his feet shot out at right angles to each other and he pitched forward on his face. It was some time before he could draw his legs under him, feeling as if they had been wrenched off at the hips, and he sat gazing at the staves standing upright in the snow where his feet had left them. The leather strap on one of them had broken loose where he had nailed it on to the wood; the strap on the other was broken in two pieces with one end still dangling from his ankle. They were impossible, and he knew it. Leaving them standing where they were, he began to retrace his steps, flailing and churning on the short way back for what seemed an eternity before he once more reached the doubtful security of the cabin.

The struggle left him winded and a little dizzy, and he dropped on the table and closed his eyes. There was no doubt about it now, he told himself, he was marooned here until a firm crust was frozen on the snow that would support his weight; then he could walk away. Might as well make myself comfortable, he said, and began bringing into the cabin all the wood that had been stacked on the front porch. Then, thoughtfully, he opened the can of axle grease, spread small daubs of it on all the walls, and busied himself with pressing sheets of newspapers tightly against it to keep out the driving wind. Pouring the barley from his pockets back into the tin container, he measured it with his eye; there was enough to last him several weeks, he was sure, if he ate sparingly, just enough to retain his strength.

It was weeks later when Karl finally abandoned the last of his fading hopes of ever getting away. It wasn't easy to admit that you had failed, when defeat meant paying with your life, but there was no other way to look at it. Each time, before the snow had crusted solid enough to support him, the temperature had risen slightly, or more snow had fallen. Still hoping, he had spread his meagre food supply to the point where he had become weaker by the day. Now it was all but gone; the last of the barley was slowly boiling in the big kettle.

He wrote for a time in his notebook, then dozed off again—it seemed he slept more and more as he grew weaker. When he awakened, his nostrils were filled with the pungent odour of barley burning on the stove, but he scraped the kettle and ate it clean. The cabin was getting cold again, and the last of the wood was in the stove. There was but one place from where the supply could be renewed, and he had dreaded the exertion it would require. Finally he opened the rear door and slowly crawled off through the snow tunnel.

Reaching the stable he managed to loosen a plank and had started dragging it across the earthen floor when he suddenly stopped. 'Hay,' he said aloud. 'There must be some strength in this stuff.' He stood a moment staring down at the little pile of hay, then stuffed both pockets full and crawled on into the tunnel. Back in the cabin he filled the kettle with melted snow and several handfuls of hay and placed it on the stove. Then he broke the stable plank into stove lengths with the shovel and fed it into the fire before sitting down to wait. The greenish liquid that came from the boiling hay proved to be rather tasteless, although it did help to fill the emptiness in his stomach. But an hour later he was cramped with a dysentery that left him weaker than before.

A howling blizzard was sweeping across the mountains next morning when Karl opened his eyes. The fire had burned itself out, and the cabin was frigidly cold. His legs were stiff and numb as he struggled to sit up, and the room swam before his eyes. But he must have more fuel for the fire or he would soon freeze. He managed to crawl across the floor on hands and knees and once more disappeared into the tunnel. At the other end he paused a moment to regain his breath while his gaze followed the efforts of a fat pack rat that was nosing through the horse droppings on the floor. His eyes greedily followed the rat as it scurried away, then he suddenly crawled forward and began a frantic search where the rat had been feeding. His fingers came upon bits of grain and an occasional whole kernel of corn. His hand was almost filled

94

when he had finished and he clenched it tight shut as he crawled back into the tunnel, dragging another plank behind him.

It was a tense, agonizing moment when he was ready to relight the fire, and he didn't breathe until flames were leaping high up in the stove. Never again would the fire be allowed to burn itself out—he had struck his last match.

It was an unsavoury mess he finally spooned from the kettle, but he ate it to the last kernel, and drank the watery broth until it was gone. When he had finished he sat staring into space until his eyes focused on the old notebook lying open before him on the table. Slowly he drew it to him and got the pencil poised between his fingers. He put the date in the upper corner—January 4, 1935, and just below, for the first time, he added his initials—K.A.B. The pencil began to slide away and he tightened his grip on it; the notebook became strangely dim and he touched it to be sure it was there. 'Strange,' he wrote, 'how things don't seem real any more. Almost like . . .'

The fire burned low, fluttered, and finally died. The darkening room grew still as a tomb. Outside, the mournful wailing of the blizzard was piling snow high over the lonely little cabin hidden between the tall mountains.

Seven

ONE morning we were lying late in bed, 7.30 a.m. It was Bill's day off duty, and I was trying to capture a few extra winks of sleep. I knew he was wide-awake, as he always is at the crack of dawn, for he was tossing about restlessly. Several times he rose on one elbow, and I could feel him peering down at me, but I didn't move a muscle. When I was almost asleep again, he slowly lifted my eyelid and looked in at me.

'You awake yet, Marge?'

I closed my eye and breathed sonorously.

'I just wanted to tell you,' he said softly, 'that the Yosemite Park superintendent and his wife are coming over tonight for dinner.'

'What!' My eyes flew open and I sat up with a jerk that rocked the bed. 'Dinner! Tonight! . . . Who?'

'Superintendent and his wife. Guess I sort of forgot to tell you.'

'How . . . W-why?' I stammered.

'I invited them yesterday, when I was in his office. Just happened to think about the prime rib roast we have in the icebox. Don't have a prime rib too often, you know.'

'Yes. But—but——'

'Nobody fixes it like you do, Marge—golden crust all over and the inside oozing with juice.'

'But I had an electric stove then,' I cried, 'not an old wood-burner.'

I never learned just what delicacies he had promised the superintendent, for, leaping out of bed, I stumbled into my slippers and dashed through the doorway with my nightgown streaming straight out behind. For a fleeting moment I was sorely tempted to fix a roast that would end all roasts—like garnishing it with vanilla sauce, or treating it to a good four-hour burn. But I couldn't do that to the superintendent and his lovely wife, or, to be wholly truthful, to Bill, either. No woman would like her husband making excuses for her poor cooking, even if she hadn't yet gained too much experience and, especially, experience cooking on a wood stove. After all, he must be a little proud of me or he wouldn't have asked them over.

Bill went outside to do some work in the fire-equipment shed, and I fell to preparing the vegetables and salad. I was taking my cake from the oven when he returned, and the telephone was ringing our number.

'Accident near Wowona tunnel,' the receiver shrilled in his ear. 'Couple of Indians ran off the road. Fellow that called in said one is dead and the other is wedged between the car and a tree—can't get him out . . . I'm sending the ambulance. Make it quick, will you, Bill?'

Bill dashed from the house and roared away; I went back to shelling my peas. I should have known it was going to be 'one of those days', as Bill calls them, when the roof falls in on you just as it's starting to rain, but I was too occupied to lend it a thought. My first interruption came while I was stemming the berries—a hiker wanted to get a campfire permit, a chore I usually perform while Bill is away.

It was Sunday, which always brings an influx of interruptions to any ranger station, so I decided to get the roast in the oven as soon as possible, while there was time to superintend its preparation. I was putting fresh wood into the stove when the telephone rang our number. The park naturalist was calling.

'Very busy?'

'Well——' I hesitated.

'I have a magazine photographer here,' he went on. 'Wants to get some pictures of a snow plant. Know where he can find one?'

I knew.

'I simply can't get away right now, and he's in a hurry. Would you mind pointing it out to him?'

With one eye on the roaring wood fire and the other straying towards the uncooked roast still resting on the table, I agreed, and managed to change into a different frock and get the roast inside the oven before the man showed up with his camera.

We climbed the steep, rough trail behind the station, for a half mile, and hiked across a mountain meadow before I pointed out the snow plant I had been watching ever since the snows had left. The man was delighted, and after replacing the barricade of sticks to guard against straying feet, we started back.

When I returned to the kitchen, the fire in the wood-burner had gone out, and the stove was cold. I got more kindling and started it once more. Bill got home about eleven o'clock, said he was late because Dr. Dewey had asked him to go along to the hospital and help put casts on the broken arm and leg of the Indian he had saved out of the wreck. We were just sitting down to a noonday snack when a strange man walked in without knocking and came up to the table.

'I've been bitten by a rattlesnake,' he said, holding his wrist. 'What do I do now?'

'Sit down and keep a tight grip on your wrist,' Bill ordered, and dashed into the bathroom.

'I was fishing in a pool near here,' the man told me. 'Must have put my hand right down on the snake when I got up.'

Bill was back. 'Don't like it,' he said, inserting the hypo needle. 'This antidote looks a little milky, not a bright amber colour like it should be. You got a car handy?'

'No,' the man said. 'Friend's supposed to pick me up later. On vacation, you know. I'm a cop—Los Angeles.'

'Better have the doctor look at this,' Bill said. 'Come on, I'll take you to the hospital.'

When they had gone, I found the kitchen fire all but burned out and rebuilt it. I had finished my solitary lunch and was tidying up the house when Mary, a friend of mine, dropped in for a few minutes. She mentioned a crowd of people she had passed on the road.

'They were watching some bears,' she said. 'A mother and two cubs. Let's go have a look.'

I put more wood on the fire, got in the car with her, and drove over to watch—the people, I mean. They're usually more fun than the bears. A prissy little woman from Massachusetts was feeding pieces of candy to the old bear while another was busy clicking the camera. She was so occupied with posing that she paid no need to the big brute as it opened its yawning mouth and snapped the morsels from her fingers. Each time I looked to make sure her hand was still there—it made my blood run cold. Then the one who had taken the pictures climbed into her car, rolled down the glass, and beckoned to the bear with another bar of candy. When it lumbered over to the car and reared up to get it, she suddenly plopped one end of the candy bar in her mouth and leaned out of the window, smiling for the benefit of the camera.

'Good heavens!' Mary gasped.

How the bear actually snatched the bar from her lips without taking half of her face with it, I'll never know. That was enough for one day, and we were preparing to leave when we saw a man with a little boy in his arms hurry over to the frolicking cubs, where he dropped the boy on the ground between them and stood grinning at the picture it made. The old bear took one look at her unprotected cubs and started after the man. When she was almost on him, he turned and tossed a handful of marshmallows at her feet. While the bear was occupied with the added sweets, the man put one in the little boy's hand and motioned for him to feed the pretty mamma bear. We were frozen in our tracks when the little boy suddenly became interested in the candy just as the big bear was reaching for it. But at that moment the man happened to toss another handful on the ground, and the bear immediately forgot the lone piece the boy was putting in his own mouth. The man smiled happily, turned on his heel, and started towards the road.

'Hey there!' Mary screeched. 'Where you going?'

The man looked our way. 'I've got more candy in the car, and I'm——'

'You get right back there!' Mary yelled like a leather-lunged top sergeant. 'Take that little boy with you!'

The man went back for the boy, grumbling under his breath about smart-aleck women. Mary grumbled, too, something about God taking care of knuckle-headed baboons and little children.

The cookstove fire was out again when I got back to the kitchen, the third time my roast had suffered from lack of heat. It was beginning to be a sickly-looking thing, and I was feeling the same. But it looked beautiful when I placed it on the table that evening, and I waited, breathless, while Bill did the carving.

When the last plate had been passed I sat there coiled up like a tension spring, ready for instant flight. Bill sampled his helping and looked at his boss. The superintendent took a small bite and looked at Bill. I was ready to explode when they finally turned to me.

'Marge,' the superintendent said gravely, 'this is, without a doubt, one occasion I shall never forget.' He paused. Then: 'This roast is simply beyond words—it's more than delicious!'

I had held my breath so long I was turning green, and I uncoiled so suddenly I knew my ears were flapping in relief.

'It is absolutely perfect!' his wife was saying. 'I hope you remember the exact temperature you kept the oven! I know it's so important.'

I smiled weakly. I did remember something, though, and I heartily agreed with Mary in doing so—God surely does protect his knuckle-headed offspring.

One wintry day Bill and I started for Fresno, where we had been invited to attend a formal ball in a large hotel. The trip to Fresno during the winter has always fascinated me. We may leave Yosemite in a swirling blizzard and within thirty minutes be driving down through a sunny valley studded with lupine, redbud, and poppies. There are flowers everywhere—it never seems quite possible, even in California. Bill had bought a pin-striped, double-breasted suit, and I was wearing, for the first time, a beautiful taffeta evening gown I had selected for the occasion. Bill was amusing himself making sly remarks about the high overshoes I was wearing—they were peeping out from beneath my gown—when he suddenly slowed the car and came to a sudden stop.

'What's the matter?' I asked.

'Tracks back there in the snow,' he said. 'Looks like a car might have skidded off the road.'

He reversed the car.

I said nothing.

'Back in a minute.' He jumped out of the car and hurried down a bluff towards the river, following the tracks.

I waited.

Five minutes later he was back, holding in his arms a small Indian boy, covered with mud and dripping water from every pore.

'Fished him out of the river,' Bill said. 'Car upset down there. There were three Indians and this kid. Open the door, Marge.'

I opened the door.

'Bill!'

Before I could do anything but gasp, he plopped the oozing youngster in the middle of my lap.

'He'd freeze down there,' he said calmly. 'Keep him warm, honey. Put your coat around him. I've got to get back to the others.' He rushed off.

I put the car blanket round him.

An hour later Bill and the three adult Indians, with the help of a tow-car, managed to get the car back on to the highway. Bill handed over the little fellow, who was fast asleep, bundled in our only car blanket, and we continued the journey.

'My dress is ruined!' I wailed. 'What will people think when they see me?'

'I'm sorry, Marge,' he said. 'Just wasn't anything else we could do.'

We were quite late getting to the hotel, and Bill dropped me at the entrance while he disposed of the car. Inside the lobby I thought I was attracting undue attention, although I held my coat close around my soiled dress.

'May I, miss?'

I spun around and stared at the grinning bellboy.

'Your arctic boots,' he said, pointing at my feet. 'Don't believe you will need them in here, miss.'

When Bill checked our wraps, the girl behind the counter seemed unable to take her eyes from my beautiful gown—the splotch on the front, I mean.

'Do you have cleaning service in the hotel?' Bill inquired.

The girl nodded. 'Through the door at the end of the hall.'

We waited while my gown was cleaned and pressed. It looked fresh as new. On our way to the ballroom we passed close by the same girl, and I noticed her eyes carefully following us. Bill stopped and leaned over the counter.

'An Indian went to sleep in her lap,' he whispered.

The girl nodded absently, then suddenly backed away as if Bill were a bearer of the bubonic plague.

'Come along, Marge,' Bill grinned. 'I think this is my dance.'

Late in May, 1931, came a day that was set aside for great rejoicing by Japanese-Americans, most of whom were to be found on the West Coast. Prince Takamatsu and his princess were to visit California's Yosemite National Park, a delightful pleasure they had tenderly nursed for many years. The impending arrival of the royal couple had been front-page copy for weeks, and the big park was made ready, as usual, for any eventuality—or so the officials thought. Colonel Thomson, who was then superintendent of Yosemite, had once made a tour of Japan while serving as assistant director of Philippine prisons and had been extended every possible courtesy by Prince Takamatsu while in that country. This was the colonel's first opportunity to reciprocate.

The route from El Portel, the railhead, through Arch Rock, along the all-year highway to the Ahwahnee Hotel, was laid out, discussed, and rehearsed. All side roads were to be blocked by rangers so that the caravan could travel directly through to the hotel without meeting any traffic, as ordered by the U.S. Secret Service. Bill was to lead the procession on a gleaming new motorcycle, and Harry Deming would be a short distance behind him, mounted on another motor-cycle. Third would be a car occupied by men with Browning automatic rifles and enough riot guns to disperse a small army. Then would come the flag-draped limousine of the Prince and Princess, followed by another car bearing their staff and servants. The final vehicle would be a patrol car manned by two armed rangers. Every precaution was to be taken to guarantee the royal couple's safety.

The great day arrived, and with it came thousands of Japanese-Americans. The park was teeming with them, each one harbouring a fanatical passion to get as near to the Ahwahnee Hotel, the terminus of the caravan, as was humanly possible. At the train the royal party boarded the limousine, and the procession immediately got under way, Bill taking off first, followed at regular intervals by the other vehicles. Everything was progressing according to schedule.

Before reaching the sharp winding road leading into Yosemite Valley, Bill glanced behind him and nodded his satisfaction. They were travelling at forty-five miles an hour, and each unit was keeping far enough behind the next to preclude an accident in case the vehicle ahead was forced to make a sudden stop around a blind curve. Taking one more quick look to the rear, the last he would have before reaching the valley, Bill leaned into the first twisting curve.

I knew Bill was approaching long before he came into sight. His motor-cycle and its wailing siren could be heard for a country mile. I was wedged into the buzzing throng directly in front of the Ahwahnee, where the royal couple would step from their limousine. Excitement was in the air, and every available ranger was there trying to control the wide-eyed crowd that was threatening to burst out into the parking area as the tension mounted. It is not often that I am caught up in a crowd if there is any possible way I can escape. Today it was different. Bill was wearing, for the first time, his brand-new uniform, including high gauntlet gloves of pure buckskin leather and a pair of brown scotch-grained boots that he had polished to a mirror brightness. I was proud of my ranger and wanted to see him as he led the caravan into the valley.

The huge throng was rapidly getting out of hand as the scream of Bill's siren drew nearer. The rangers were shouting for everyone to stand back, please! U.S. Secret Service men were everywhere, searching for a fanatical face that could spell trouble, a nervous hand that might suddenly reach for a gun. Then the crowd let loose a wild roar as Bill swung around the bend and headed down the middle of the road towards us. I found myself standing on the tip of my toes, without realizing that not one of the people around me reached as high as my shoulder.

Then Bill was upon us, eyes looking neither to right nor left, like a general on dress parade, and a thrilling sight he was in his neatly pressed uniform, gleaming boots, and spotless white gloves. I was tingling all over as he came to a sweeping halt, switched off the moaning siren, and cut the engine. Expertly he climbed from the motor-cycle and with a grand flourish removed his gloves. Then he straightened to his full height, nonchalantly slapped the gloves across his glittering boots, spun around, and stood at attention.

The first inkling I had that something was amiss dawned on me when I saw the look of disbelief slowly spreading across Bill's face. I turned to look where he was staring. The roadway was as barren as the middle of the Sahara—the royal procession was nowhere to be seen! The cheering had died to a frantic whispering, and the enormous crowd was standing transfixed. The only movement I could see anywhere was the headlong flight of Secret Service men converging from every direction on Bill, who stood uncertain, as if debating whether to stay and fight or take to the tall timbers.

'What's happened?' they were demanding.

'What's wrong?'

'Where are the Prince and Princess?'

Bill shook his head. 'I don't know,' he said, still peering with wide-eyed incredulity down the empty highway. 'I just don't know.'

'When was the last you saw them?'

'Just before I left the straight road out there.'

'Could they have dropped behind?'

'Not supposed to,' Bill said. 'We were to keep a proper distance from each other, to avoid collisions around the curves. Every driver was to maintain a forty-five mile speed—I did.'

Just then another shout went up from the anxious throng. Ranger Deming was appearing around the bend in the road, and necks were craned in his direction. He halted his motor-cycle beside Bill's and swung off. The commotion had again just begun to fade when the car bearing the armed guards showed up in the distance. It, too, rolled up and stopped before the hotel. Necks immediately swivelled back as the crowd eagerly waited for the royal carriage to come into view. Then, after a longer wait, the next car put in its appearance, and the crowd went wild. The car was overflowing with little men, thin ones, fat ones, and medium ones. But the crowd became silent as death when the car drew near. The Secret Service men turned to Bill.

'Is the Prince in there?'

'Is that the royal car?'

'No.' Bill looked as puzzled as anyone else. 'Those people are his servants.'

'Servants! Where's Prince Takamatsu and the Princess?'

'Servants don't ride in front of their prince.'

'They weren't in front of him when I last saw them,' Bill said. 'This car was behind the Prince's limousine.'

'Then that means . . .'

Another car was coming around the curve driving rapidly with siren screaming. It was occupied by two rangers, the rear guard.

'That was the last car,' Bill yelled, running for his motor-cycle. 'The Prince's car has disappeared!'

His motor-cycle burst into a roar and Secret Service men raced for their cars. But they were stopped in their tracks by the tumultuous cheer that suddenly went up from the crowd. Sweeping majestically around the bend in the road, another car was approaching—the flag-draped royal limousine—with the bowing Prince Takamatsu and his smiling princess acknowledging the welcome of the huge crowd.

The answer to the riddle was really quite simple, if irregular.

With his first glimpse of the Bridal Veil Fall, Prince Takamatsu was carried away with its beauty and asked—demanded by royal command—that they leave the procession for an immediate inspection. They had crossed over the Pohono Bridge and had come up the South Road without the escort. Unable to be seen leaving the caravan, because of the many sharp turns in the road, his absence was not discovered until Yosemite park officers and men of the Secret Service were convinced an international incident was surely in the making.

Eight

WHEREVER we live in the national parks we always seem to fall heir to a collection of wild animals, with some repeaters following from one station to another. During one period we moved eleven times within two and a half years, but there was never any deficiency of animal life around us. We love them all, from our lumbering five-hundred-pound bear to the perky little chipmunk who now dines with us from the window-sill each morning—so long as we provide the breakfast. During the snowed-in winter months we sometimes learn to know them best, the bullies and the shy ones, the bluffer and the clown, they're all here, the counterparts of our own human family.

We inherited Porky a few years ago when we moved into the station at the south entrance to Yosemite, although we didn't know it immediately. Moving day is a busy time for anyone. However, a ranger is rotated so many times—a custom intended to familiarize him with all park locations—that it makes the chore less troublesome, especially when the house is one in which he has previously lived. So by evening we had everything in place and were enjoying a late dinner when Porky first announced his presence.

It started as a sort of nibbling sound, as if something or someone was taking a few experimental bites from the timbers somewhere beneath the floor. After a few minutes of nipping here and biting there, whatever it was chose a favourite spot and pulled out all the stops. It wasn't quite like anything I had ever heard before, and we grow accustomed to many eerie night sounds that the city dwellers never hear. It filled the house to overflowing, it bored into my ears and distracted me from my newspaper. Bill said nothing about it, and I remained silent as long as I possibly could.

'For heaven's sake!' I finally exploded. 'What on earth is making that horrible noise?'

Bill looked up from the sports section. 'Porcupine under the house,' he said calmly, and turned to the fishing news.

All evening it kept up, never ceasing for one second—gnaw, grate, crunch! I couldn't get away from it; the book in front of me became a blur, and at any instant I expected to feel the house crashing down around my ears. But it didn't—gnaw, grate, crunch! We went to bed, and Bill, as usual fell asleep at once. I lay in a nerve-bound knot waiting for the first quivering dip when the floor would give way. At least a million sheep went over the fence while I counted their curly little tails—gnaw, grate, crunch! I got out of bed, walked unsteadily to the bathroom, where I got a drink of water—and the noise stopped.

It was like the end of hostilities, and my ears rang with the silence, but before I could reach the bed it started all over again. I went back to the bathroom and experimented: each time I turned on the tap Porky would stop chewing, when I turned it off he would begin. I left the tap full on and went to bed. But it didn't work. When I was just beginning to think I had masterminded him—gnaw, grate, crunch! I shook Bill; he grunted, turned over, and continued to snore. I swung out of bed and marched defiantly back to the bathroom. 'All right, Mr. Porky,' I hissed. 'If a little water frightens you, I'll scare your pants right off!' I pulled the chain above the bowl.

When the water stopped running the house was quiet as a

country graveyard at midnight. But I waited . . . waited . . . It was so still I could hear the ticking of the big clock in the front room. It had worked, I was sure of it now. I could almost see Porky scurrying away through the forest with his quills tucked between his legs. Dashing across the room, I leaped into bed and pulled the covers over my head.

I was working on my three hundred and sixth sheep when it started again. I groaned, burrowed deep under my pillow, and pulled it down tight around my ears—gnaw, grate, crunch! I sat up in bed and glared at Bill—nothing on earth could waken him but the ringing of the telephone bell. He always came alive with the first note. I prayed for it to ring . . . It didn't ring. I got wearily out of bed, recovered my book from the mantel, and made my way back to the bathroom. The rest of the night was calm and peaceful—at the end of each page I automatically pulled the chain.

'We'll have to do something about that porcupine,' Bill said next morning. 'I'll take care of him this evening when I get home.'

Not a sound came from Porky all day long—I suppose a porcupine has to sleep sometime—and I was quiet as a mouse while I tiptoed around doing my work lest I waken him to re-newed activity. It was dinner-time when he again took his first warm-up bites.

'I'll scare him away,' Bill said as he sprang up from the table. 'When I shoot under the house he'll come out back here. You watch for him.'

He darted out of the front door, and almost immediately I heard the reports as he fired repeatedly beneath the floor. When came he back inside, I was still seated at the table.

'Where did he go?' he asked. 'Didn't you watch for him?'

I merely turned my thumb towards the floor—Porky hadn't missed a juicy bite.

'Have to set a trap,' Bill finally decided. 'Didn't want to do it.' He hurried out of the rear door.

It was after eleven, and I was beginning to have visions of another bathroom vigil, when we heard the trap snap shut. Porky was a nice fat fellow, and he was held in the trap by the toenails of one back foot. Bill dragged him out and upended a garbage can over him before releasing the trap. 'You sit on him, Marge,' he called. 'I'll get something to hold the can down all night.'

The next morning Bill loaded Porky into a big box waiting in the car and drove away. He said he would turn him free far off in the forest where he could never find his way back to us. After they were gone I didn't feel as overjoyed about it as I had thought I would—in fact, it sort of bothered me. Come to think of it, Porky undoubtedly had been here long before we came, probably was born under this very house. What right did we really have to drag him off like a sack of garbage and dump him somewhere in a strange world? He was a perfect nuisance, I reminded myself, and only a porcupine, but somehow I couldn't make myself feel the way I wanted to about it. When Bill came home an hour later, he was wearing that little-boy look that always sets me back on my heels.

'I couldn't do it,' he said, a little embarrassed. 'This is the only home Porky knows. I just couldn't do it, Marge.'

I nodded my head, relieved in spite of myself.

'He won't be here much longer, anyway,' Bill added. 'He's about big enough now to take to the woods.'

The gnawing continued for several more weeks, and gradually we became almost immune to it. Then one night I found myself sitting bolt upright in bed, wakened from a sound sleep. Bill actually stirred and got up on one elbow. Something was wrong, but we didn't know what it could be. Then it dawned on both of us at the same instant—the gnawing wasn't there. It had stopped. Bill jumped out of bed and hurried across the room.

'Come, Marge,' he whispered. 'Look.'

I joined him at the window. Porky was waddling off through the moonlight, with a Mrs. Porky and two little ones close behind. They disappeared into the forest, and we never saw them again.

In 1949 we were transferred to Olympic National Park. This wilderness park, located in the Olympic Peninsula at the northwestern tip of the state of Washington, abounds with types of wildlife not found at Yosemite in California. During the first summer months at Storm King station we became aware of a small flock of mallard ducks that appeared in the sky each morning, flying in their usual formation. They would make a beautiful landing on Lake Crescent, which ended in our front yard, and ride the little waves in almost to our doorstep. Bill began feeding them scraps of bread which he managed to toss on the lawn without frightening them away, and it gradually became a morning chore that lasted throughout the summer. Two of the ducks, which we named Donald and Molly, became our favourites, for no reason except that Donald had a peculiar note in his quack, a sort of off-key tone, that set him apart, and Molly, his mate, was always with him. They never became domesticated, of course, but Donald did learn to answer when Bill called to him.

When that first winter closed down on us in what was to be one of the most severe seasons the North-west had suffered in years, the ducks came in one morning, circled the lake several times like a formation of aircraft saluting the home base, and wheeled off to the south. After they were gone we missed them terribly; their quacking in the front yard was something we had daily looked forward to all summer. Then one morning, a short time later, Bill called for me to come quickly. I found him with his nose pressed to the frosty window-pane peering out towards the lake.

I searched for a peephole. 'What is it?'

'Not sure. Could have been mistaken,' he said slowly. 'I thought I saw some ducks on the lake, but . . . Hey, look! It is ducks, and they're coming this way.'

We rushed on to the front porch. The lake was rough and bitterly cold, but out there, bobbing up and down as the waves sometimes rolled completely over them, were two mallards headed in our direction.

'Do you suppose . . .?' I seized Bill's arm. 'Do you think it could be——?'

Bill cupped his hands to his mouth. 'Donald,' he called. 'Hello, Donald!'

The drake lifted his head, waggled his tail, and gave forth an off-key quack. Donald and Molly had come back to us.

Why they returned we don't know, of course; perhaps the free meals we handed out had a lasting effect. But when they reached the shore they could come no farther, as the yard was covered with snow far too deep for their short legs to manage. Bill tried to feed them by tossing bread into the pounding waves, but this wasn't very satisfactory. He was really concerned about feeding them, too, as their natural food was buried far beneath the heavy snow. Although Donald would answer Bill's call, he was still a wild mallard and wouldn't come near enough to get the bread he was offered. The problem was solved a few days later in a most peculiar way.

We were wakened early one morning from a sound sleep by the sharp rapping we heard at the front of the house. At that time of year we were just about the only family living in the entire lake area, and we both sprang out of bed, certain that an accident had befallen someone. Bill hurried to the front door and threw it open —there was no one there. He tried the kitchen door with the same result. But we were no more than comfortably back in bed, half-convinced we had dreamed it, when the rapping started all over again. Several times we were summoned to the door, and each time it was the same: no one was there.

The following morning at the same time we were again wakened by the loud rapping. We were mystified—it didn't make sense; a practical joker is not likely to be at your door in below-zero weather at 5.30 a.m. Still we couldn't discover what was happening.

The third morning Bill was determined to get to the bottom of the mystery, and reluctantly scrambled out of his warm bed when the alarm rang at five o'clock. He was shivering in a chair facing the door a half hour later when we heard the whir of wings outside. Jumping to his feet he ran to the door and stood waiting, his hand on the latch. A moment later the rapping began. But it wasn't at the door—it was coming from the window nearby. Through the frosty pane we could make out the figure of a sea-gull standing on the window-sill rapping sharply against the glass with his strong bill.

The bird had evidently been nearby the preceding days when Bill had tried to feed the ducks—the Straits of Juan De Fuca being but four miles away—and undoubtedly had decided to crash the party. Bill slid the door open, tossed out a handful of bread, and was rewarded with immediate action as the gull ate ravenously while Donald called wildly in his off-key salute from the shore, where he and Molly were riding at anchor. A few minutes later, with Bill and me watching from the window after we had thrown more bread on to the porch, the two ducks finally made a wary landing on the porch railing and soon were joining in the feast.

That was the beginning of our front-porch free-loading parties that lasted throughout the severe winter, although they didn't continue long in the same proportions.

The sea-gull would arrive each morning at about five-thirty, alone, and rap out his call for breakfast, but Donald and Molly soon began flying in with all their poor relations. Every day found more mallards added to the party, and our bread supply eventually became a major problem. Finally Bill began buying stale bread in the bakeries at Port Angelus and bringing it home in large grain sacks, but the demand gradually became greater than the supply of stale bread he was able to find. The morning that we counted fifty-four ducks on the porch gulping down our hard-to-get bread Bill took off in search of help from the state game department.

When the snows left in the spring the mallards disappeared with it—all but Donald and Molly. We saw them almost every day; they would show up for a handout or stop by for a few minutes, when they were passing over the lake, to bob on the waves. We never tired of watching them come in for a graceful landing on the water, like amphibious planes swooping down from the sky, except that they lowered their undercarriage only a second before meeting the water. But before long, Donald became too engrossed in his spring courting to waste much of his time on us, although he still answered with his peculiar quack when Bill called to him. Most of the day he was busy bowing, preening his vivid feathers, and just plain showing off for his lady-fair's benefit. Molly, for her part, liked it immensely and said so in a quacking chatter.

Then one morning Molly ate her breakfast alone, looking a

little sad. When any of her winged fellows soared overhead she raised her head expectantly, then continued her solitary meal. But Donald didn't show up, and a week later Molly, too, disappeared. I missed them as I do any of our wild pets that one day go out into the forest and never return. When I mentioned it to Bill, he just grinned and said nothing. One morning a few weeks later I stepped out on the front porch for something and happened to glance towards the lake.

'Molly!' I cried, barely restraining myself from running down to the water. 'You've come back again!'

I hurried to get a slice of bread. She was still sitting there on the sand when I came back, almost at the water's edge, and didn't move as I drew near.

'Are you hurt?' I asked. 'Has something happened to you?'

Slowly she got to her feet and proudly looked up at me as eight fuzzy little babies appeared from beneath her wings. If she could have talked I'm sure she would have said that this was proof of what she had been doing while away. Never have I seen a mother display more love and tenderness towards her offspring than Molly did that day. Her habits became regular again after that, and she never failed to bring her youngsters around for their early feeding. A few days later two of her brood were missing— probably prey to a racoon or weasel—but she proudly carried on with what she had left.

Their training period began almost at once. It started in a shallow pool where Molly led them for their first swimming lesson. I was surprised to learn that they didn't know how to manœuvre in water instinctively, but Molly knew she had the job to do and how to go about doing it. She was a stern disciplinarian who stood for no foolishness from her pupils. I spent several days watching them through Bill's binoculars, and it was quite a sight to see her teaching the little brood. With the babies on her back she swam into a shallow pool and nonchalantly dumped them in. They sat like tiny tufts of cottonwool on the water while Molly went through her bag of tricks, treading with her left foot while she made right turns, using the right foot for left turns, and both feet for straightaway speed; and if she detected any woolgathering on the part of a pupil, the culprit received a swift bat on the head from her hard bill. She even taught them to drink. It was laughable to see them dunk their bills, then raise their heads in unison while the water trickled down their throats. It was also a little startling to see them come walking out of the water dry as powder.

Molly appeared on the lawn one morning with an addition to her troop. She had adopted a stray baby from somewhere, and he displayed his lack of discipline at once. I saw them waddling up from the lake and the stepchild—which was a few weeks older and more yellow than the rest—was for ever breaking ranks. Wild mallards swim in just about the same V formation they maintain while flying, but on the ground a brood of babies follow behind their mother in a perfectly straight line. Stepchild had no time for such fiddle-faddle and was for ever running over the smaller fry in his effort to reach the front of the column. Molly would upend him with a whop from her powerful bill and send him scurrying back into line. It took days of chastising before the overgrown ruffian recognized his place and was willing to stay there.

As the babies grew older and sprouted feathers, Molly began their final lesson—flying. When one sees mallards wheeling gracefully through the sky, it's almost impossible to imagine they ever had to be taught the art, but it was several days before Molly could even get one of her brood to attempt a take-off. When they finally did try, they almost immediately nosed back into the water. Stepchild was the first to make it, and he flapped excitedly around over their heads, quacking wildly for attention, exactly like a young boy with a new bike showing off before his admiring family.

One morning Molly and her brood, which were now nearing maturity, were finishing their breakfast on the front lawn when a large mallard flashing in vivid colours swept down over them and landed on the lake nearby.

'Believe that's Donald,' Bill called and hurried outside.

'But it doesn't look like Donald,' I said, running after him.

'Got his new plumage now,' he explained. 'They always hide out while moulting.' He cupped his hands to his mouth. 'Hello, Donald!' he called.

The beautiful drake raised his head, looked towards Bill, wiggled his tail, and emitted an off-key quack.

As if answering the signal for which she had so long been waiting, Molly started immediately for the lake, her troop of youngsters bringing up the rear. Once on the lake they swam rapidly towards the waiting drake, and Molly didn't pause until she was at his side. For a moment they chatted and waggled their tails in pure joy while the children remained at a respectful distance. Then Donald turned into the wind, and they all moved into position behind him. They were like a squadron of jets as they raced through the water and on up into the sunny sky. We last saw them disappearing over the mountains, heading south in perfect formation.

Bill has taught me many wonderful things about nature and wildlife. From the time we were married he insisted that I get outdoors every day for long walks, and he always accompanied me when he was free from his work. We tramped through summer and winter, rain and snow—nothing was allowed to interfere. A new world gradually unfolded before me, fascinating, and at times almost incredible, one that a city-bred girl could never dream existed. Bill is an excellent instructor, and nothing was ever too much trouble to explain.

One learns from other sources, too. One day at Yosemite, for example, I had a chance to watch animals behave in a way you would have to see to believe. A skunk had been struck by a car in front of our house; it was paralysed with a broken back and had to lie there beside the road in the hot sun until Bill came home in the evening to destroy it. All day long its mate made countless trips to the nearby stream for water which it carried back in its mouth and transferred to the mouth of the injured skunk. When Bill arrived and made ready to shoot it, the uninjured one spread itself protectively over its mate and Bill was forced to shoot them both in order to put the injured one out of its misery. I sometimes get a bit impatient with people when they talk about 'dumb animals'.

I have never known a ranger who failed to display a remark-able affinity for the wild creatures, and there are certain unwritten laws in dealing with them that he hesitates to violate. Bill had a demonstration of this one day while he was training a new ranger.

It was in the dead of winter when he and the young ranger, Frank Fish, arrived at Alder Creek station on the outer fringe of Yosemite late in the evening, weary after a twenty-three-mile trip on skis. The station at this season was not occupied, but was well stocked with food, as were all the outlying stations, in case of emergency. They had just removed their skis when a young skunk moved out from behind a stack of stove wood by the door.

'Get away from here!' Frank yelled, hurling a stick at the animal.

'Don't!' Bill yelled. 'Don't ever do that, Frank.'

But Frank had no intention of sharing the porch with the odoriferous little stranger, and he rushed towards it, stomping his feet as he went.

'Stop!' Bill yelled, pushing him to one side. 'We have to sleep here tonight.'

'I don't intend to sleep with any skunk.'

'You won't sleep anywhere if it sprays you,' Bill warned. 'Might have done it when you rushed him. Must be too young, or else he's used up his scent.'

They trooped into the station, started a fire, and put on a can of stew to cook. While the food was heating over the fire, Bill stepped outside to retrieve their skis, and while the door was open the skunk slipped into the room. After telling Frank not to touch it, Bill proceeded to bring in the skis and stand them against the wall; he then scooped the skunk into a two-pound coffee-can and deposited it outside on the front porch. After they had eaten and while Bill was washing the dishes, Frank had a change of heart and opened the door for the skunk to come in out of the cold.

'He's such a friendly little fellow, after all,' he said, closing the door. 'And he acts like he's hungry, too.'

Bill gave Frank a quizzical look but said nothing. They fed it scraps from the table and allowed it the run of the place until they were ready to retire, then Bill got a broom and gently nudged it outside. Next morning when Frank was going for wood, the skunk again darted inside as soon as the door was opened. Again they fed it and paid it no more attention until they were ready to leave for home. But this time the striped little fellow had its own ideas about being put out in the ice and snow.

Bill first tried to recapture it with the coffee-can, to no avail; then Frank urged it with the broom, but the skunk showed no inclination to leave.

'Can't leave it in here,' Bill decided at last. 'It would soon starve.'

'Maybe if we opened the door,' Frank suggested, 'and I made a loud noise to scare——'

'No,' Bill said quickly. 'We'd get sprayed for sure.'

'I read once in a magazine,' Frank said, 'that if you pick them up by the tail it prevents them from spraying.' He hesitated. 'Open the door—I'll try it!'

Easing carefully over to the skunk, he gently lifted it by the tail, waited expectantly for a second, then, grinning broadly, started for the door. He was stepping over the threshhold when the skunk struck back with the only weapon it possessed. Dropping it suddenly, Frank clawed wildly at his eyes while stumbling outside where he buried his face in the snow in an effort to regain his breath and lessen the horrible burning in his eyes. When he could breathe again, he shouted for Bill to open a can of cream, and he bathed his eyes in the heavy liquid until the burning stopped. But he was entirely blind until almost noon, when his sight slowly returned. After rinsing his new ninety-eight-dollar uniform in a solution of vinegar water to destroy the odour, he and Bill started for home.

'That writer who said you should pick them up by the tail sure never tried it himself,' Bill remarked. 'This one was a dead shot.'

'Not only that,' Frank snapped, 'he used an automatic and a repeater!'

I had just taken Bill's lunch to him one summer day when a car drove up in front of the south-entrance checking station, where he was on duty. A man climbed out and hurried to the window where Bill was sitting checking the cars as they entered the park.

'See here, young man!' he wheezed, glaring at Bill. 'Just what are your duties around here?'

Bill grinned and glanced over at me. Another crank, I thought, or some cheap politician throwing his weight around. 'Right at the moment,' Bill said, 'I am checking cars—making a record of licence numbers, searching for firearms, seeing that no dogs or cats are brought in to frighten the park animals, looking out for criminals and drunks. Does that answer your question?'

'It does not! What about the bear and deer? You rangers are supposed to look after them when they need attention, aren't you? That's what we're paying you for. I'm a taxpayer, and I demand to know why you're sitting around here all day long when——'

'Just a minute, sir,' Bill snapped. 'I'm doing the job I was instructed to do. But I am not the only ranger in the park, and if you will tell me what it is you want——'

'You just bet I'll tell you! Early this morning, when we got to the park, I saw a young deer lying along the side of the road, not a mile from here. My wife was driving and she wanted to stop, but I told her not to because the rangers would take care of it, that's what you're paid for. I came by there just now and that young deer was still lying there! Where are your fancy-pants rangers, up at the hotel playing tennis?'

The grin disappeared from Bill's face. 'Listen, mister,' he said shortly, 'every road in the park is patrolled regularly. Someone would have taken care of the deer if it needed our attention.'

'Needed attention!' the man fairly shouted. 'I'm from Topeka, Kansas, and I never saw a deer in my life before outside a zoo, but even I have enough sense to know a deer isn't going to lie there alongside the road unless there's something wrong with it!'

'Think it was struck by a car?' Bill asked. 'Broken leg or——'

'How should I know?' the man fumed. 'That's your job around here. You're the ranger. Believe me, my congressman is going to hear about this!'

Bill turned to the telephone. 'I'll call headquarters and have a patrol car sent out to investigate. Just where is the deer located?'

'Right there on the back seat of my car!' The man pointed. 'I wasn't going to leave him——'

Bill hurried outside, and I followed. When he opened the car door, his look of concern forced me to peer inside. It was a baby fawn that had been born but a few hours ago; its spotted coat was still uncleaned. Curled up in a corner of the seat, it was as quiet as if it were still hiding from the prying eyes of the forest; a fly was crawling up from its nose and walked directly across one eyeball, and the fawn didn't as much as move a muscle.

'You touched it,' Bill said to the man.

'Know a better way to get it in the car?'

'This fawn was probably born this morning,' Bill explained, closing the door. 'They're perfectly odourless at first, which is Nature's way of protecting them until they're strong enough to get on their feet. But now that you've touched it with your hand you've changed all that. The mother probably will have nothing more to do with it, and every carnivorous animal in the forest will be led straight to it before morning.'

'Oh . . . Oh.' The man was at a loss for words. 'I—I didn't know.'

'These matters should be left to people here who do know,' Bill said evenly. 'For instance, the rangers.'

'I—I'm sorry, truly sorry. I guess I lost my head: I didn't understand about deer. As I told you, I'm from Topeka.'

'I understand,' Bill nodded. 'I know just how you must have felt about it. Now, if you will take it back and place it as near as possible to the place where you found it, we'll hope the mother will come back and claim it.'

'I'm awfully sorry.' The man pumped Bill's hand. 'I found it back there where the road bends, near that big tree. I'll take it right back.'

That was our introduction to the little fawn that was to become probably the best-known, the most photographed, deer in the country, petted by princes and presidents, fondled by queens and your Aunt Abigail from Timbuktu. But, at the moment, Bill was worried about leaving the little fellow alone in the forest. It was almost a certainty that the doe would desert her baby now, and, if she did, there could be no doubt about its fate during the night. I wasn't at all surprised just before dark when I saw Bill drive off in the patrol car. A half hour later he was back, pounding at the kitchen door.

'Let me in, Marge,' he called breathlessly. 'Open the door.'

He walked inside with the little spotted fawn nestled like a baby in his arms. I made a pad on the floor with some rugs, and Bill got to his knees while he put it down and innocently covered it with one of my very best guest towels. I should have known right then what was coming—his pets had already ranged through most of the menagerie Noah had trotted on to the ark—but I contained myself with a deep growl and a few well-chosen words concerning hand-embroidered linen.

'I couldn't leave him out there,' Bill said. 'I just couldn't, honey. The mother didn't come back for it.'

I agreed. 'But remember one thing, deer have a habit of growing a lot bigger than this little fellow—and fast. I'm not going to have a spreading hat-rack galloping around through my house.'

'Of course not,' he said, grinning up at me. 'Soon as he can stand on his feet—out he goes.'

'You mean——'

'I don't mean I'll turn him loose that soon, no; he wouldn't last overnight. But I'll build a pen in the garage tomorrow, where we can shut him up for the night, away from the coyotes. He'll soon take to the woods, though—they all do.'

For an hour or two the fawn was perfectly quiet, and we disposed of our dinner and retired to the living-room to read the evening newspaper. Bill seemed to think the little fellow was too quiet, and every few minutes made an excuse to go to the kitchen, to wash his hands, to polish his shoes, to get another drink. I noticed he lifted my fancy towel each time to peer underneath before coming back to his sport section. I was just getting comfortable with a good book when the fawn raised its head and let go with a plaintive wail that sounded exactly like a human baby, but one equipped with cast-iron lungs.

'It's hungry!' Bill cried, springing from his chair. 'Heat some milk, Marge.' He was on the floor, lifting the fuzzy head into his lap. 'He'll be all right now.'

'Fine.' I had to smile at him. 'Tuck the towel right under his chin. Warm milk coming up.'

But we couldn't get him to drink. He would root helplessly around in the pail Bill held for him, then lift his big innocent eyes to us and cry in frustration. When Bill forced its nose down into the milk, the fawn amused himself by blowing bubbles all over my clean kitchen floor, but he wouldn't drink. We tried a medicine dropper with no success and, when Bill was exasperated and I was ready to throw out the pair of them, Bill's finger accidentally slipped into the fawn's mouth while he was wiping the milk from its face—it began gulping on it like a well-oiled suction pump.

'Nipple,' Bill said slowly. 'That's what it needs, a regular baby nipple.'

'That,' I declared, 'is the one thing we are fresh out of.'

He nodded his head. 'I'll get one.'

'Do you mean you would drive thirty miles to the store to-night to get a nipple for that stubborn little mule?'

'Looks like I'll have to,' he said. 'Nature always provides one, and his instinct tells him he has to have it. He doesn't know how to drink.'

Bill made the trip to the store, thirty miles over and thirty miles back, and got the storekeeper out of bed, but it was worth it. Inserting the nipple into the fawn's mouth, Bill pushed its nose down into the pail, and the milk disappeared like the bottom had fallen off the container, accompanied by the fawn's happy gurgles, shivers of delight, and occasional gasps for breath. Bill was fascinated and as pleased as Punch.

'You know, Marge,' he laughed, 'I've always imagined Jiggs making a noise just like that when he sits down to a big plate of Dinty Moore's corned beef and cabbage.'

From that moment we always referred to the baby deer as Jiggs, and he later learned to respond as faithfully as any well-trained dog when his name was spoken. But our troubles were far from being over; Jiggs would dispose of all the milk in sight and clamour for more; he was for ever hungry. The following day Bill brought home some canned milk and we added only enough water to allow the rich mixture to flow through the nipple—that did the trick, except that he demanded a fresh feeding every two hours, day and night, for six long weeks.

Eventually Jiggs learned to eat raw potatoes, celery, and apples, but he never outgrew his fondness for milk; even water was coldly disregarded unless coloured with a few drops of his favourite beverage. He was an adorable little fellow and at the same time a full-blown nuisance—a sort of pet to end all pets. But Bill lived up to his promise and stowed him safely away each night in the pen built inside our garage. It was during the day that he became a pest, always underfoot, tagging at our heels like a gun dog. When he wanted to come inside the house he would announce his presence by striking the door with his front hoofs, and many of our guests were considerably startled when they answered the summons and had to leap to one side as Jiggs bolted wildly through the doorway.

Jiggs grew rapidly and was quite a handsome fellow, fat as butter, but he never showed any inclination to join his brothers in the forest as our other pets eventually had done. We had a star boarder on our hands. I have always thought that Bill would probably have been a successful circus trainer of wild animals if he hadn't first become a ranger, but I'm sure no great amount of credit is due him for educating our deer. Jiggs never realized that he was born to be a wild animal; he never knew he was a deer, either. When his wild brothers crossed our back yard every day on the path they had worn there, Jiggs would give them no more attention than he showed a bear or a flock of noisy birds. Taking his meals in the house was something he didn't outgrow, either, and if Bill let him inside before his dinner was quite ready, he always made a dash for the bedroom where he would bounce stiff-legged on my pretty blue bedspread like any spoiled brat.

I think the only thing Jiggs ever really hated was a pair of bear dogs Bill had at the time. He simply detested the sight of them and never failed, sometime during the day, to corral them on top of the woodpile, where he would stand striking at them with his sharp hoofs while the dogs tried hard not to disregard the vigorous training Bill had forced on them. Jiggs loved to ride in the patrol car, or lie sleeping on a mat Bill always placed on the floor in the checking station while he was on duty. Many park visitors got a first-hand taste of wildlife that left them a little goggle-eyed, for Jiggs would often rear up to meet them face to face at the open window. Other days he would stand for hours beside the park entrance, trying to beg a ride while the cars were halted at the station, and if a car door was ever left open for a minute, he would leap inside, to the howling delight of the children, and the startled dismay of the parents.

During the winter season he would wade the deep snow—which is foreign to any deer's nature—to the roadway in time to meet the approaching snowplough crew, and climb in the cab while they held open the door. Off they would go, opening the road to the park entrance, while Jiggs dined royally on the choice morsels they always fed him from their lunch pails. When we took down our skis, he was as excited as a hunting dog seeing a gun in his master's hand and would jump excitedly about the room while we put them on. Outside he would dash ahead and disappear behind clumps of shrubbery, then come bounding out as we drew near. And if you took a spill in the snow, he was on you in a flash, jumping up and down and licking your face. During the hunting season I tied a sheep-bell around his neck with a bright red ribbon. He was like a kid with a fascinating toy and never seemed to tire of bobbing his head to hear the little bell ring.

Jiggs never left us for any length of time. For an hour or two he might be gone on an exploratory trip down the road or even into the forest, but he never stayed long; so the day he was missing all morning and still hadn't returned by noon, Bill was as worried as an old mother hen and called everyone he knew in an effort to locate him. It was midafternoon when an open touring car drew up at the checking station with Jiggs holding down the rear seat. Unknown to the driver, Jiggs had jumped inside the car sometime before it left the park, and the driver was miles away, on the road to Fresno, when he suddenly felt a cold nose pressed against the back of his neck. The car nearly went over a high embankment before the man recovered from the shock and surprise. He returned Jiggs to our front yard, where he knew he belonged.

At this time we were living on the highway near one of the main park entrances, and our front yard gradually became a regular unscheduled stop for traffic. Stages and big sightseeing buses would roll up in front and disgorge fifty or sixty camera-happy passengers on to the lawn, and it never seemed to matter what I might be doing—scrubbing the floor, baking a cake, or entertaining guests—it always followed the same pattern: 'Mrs. Merrill,' the driver would shout, 'how about calling Jiggs?' For a time after this started I wouldn't appear until I had changed into a fresh dress and combed my hair, but I soon learned that I couldn't cope with Jiggs' popularity, change clothes forty times a day, and take care of my housework too. So the costume for my Grand Entrance before Jiggs' public soon depended entirely on what I might be doing; it often included a wrinkled apron and was frequently highlighted by a flour smudge on the tip of my nose, as I am for ever baking cakes.

Once every week Jiggs got a bath in our tub. He didn't exactly approve, but there wasn't much he could do about it with Bill sitting on him while I scrubbed. He was getting larger by the minute, but he still demanded his milk and the nipple through which he would drink it. Then one day Bill decided that this foolishness had already gone too far. From now on Jiggs was to take his milk the same way as any other self-respecting deer. He wouldn't deny him the milk but, as of right now, the nipple business was out, gone, all over, and for emphasis he hurled the thing as far as he could out into the bushes. Jiggs wasn't inclined to agree with this odd arrangement; in fact he would have nothing to do with it at all—or the milk, either. Two days later —with a sulky, fast-dehydrating deer on our hands—I noticed Bill searching through the bushes out behind the house. I'm sure he didn't find the discarded nipple, for he suddenly remembered an urgent errand he had to attend to at the store. And since he would be there anyway, he thought he might as well get a new nipple. 'Never can tell when we'll need one.'

The day I discovered that Jiggs had inherited a flock of ticks, I thought I had reached the end of the line. I simply couldn't have him running through the house dripping with ticks. The ticks just had to go, now. The only cleaning fluid at hand was a can of kerosene, and I sponged him thoroughly, even swabbing the inside of his big soft ears. When I finished he sniffed for a moment, stamped his front hoofs, and gazed inquiringly up into my face. Then, with a wild leap he suddenly exploded all over the front lawn, dashing around in circles, bawling, rubbing against the trees, and dragging himself frantically through the tall grass. I

125

never dreamed the kerosene would burn his hide, but I could see he was nearly insane. I ran after him, calling his name, pleading, bawling louder than he, but he suddenly took off for the woods and disappeared in a cloud of dust. I felt terrible about it, and knew I should have asked Bill before taking the matter into my own hands, but it was too late now. I was sure he would never come back, but he did. Most of his glossy coat was gone when he returned, and he resembled nothing so much as a big Mexican hairless dog, but he was back. It was weeks before a new coat grew out, and he could once more appear before his public.

One night I was wakened by a wild commotion outside in the yard. It was a peculiar, frightening sound that I couldn't quite place. I was sitting up in bed, listening, groggy with sleep, when it broke forth in all its fury. It sounded like a pack of wolves racing around the corner of the house, yelping and snarling, in wild flight. Again they circled the house and were rushing around the corner a third time when I heard Jiggs' pitiful cry as he bounded past the window. My heart was in my throat, and I snatched for Bill's arm to waken him, but he was already out on the floor.

'Dogs!' I gasped. 'Dogs are after Jiggs!'

'Coyotes,' he muttered as he dashed outside.

There were several rapid shots, and after a short silence Bill walked in with Jiggs in his arms and put him down on the kitchen floor. Jiggs was utterly exhausted, his tongue hanging from his mouth, and he staggered as he rose and made his way to me, resting his head in my lap like any frightened child that needs comforting.

'Jumped out of his pen,' Bill said. 'Got to build it higher.'

I didn't answer; I was busy arranging a soft bed on the floor.

'He isn't hurt,' Bill said presently. 'No reason why he can't sleep out in his pen.'

I knew what he was remembering—that I had said Jiggs was never to sleep in my house—but I couldn't do it, not this night. I knew he was grinning at me, with that little-boy look on his face, but I had made up my mind, and I made a pad from some rugs and spread my fancy guest towel across Jiggs' quivering head before getting to my feet.

'Know something, honey?' Bill said, and kissed me a little harder than usual. 'We'd better get to bed.'

One morning a few weeks later Jiggs strolled away and never came back. He went over to the schoolhouse nearby, where he loved to stand watching the children at play. Attracted by the bright red ribbon around his neck, a little boy came over to pat his silky head—Jiggs never understood that he was a deer and should be afraid of people. When the little boy playfully tied a short rope around his neck, it was something that never had happened before, and he was suddenly frightened. He whirled and lunged away, raced blindly towards the schoolyard fence, and leaped high into the air. But he didn't make it; the trailing rope lodged beneath one hind hoof as he leaped, and his head suddenly snapped back against his side. His neck was instantly broken.

Jiggs lies today in his little grave close beside the Wawona schoolhouse in Yosemite National Park, where he knew his first fear of a human being and lost a freedom he had never learned to question.

Nine

EARLY one morning a lone horseman rode up to the Mather ranger station and slid to the ground. That he was an Indian there could be no doubt; his sharp, piercing eyes, his straight black hair, and his way of walking—on the balls of his feet like a cat ready to spring—told their own story. Bill was on the telephone when he walked in, and the young buck stood waiting, disregarding me as completely as he might a rock beside the trail. When Bill finished talking, he turned towards the Indian.

'Well, what brings you here, Strong Bear?'

For a time the buck made no reply. Then, without looking at either of us: 'Me sick. Heap bad cold.'

Looking closely at the Indian, Bill had no compunction about treating him; you could see he was suffering from a severe cold. Since he remembered when the doctor had removed the Indian's appendix, he felt free to recommend a good laxative, which was plainly indicated.

Bill went to his first-aid kit and drew out two bottles. From one he extracted some small pink capsules, from the other, a large brown pill.

'Take two of the pink ones every four hours,' he instructed, placing them on the table. 'This one,' he said, holding out the brown pill, 'you had better take right now. You'll find some water in a bucket on the back porch. Then Strong Bear will feel better.'

All of a sudden I realized who our visitor was. Most of the Indians one meets answer to white men's names, like Charlie or Joe. This young buck was the one I had heard about who would accept only his true Indian name. Half Piute and half Digger, he claimed to be the son of a famous chief. But Strong Bear was also known to the rangers by a much more familiar name, one that he had well earned—Bad Indian. When he returned to the room, Bill was waiting, an envelope in his hand.

'Give me the pink pills,' he said, holding out his hand. 'I'll put them in this envelope for you.'

Strong Bear sullenly shook his head and started for the door.

'Wait,' Bill insisted. 'You'll lose them. Where are they?'

'Me take-um,' Strong Bear muttered. 'Take-um all. Get better heap fast.'

'Look,' Bill called. 'You can't do that. Put your finger down your throat and raise them. Those pills are laxatives and mighty powerful.'

'Two-gun say take-um,' the Indian grumbled.

Bill shook his head. 'I didn't tell you to take all of them at once. You'll get sick, Strong Bear. Mighty sick.'

'Me no get sick now. Strong Bear take-um pills.' He swung up onto his horse and galloped away.

A few days later, at the small town of Sonora, Strong Bear was overheard telling another Indian that he had been 'heap sick' and that Two-gun's pills were bad medicine. He also swore that he intended to kill Bill on sight. The local deputy sheriff notified Bill of the threat.

A month later we were transferred back to headquarters, and Bill had to take his turn on the 12 to 8 a.m. patrol. One night, shortly after going on duty, he was ordered to hurry over to Indian Village to quiet an uprising. What probably had started as a sociable powwow for a group of young bucks had suddenly flared into a drunken brawl that already was out of control. Bill rushed outside, calling to Ranger Martin to accompany him, and they roared away.

Indian Village in Yosemite Valley was never intended as a park attraction for visitors; it is made up of a number of neat little houses provided as permanent homes for a sizable group of Indians who are employed at all sorts of jobs inside the park. All the houses save one were dark as the patrol car swung silently from the street and came to a stop. Bill and Ranger Martin slid out and cautiously made their way towards the lighted house. One minute the night air was being pierced by wild war whoops and bloodcurdling yells, and the next it was as quiet as an Egyptian tomb. An Indian may become a bit careless while in his cups, but his sense of hearing never seems to desert him.

'They've heard us,' Bill snapped. 'Come on!'

They dashed across the yard and headed around towards the rear door. Indians were cursing and falling over each other as they came stampeding from the house. Two young bucks had made it to the far edge of the yard when the rangers appeared. One immediately lost himself in the shadows, but the other suddenly stopped, spun around, and raised his hand. Bill caught a fleeting glimpse of the sullen face as Strong Bear's arm lashed out, and he dropped to the ground as a knife whistled over his head. Then Strong Bear, too, disappeared into the darkness. There was no time to follow them now, and they quickly herded the remaining Indians back inside the house, where Bill guarded them while Ranger Martin sped off towards headquarters for reinforcements and the paddy wagon.

'Send the ambulance, too,' Bill called after him. 'We're going to need it.'

There were great splatterings of blood on the floor and walls, even on the ceiling. The broken blade of a butcher knife protruded from the wall where someone had hurled it, the bloody handle resting on the floor. On the table was a straight razor, red and still dripping; the floor was strewn with glass from light bulbs the Indians had crushed with their bare hands in their haste to darken the room and escape when they heard the rangers approaching. The only bulb left intact was in the kitchen, where Bill was holding his captives.

When help arrived, the rangers found several Indians in other rooms unconscious from blows on the head and loss of blood. One buck had been slashed severely across the neck and head and was discovered under a bed where he had been kicked out of the way, a pillow doubled over his head and a length of clothesline wound around his neck to stop the bleeding. Soon they were on their way to the hospital, where they were sewn up and given transfusions; then those who had not been too badly cut up were jailed.

Before Bill could get away from the hospital, another call came in for him to rush down to Arch Rock entrance, eleven miles away, and assist Ranger Schilling, who was having a bad time trying to control two more Indians who had run afoul of some fire-water. Arriving just in time to see Ranger Schilling go down from a blow on the head, Bill dashed after the culprit, who leaped in a car with his companion and took off. Bill managed to get a toe-hold on the running-board and was reaching for the ignition key when he was knocked sprawling into the roadway. He got up, saw that Ranger Schilling was getting to his feet, and ran back to his patrol car and roared away after them.

The car ahead was almost impossible to follow, as the Indians had switched off their lights, and Bill wasn't at all sure he hadn't been outmanoeuvred until he saw their stop-light flash on in the blackness ahead as they slowed their car before careening from the main highway into a secondary road leading to Camp 6. Bill bore down on the accelerator. The road the Indians had chosen was a short one that didn't leave the park, and if only he could get there before they could backtrack, he would have them trapped. He made it; they were turning their car at the end of the road, and before he could reach them, their rear wheels skidded over the edge of the river bank. The young Indians sat there cursing as their wheels spun helplessly in the air.

'Get out,' Bill said as he hurried over to them. 'You're coming with me.'

The driver shook his head and stamped down on the accelerator.

'You can't drive this car,' Bill insisted. 'You're drunk.'

He reached inside to remove the ignition key and ducked

sharply as a bottle whizzed past his ear and crashed against the wind-screen. Not waiting to dodge any more, he dragged the driver out on to his feet. Then the Indian swung a tyre iron, but Bill met the thrust by giving him a sharp blow across the wrist with the side of his hand. The iron clattered to the ground and the buck staggered backwards, fell, and struck his head against a large boulder—he was out cold. Bill spun around as the other Indian darted out from behind the car.

'Well,' he said, bracing himself. 'You again.'

Strong Bear paused long enough to draw a long glistening knife from his belt.

'Two-gun make Strong Bear heap sick,' he said, inching forward. 'Me no like. Ever'body laugh. Call me "Sitting Bull".'

'That was your fault,' Bill said. 'You didn't do as I told you.'

The big Indian was creeping towards him like a cat. 'Nobody laugh at Strong Bear,' he grumbled. 'Me kill you plenty, right now!'

'Wait!' Bill whipped out his gun, and Strong Bear paused, balanced on his toes. 'You're drunk. I don't want to shoot you.' He levelled the barrel at the Indian's stomach. 'Now, drop that knife!'

Still on his toes, Strong Bear released the weapon.

'No need knife,' he said through his teeth. 'Me kill you with hands. You drop-um gun. Me show you!'

When Bill's gun slid into its holster, the Indian sprang. They went over in a tangle of legs and flailing arms, rolling across the grass and down the steep bank of the river like actors in a western movie. When they regained their feet they stood trading blows—panting and grunting—then closed again, and finally toppled off the bank into the river, where Bill shoved Strong Bear's head under water until all the fight had gone from him. Then he put the cuffs on his wrists, led him up the bank, and deposited him in the patrol car. The other Indian was revived, handcuffed, and pushed in beside his partner.

'You've got a bad cut on your head,' Bill said to Strong Bear. 'Sit as still as you can and I'll take you to the hospital.'

It took sixteen stitches to close Strong Bear's torn scalp, and he never as much as flicked an eyelash, but it required the services of four men to hold him down so that his head could be shaved. As his long black hair fell to the floor, he cried like a baby.

Strange people, these Indians. One ancient Indian who had spent most of his life fighting rangers made one final request before he died: he would like the ranger quartet to sing at his funeral—they did. Once when we were being transferred from Yosemite, a big farewell party was arranged for us at the Ranger Club. The party was at its height when someone reported that there were several carloads of Indians waiting out in the parking area to say good-bye to Two-gun. Bill invited all of them inside, many of whom he had fought, arrested, and shared his lunch with. The festive board was set once more, and after they had eaten their fill, Bill danced the squaws around the polished floor till the rafters bounced. Strange people, these Indians. We thought it quite an honour that they respected Bill enough to honour him by coming to our farewell party. It was not a usual custom, and indeed they had never extended such an honour to a ranger.

Although Bill was born in Chicago, he has no recollection of ever having lived there. His father died when Bill was a baby, and when he was six he met the one person most responsible for moulding his life and character. George Suttle lived in Portland, Oregon, and was an old man when Bill first discovered him sitting in a swing on the wide veranda across the street. The old man's eyes must have twinkled as he beheld the stealthy approach of the youngster, gliding from tree to bush across his front yard. When the serious, wide-eyed face regarded him from beneath the bottom porch rail, he carefully leaned forward.

'They went that-a-way,' he whispered.

Little Billy regarded him evenly. 'Who did?'

'Them cattle-rustlers you're after.'

'I'm not after rustlers,' Bill explained. 'I'm Kit Carson and I'm chasin' Indians.'

'Of course,' the old man said with a grin. 'Didn't recognize you, Kit, without your coonskin cap. You come up and sit here beside me and we'll make some battle plans—like me and Buffalo Bill used to do.'

133

That was the beginning of a friendship that could exist only between a little boy and a white-haired man who had forgotten to age with the years. The front yard and the houses across the street had a way of disappearing while Mr. Suttle spun his tales from the porch swing, and little Billy Merrill grew to know the beauty and solitude of the deep forest and became intimately acquainted with every wild creature it sheltered long before he met them in real life. It was a lesson that became so indelibly impressed on his mind that he never forgot. From that date on, his whole life and all his ambition were directed towards living and working in the great outdoors.

I have never known a ranger who didn't love children. It's something that seems to be as much a part of rangers as their love for the forest or the mountains. I have often seen them take hours of their own time to explain the peculiar habits and traits of wild animals to a group of eager youngsters, or to a single boy who showed an interest. Often, after a long tour of duty, Bill will spend the entire evening leading a party of little fellows back along the dim trails where, during the day, he has spied a little fawn or some woolly bear cubs. He never becomes too occupied to stop and explain anything to children that arouses their curiosity. He shows them how to balance kyacks and fit them to the backs of pack animals, allows them to handle his riata, shows them his guns, and often lifts them up to the driver's seat on the red fire truck, from which they take off on an imaginary wild flight through the flaming forest. Little boys often inquire if he is the real Lone Ranger, and I have never been surprised to find him posing for them on his white charger, Blue Jay, while the small fry snap pictures like mad.

It seems Bill is always on duty. If we are making a social call, driving into the city—inside the park or out—he never passes up anything that looks suspicious, or a person who might be in need of help. We were on our way to church one Sunday when he spied a car parked on a deserted stretch of road, and he stopped to look it over. The car was unoccupied, and nothing about it appeared unusual—I would have guessed that it belonged to a fisherman who was down at the river teasing the trout. But before continuing, Bill paused for a quick survey of the surrounding area—

and stopped. Barely visible through the dense shrubbery was the deathly white face of a woman staring directly at us.

'You all right?' Bill called.

The woman's lips moved spasmodically, but she made no reply.

'Don't move!' he yelled, seizing his gun from the seat beside me.

He disappeared into the brush, and a moment later I heard a shot. Then he was making his way back to the road with the woman, unconscious, in his arms.

'Fainted,' he said, laying her on the pine needles while he treated her for shock.

'What happened?'

It seemed the woman had been attracted by the profusion of wild flowers growing off the road and while preoccupied had stepped on a rattlesnake. Luckily her foot rested so near the snake's head that it couldn't strike, but she knew the second she raised her foot to make her escape it would instantly sink its fangs into her ankle. She had stood there with the snake rattling and curling about her legs for what must have seemed hours before we happened along. When Bill shot off its head, her relief was so intense she fainted in his arms. When Bill asked her afterwards why she didn't jump when she stepped on the snake, she said she had been too frightened to move.

The following summer Dianne, one of my friends, came to spend a few weeks with us. We were passing through one of those periods where everything unexpected seems to have been lying in wait to happen to us all at once. From the first, Dianne was far from impressed with our lack of the modern conveniences to which she was accustomed. Our station at the time was not one of the chosen few which boasted inside plumbing. When she mentioned wanting a bath, however, I was prepared for her. I had it all worked out in advance.

We packed a bag with towels and fresh clothing, and I took her down into the valley, where she could bathe to her heart's content at an unoccupied station equipped with a modern bathroom. What we didn't know, of course, was that a work crew was preparing to flush out the plumbing and had attached a fire hose to the cleanout valve behind the building. I heard Dianne step into the water, and she must have just had time to get comfortably seated in the tub when the workman turned on the pressure. Immediately I recognized the sound for what it was, and there was an ominous note added to the usual rumbling which warned me an inexperienced workman had released the full pressure of water and it was time to take cover. The rumbling grew to a gurgling roar that chattered the windows like a miniature earthquake.

'Marge!' Dianne yelled. 'What's happening?'

Before I could answer, I heard her scream as cold water from the drainpipe shot up under her with a force that must have raised her from the tub. The house shook, and water from the kitchen sink erupted to the ceiling, while Dianne gasped and screamed for mercy. When the commotion died down, she unlocked the bathroom door and stumbled outside, looking for all the world like a drowned rat. My suggestion about coming here for a bath had been offered in perfectly good faith, but something about the set of her clamped jaw dissuaded me from mentioning it.

Dianne would never be mistaken for a Nature Girl, and it seemed the Great Outdoors never allowed her to forget it for a second. One bright sunny morning she decided to take the bit between her teeth. She insisted on walking up to Little Yosemite Valley in the Half Dome area and spending the day communing with nature. I am sure she deliberately chose the day it was simply impossible for me to accompany her; she was determined to prove to us, and herself, that she could adapt herself to her surroundings with help from no one.

She took off about nine in the morning with a lunch tucked under one arm and a grim and resolute look in her eye. Long before reaching her goal, she was plodding through a sudden downpour that quickly drenched her to the skin, but this time she would not turn back. Reaching her destination at last, she defiantly sat on a boulder while thunder and lightning crashed around her. When the sun again showed its face, she glared at it and smirked at all she beheld. The strange, eerie cries reaching her ears were not the tortured gasps of hobgoblins or the wailing of disembodied spirits, she told herself—merely the calls of strange wild birds with which she was unfamiliar. The occasional rattling she heard nearby could be the sound of dislodged pebbles trickling down the dripping mountainside, and busily working honeybees could easily account for the buzzing in the grass, even if it did seem more rational to conclude that rattlesnakes were wriggling about her feet.

Then it happened, a whooping sound so close behind her that she was on her feet and dashing wildly down the path with no time or inclination to look back. It was unlike anything she had ever heard, a full-grown bear couldn't have been more terrifying. For all she knew the horrible noise might have been made by an angry lion, but she wasn't losing any time in idle speculation. Bill met her half-way up the trail, where she collapsed on his shoulder, and brought her down to the station before going back to investigate. He hadn't yet reached the little valley when he heard it—a whooping, growling roar, the mating call of the blue grouse. You could have tucked the little fellow into your handbag with only the tail feathers showing. Bill hesitated to tell her what he had found, and she never asked—she was so gratified at having escaped with her life.

On the final day of her stay with us Dianne received one last blow. We were preparing to leave for Fresno when she made her farewell excursion to the little plank outhouse with the crescent cut in the door. She had scarcely entered when the door again flew open, and she dived outside in a blur of flying petticoats and churning legs. She was off and running, her skirts swirling almost over her head, feet straining to put vast distances between her and the outhouse, while her ear-splitting screams could have served a steam locomotive. A large sight-seeing bus had just halted at its regular stop before our station, and craning necks leaned from every window while passengers shouted and urged her on to the finish wire, gleefully applauding the most exciting spectacle the park had offered that day. We were well on our way to the city before Dianne regained enough breath to tell us that just inside the outhouse door she had nearly stepped on a coiled rattlesnake.

In Fresno we learned that Dianne's train was two hours late, and Bill immediately suggested that she and I have our finger-prints taken and registered as a means of identification in case of accident. We had no objections, although, if he hadn't mentioned it many times before, I might have been suspicious that it was merely a deft manœuvre on his part to get us to the sheriff's office, where Dianne and I would count the cracks in the ceiling for two hours while he visited with his uniformed pals. It didn't quite work out that way.

Just inside the entrance we met the identification superin-tendent, and he conducted us to the finger-print room, where we were told to wait for the officer who would take care of us—he would send him in immediately.

'Call me when you're finished,' Bill said to us. Then he and his friend stepped into another office and closed the door, as always happens when they have something private to discuss. A few minutes later Dianne and I were descended upon by at least twenty girls of about our own age who seemed to arrive in a body. They were a friendly lot, chatting and laughing with each other—a club group, was my guess. Then several police officers and deputies arrived, and the work began.

'Line up along that wall,' an officer directed. 'We'll get this over with as soon as possible.'

Everybody got into line, Dianne and I falling in at the rear end. The girl in front of me turned around and smiled.

'I like your hat, dearie,' she said.

'Thank you.'

'Almost bought one like it myself. Glad I didn't, now.'

I waited.

'You're not afraid to wear it?'

I felt myself beginning to fry around the edges. 'What do you mean, afraid to wear it?'

She smiled sweetly. 'I guess I talk too much, dearie. I meant you don't exactly melt into a crowd when you're wearing that hat. That's the reason I didn't——'

'You're next,' the officer said, and the girl turned away.

She couldn't have struck me at a more vital spot. I was extremely proud of my new hat and wore it on every occasion where I thought it proper. Bill, for some unknown reason, had detested it from the first and had been urging me to throw it away, said it reminded him of an ice bag with a red rooster tacked on one side. I stood by my guns. Actually, it was the cluster of vividly coloured feathers that had sold me on the hat and . . .

'All right, sister,' the officer snapped. 'We haven't got all day.'

I glared at him while he rolled my freshly manicured fingers on to a messy ink pad and made my prints.

'In there.' He pointed towards the doorway through which the other girls had disappeared.

I waited for Dianne.

'Let's go, sister,' he said, after smudging Dianne's fingers. 'Make it snappy.'

I was surprised by the officer's attitude and quite annoyed. We took our time strolling through the doorway and drifted casually into the long hall beyond. The officer stayed close behind us, mumbling pointed words under his breath, while another was holding the door open at the far end of the corridor. As we stepped outside, I noticed that the other girls were climbing into police cars that were waiting in the courtyard. I suddenly halted.

'Shake it up,' Old Grumpy mumbled, pushing us gently from behind. 'In the wagon with you.'

'See here!' I whirled around. 'We came in here to have our prints taken and——'

'And you had 'em taken,' the officer finished. 'Get going!'

'Marge, there's something wrong here!' Dianne exclaimed.

'There certainly is!' I cried. 'We're not getting into any paddy wagon,' I snapped at Old Grumpy.

'Listen, sister. You're in no position to say what you're not going to do.' He seized us by the arm. 'March!'

We were propelled up the steps and dumped unceremoniously into the crowded wagon. The other girls seemed to be enjoying the fight we were putting up.

'Why didn't you bite him?' one yelled.

'Good try!'

'It's no good, dearie.' I looked around. It was the girl who had spoken to me in the finger-print room. 'In this racket you got to expect this sort of thing, you know.'

'What?' Dianne demanded.

'Say,' another girl called sharply, 'how did you innocent fillies get mixed up with us? Looks like you're in the wrong racket.'

Everybody was talking and laughing at us, and the whole glaring truth suddenly dawned on me. These girls were, of course, ladies of the street, and as we later learned, they represented the net result of a series of raids made on every known red-light resort in the city and county. Dianne and I inadvertently had fallen in line with them in the finger-print room, and under the circumstances it was a perfectly natural mistake for any of the officers to include us in the group.

'Let us out!' I yelled. 'We're not supposed to be in here.'

The wagon started to move, and I heard Dianne begin to cry.

'First time's the worst,' one girl comforted her. 'You'll get used to it.'

Then I heard Bill yell. 'Wait!' he shouted, running towards us. 'Hold up there!'

The patrol wagon stopped.

'What is it, Ranger?'

'Have you got my wife and her girl friend in there?'

'Here I am, Bill,' I heard Dianne sob from near the door.

All the girls were cackling and waving, trying to attract Bill's attention. He and the police officer jumped on the back step and peered inside. I stood on my tiptoes and waved. So did all the rest.

He saw me at last.

'There she is,' he said. 'Back there in the corner.'

The police officer craned his neck. 'Which one?'

'Over there,' Bill pointed. 'The one with the red rooster on her hat.'

From the way the girls shrieked and crowed you would have thought it the most hilarious thing they had ever heard. It wasn't funny to me; I was fighting mad as I followed Dianne outside. As I stepped to the ground, the same familiar voice reached down to me from the paddy wagon, as it started to roll away.

'It's the hat, dearie. Draws too much attention to you. Glad I didn't buy the one I——'

Back at the station that night the red rooster joined his honourable ancestors as I hurled the hat into the roaring fireplace. I meant to dispose of it while Bill was out of the room, but he walked in just as it burst into flame. He grinned to himself but made no comment. He never did like that hat.

One evening, about a week later, I was in the living-room glancing through the newspaper when I came across a headlined article under a Washington dateline stating that the First Lady of the land was planning a summer trip to Yosemite National Park.

'Bill!' I called excitedly. 'Did you read this? Bill!'

He came to the door of his office and peered out at me. 'Anything wrong?'

'Here in the paper! Bill, look. She's coming to Yosemite!'

'You mean the President's wife?' he asked.

'Of course. She's spending her vacation right here in the park!' I stopped suddenly. 'Bill,' I said evenly, 'you knew it and didn't tell me.'

He grinned. 'Sort of slipped my mind, I guess. She won't be here for a month yet.'

'But, Bill,' I chattered. 'Think of it; this will be the highlight of the season!'

'She's coming here to do some fishing,' he said. 'We're going into the Back Country where she won't be pestered with hand-shakers and autograph hounds.'

'You're going with her?'

He absently nodded his head. 'I'll be in charge of her party.' And in the same breath: 'Save the sport page for me, will you, Marge? I still have another report to make out.'

I was exasperated. The wife of the President of the United States was coming here to be conducted on a tour of the Back Country by my own husband, and it 'sort of slipped his mind' to tell me about it! I couldn't quite understand his attitude. Famous people, renowned people the whole world held in awe, were just people to him—a good fellow or a washout. Once when I asked him to tell me about his experience with President

Hoover, he merely said the President had gone fishing in a business suit. When a young man showed up at our door one night with a Coleman lantern that had gone awry, Bill quickly fixed it and then said good night to him. The next day he just 'happened to remember' that the young man was a fellow named Frederic March. And when I remarked that I would have given six fingers off my right hand to have met him, he brought Mr. March around the following day—when I was scrubbing the kitchen floor and looked like the wrath of God.

Soon orders began flowing in from Washington, detailed instructions pertaining to Mrs. Roosevelt's visit. A complete itinerary of the Back Country, which comprises the beautiful, far-flung regions of the park that are practically inaccessible without a seasoned ranger guide, was worked out and approved. Accommodations were arranged for the entire party, including helpers, secretaries, and members of the Secret Service. These problems were pretty much routine. What kept everyone awake nights was the order for the one thing no one ever had heard of— a portable comfort station.

That one item must have been responsible for nearly as much blood, sweat, and tears as was expended on the atom-bomb formula. Everyone was consulted—architects and engineers—all sorts of little men with big slide rules. The problem was maddening. Not only was it necessary for the comfort station to be built in such a manner that its assembly during the trip would be swift and simple, it must also be collapsible, folding into a compact bundle suitable for placing on the back of a pack horse. When it was made sturdy enough to stand on its own four feet, it simply refused to be collapsed into a bundle smaller than the horse itself; when it was made flexible enough to fold easily, it sank to the ground like a deflated blimp. But they finally succeeded—I never knew how—just before the deadline arrived.

If I had been unduly amused by the big brass struggling with a portable comfort station, my hilarity ended late the same day when the chief ranger strode into our living-room and dropped his hat on the mantel.

'Like to have some company, Marge?' he asked. 'Tomorrow, I mean?'

'I'd love it. Grace hasn't been over for weeks.'

'I don't mean my wife; she's in San Francisco,' he said slowly. 'I'm speaking of the President's wife.'

I thought the chief was having his little joke and waited for him to laugh—he didn't.

'I'm serious, Marge,' he said. 'And no need to look so frightened; she won't bite you.'

'Serious?' I managed. 'You really mean she . . . No. I don't believe you. She's never even heard of me——'

'That's probably right,' he broke in. 'But I thought you might like to meet her.'

I smiled then and came up for air. 'You had me for a moment,' I said, relieved. 'I suppose Bill put you up to this. It was a good try, too, but I'm not having any, thank you.'

'Listen, Marge. Wouldn't you enjoy going to the White House and have her show you through her home, explain how she meets her daily obligations, and what it's like to be the wife of the President?'

I nodded, waiting, tongue in cheek.

The chief stood up and reached for his hat. 'Well, she's just a woman the same as you. Washington called this morning and said she had expressed a desire to visit a ranger's home and meet his wife. I chose you, Marge. Mrs. Roosevelt will be here tomorrow. See you then.'

When I emerged from my trance, I felt that I was suffering from shock or complete paralysis. What had I ever done to deserve a fate like this? How did one go about entertaining a President's lady? What did you say or do? I looked about me. This was Chinquapin ranger station, and nothing I could do would ever make it anything other than a comfortable but plain cedar house that a ranger came home to each evening for a dinner prepared over a wood fire by his wife. Would she understand or be interested in knowing how we thrill to the glimpse of snow flowers, or how we drive miles to see the first dogwood blossoms in the spring, when she could have an armful of orchids by merely picking up the telephone? Bill said: 'Just be yourself. Pretend she's Mrs. Jones.' That didn't help. I was completely stunned.

The party arrived at our station next morning about ten. Five carloads of them. I recognized officials from the National Park Service, and high California state dignitaries; a very erect ranger escort stood at attention while Secret Service men swarmed everywhere. Mrs. Roosevelt was helped from her limousine and escorted towards the house by two Secret Service men. I ran to the front door, all atwitter, and stood there waiting, battling an overwhelming impulse to take to my heels and join the bears in the deep forest. Then the rap sounded on the door.

I waited a respectful few moments—to prove I hadn't been standing goggle-eyed at the window—and opened the door. Her level gaze met mine, and she smiled. She looked exactly like the pictures I had so often seen of her in the newspapers. We were introduced, and I invited her inside and asked if she would like to see the station. She would love to see it, as she never had been in a ranger's home. As I hesitated, wondering whether I should precede her, she said for me to lead the way, she would follow. She seemed to enjoy what she saw and was immensely impressed with Bill's guns and fishing tackle, which is always hanging all over the place. Returning to the living-room, she thanked me for my courtesy and assured me she hadn't meant to intrude on our privacy, her interest had stemmed from nothing more than a woman's natural-born curiosity. I said I hadn't been slighted in that department, either, and we both laughed. Suddenly she sank down in Bill's pet chair, I curled up on one end of the couch, and we fell to like Mrs. Jones and that O'Rafferty woman chatting across the back fence.

She was gracious and witty, possessed of a manner that put me immediately at ease and made me feel she was an old and tried friend. I enjoyed her immensely and was sorry when she rose to leave. As she was handed into the limousine, I caught sight of Bill, mounted on his shining charger at the head of the procession. He nodded and grinned his approval. I was beginning to understand his philosophy—the First Lady might be the renowned wife of the President of the United States, but she was also a human being. 'Just people,' as Bill had put it—and I liked her.

Ten

THE telephone rang at 5.45 a.m., and Bill, as usual, was out of bed at the first jingle.

'Ranger Merrill speaking.'

'This is one of the waitresses at the restaurant. There's been an accident near here. A man is hurt.'

'Be right over,' Bill said, reaching for his clothes as he replaced the receiver.

A few minutes later he spun out of the drive and headed down the highway, siren screaming. The accident had occurred not far from our station, and he soon pulled up at the scene. A light pickup truck had left the road and crashed head on against a solid fir tree well off the pavement. Sitting on the dangling running-board was a dishevelled young man nursing his left arm.

'Are you hurt?'

The man nodded.

'Your arm?'

'I think it's broke,' the man said. 'At the elbow.'

'What happened?' Bill walked close to the man. There was no odour of liquor about him. 'Why did you run off the road?'

'I—I guess I fell asleep.'

'I'll take you to the hospital,' Bill said, and pulled out his pad. 'Your name?'

The man made no reply.

'What is your name?' Bill demanded.

'Er—Jones. Er—William Jones.'

Bill peered closely at him. 'You're sure it's not Doe—John Doe?'

'I said my name is Jones. William Jones.'

Another car stopped, and the driver hurried across the road. 'Anything I can do?' he asked. 'Is this man injured?'

Bill looked up from his pad.

'I'm a doctor,' the man added.

'Good,' Bill said. 'Would you mind looking at his arm?'

While the doctor was getting Mr. Jones's coat off, Bill looked over the truck. It somehow had escaped serious damage and probably would run again. From the clip on the steering column he learned that the car was registered in the name of William L. Jones. The driver's licence was also in order. The faltering manner in which the man had spoken, Bill decided, was due to a natural hesitance in speech, or possibly to shock. Unless . . . He turned to the doctor.

'Any evidence of narcotics, Doctor?'

'None whatever. But there might be a fracture of the elbow. I've splinted the arm and put it in a sling. Pretty crude job, but it will hold it in place for the present.'

'I'll get him to the hospital,' Bill said, making out a summons and handing it to the injured man. 'This, Mr. Jones, is for negligent driving. You could have killed yourself.'

Mr. Jones got to his feet. 'I wasn't careless. I told you I went to sleep.'

'That is negligent driving,' Bill snapped. 'You also could have killed someone else.'

The doctor interrupted. 'By the way, Ranger, I could go right by the hospital. I'll drop him off, if you like.'

Bill agreed readily and informed Mr. Jones that his personal

146

effects and the truck, in case it would run, would be at the ranger station when he returned. After the two men had gone, Bill decided to search further—a practice carried over from Prohibition days. In the brush back of a log twenty yards off the pavement, he found a 30-06 Remington rifle that had recently been fired and two boxes of cartridges.

Mr. Jones returned from the hospital to our station shortly after noon and explained that his elbow had not been fractured after all. Just an injured nerve. Bill turned over his personal things.

'I—I see you found the gun,' the man said.

'When,' Bill asked, 'did you use it last?'

'Yesterday. Done a little target practice.'

'In the park?'

'No. Not in the park.' Mr. Jones smiled engagingly. 'That's the reason I got rid of it after the accident. I thought I wasn't allowed to have it in the park.'

Bill explained that it is permissible to bring a rifle into the park but that it must be sealed; this Bill had done. The man thanked him and drove off in the pickup and, before Bill could get away, the telephone was ringing.

'This is the hospital,' a voice said. 'Has Jones shown up at your station yet?'

'Yes,' Bill said. 'He collected his things and drove away in his truck. Anything wrong?'

'What did he have with him?'

Bill detailed his personal effects.

'Rifle? Good heavens! We gave him a strong sedative before treating his arm, and then he disappeared from his room. The sheriff called just now. This guy escaped from a mental institution. He's a dangerous criminal!'

Bill dropped the telephone and ran from the house. A moment later I heard the patrol car roar off down the road. He didn't have far to go; the pickup truck was parked in front of the nearby restaurant. The escaped prisoner turned around from the counter as Bill walked up behind him. The rifle was cradled between his knees. The seal, Bill noticed, had been removed.

'I'm hungry,' the man said simply.

'This is a good restaurant,' Bill replied.

'I ain't got no money.'

'That's the reason you brought the rifle in with you?'

Several people eating at the counter began edging away as the man deliberately raised the gun and rested it across his knees.

'I'm hungry,' he said again.

'Sure takes money to eat,' Bill said evenly. 'Why not trade some of your things for a big plate of ham and eggs?'

The man made no reply, but his fingers suddenly tightened around the stock of his rifle.

Bill caught the chef's eye, and a moment later a big slice of ham and two eggs were sizzling on the griddle behind the counter.

'I'll buy the rifle if you'll sell it,' Bill said carefully. 'Ten dollars?'

The man shook his head, and a wild look came into his eyes. 'No.'

'Twenty-five and that's all.'

Again the man shook his head, then suddenly extended his hand. 'Give me the money,' he demanded, his right hand still gripping the gun.

Bill said: 'I don't have it with me. We'll have to go to the station to get it. But,' he motioned to the chef, 'give him what he wants to eat.'

The tempting platter of ham and eggs was placed before the man, and it was more than he could resist. He turned to the counter and ate ravenously, awkwardly spearing the eggs with his fork and taking huge bites from the slice of ham which he picked up in his fingers. His movements were noticeably laborious because he was feeding himself with his left hand, his right still gripping the gun resting across his knees, his finger on the trigger.

Bill made no move, except to motion the frightened diners out of the way. He continued to wait. Twice the man's head nodded over the plate—the sedative administered at the hospital was beginning to take its toll—but he continued to eat. When he was all but finished, his head slowly sank to the counter. He was fast asleep. Bill picked up the rifle, slipped the handcuffs around the prisoner's wrists, and steered him out towards the patrol car.

When Bill returned to our station, he got the man inside and placed him on a couch in his office. While he was notifying the sheriff's office of the capture, I went to answer the front door. It was the doctor, the one who had splinted the arm and taken the escaped man to the hospital.

'Thought I'd drop by before they took him away,' he said, peering at the sleeping man. 'Dangerous criminal, eh? Never can tell by the way a man looks.'

Stooping over the sleeping prisoner he took his pulse, lifted the eyelids, then beckoned to me.

'Would you mind boiling some water?' he asked. 'And I'd like some alcohol, too, if you have any handy.'

I nodded and hurried to the kitchen, where I happened to have a kettle of water boiling on the stove. I was just reaching for the bottle of alcohol on the shelf when the doctor entered behind me.

'Could I also trouble you for some cottonwool?' he asked, apologetically. 'I'm sorry, but I don't have my bag with me.'

I had to go to another room to get the cottonwool, and was returning to the kitchen when I came to a sudden halt. The doctor, with his back to me, rummaging through his pockets, seemed as I reached the doorway to find what he was searching for —a hypodermic needle. I turned quietly and slipped away to the office.

'Are you sure that man is a doctor?' I whispered.

'What do you mean?' Bill asked.

'He doesn't carry his syringe in an antiseptic case, like they all do. It was loose in his coat pocket and——'

I stopped speaking as the man strode into the office, the hypodermic in his hand.

'I'll give him an injection before they take him away,' he said, raising the prisoner's arm. 'Won't give you any trouble that way.'

'Just a second,' Bill said quickly. 'As a matter of form, Doctor, would you mind showing me your credentials?'

The man reached inside a breast pocket and brought forth a leather folder, which he placed in Bill's hand.

'I don't think it will be necessary to give another injection under the circumstances,' Bill said, after carefully inspecting the folder. 'I have the prisoner securely handcuffed, and I'm sure he won't cause any trouble.'

'Very well.' The man hesitated, then picked up his hat and without another word walked out.

'I don't understand it,' Bill said to me. 'No doctor would carry a hypo syringe loose in his pocket like that.'

'If he did, for some reason, he certainly wouldn't use it without sterilizing it and he didn't have time to do that,' I said. 'Whoever he is, he can't be a doctor.'

'But he is a doctor,' Bill nodded emphatically. 'I saw all his papers. No doubt about it. I just don't understand it at all.'

We learned the answer two days later—after the escaped prisoner was safely back in his cell—from an article in the newspaper. The doctor had recently disappeared from his home in a distant city. Ill and overburdened with domestic affairs, he had become mentally unbalanced. Worried over his condition, he took the short way out—suicide.

Another hectic few minutes were laid in our lap late one evening while we were living at Chinquapin station. It was well after the dinner hour, and we were in the living-room where Bill was industriously thumbing through the newspaper and I was deep in a new historical novel. It had been a peaceful evening, entirely too calm; one of those peace-on-earth-good-will-to-everybody evenings that usually end with an atomic explosion. I heard a car stop out front, and the rather strident voices of the occupants reached my ears, but I was too immersed in my book to pay any attention. Presently Bill laid aside the sport section and got to his feet.

'Quite a rumpus out there,' he said. 'Sounds like a couple of drunks.' He went to the open door and peered outside. 'Be back in a minute.'

I flipped the page and once more became lost in the Deep South of my novel.

When Bill came back inside he was grinning and chuckling to himself. The couple in the car out front were something he hadn't been quite prepared for, and he had thought himself braced for anything. Their beat-up old touring car was of a vintage rarely found even in antique museums, its longevity perpetuated largely by binder twine and yards of bailing wire. The two people, a fairly young couple celebrating their honeymoon, had become embroiled in a heated discussion, and the man had parked beside the road to give his undivided attention to the business at hand—which was rapidly developing into a brawling free-for-all. But Bill had got them quieted, and everything seemed to be under control.

'Just like a bantam rooster tangling with a hawk,' he said, and laughed. 'He isn't any bigger than a June bug.'

I was sorry I had missed them; people always fascinate me. But I needn't have been so concerned, for, about an hour later, we were brought to our feet by a wild commotion outside that propelled Bill through the doorway before I could recover my book from where it landed in a heap on the floor. From the yelling and screeching it sounded like the final charge on the Alamo, and I dashed out after Bill.

It was the same couple he had talked to earlier. Instead of driving on, as we had supposed, they had apparently stayed right where he left them. Broken liquor bottles lay beside the road where they had been tossed; the man was surly and belligerent, while the woman appeared to be entering a dazed, poker-faced state of oblivion. Bill brought them over to the station and unceremoniously dumped them both on the porch. Headquarters was calling on the telephone and, after a cursory glance at the blinking couple, he hurried inside. There certainly didn't seem to be any great chance involved in leaving them for a few seconds. The man was slumped against the wall like a sack of meal, and the woman sat with her head pressed down on her knees. Anyway, Bill had their car keys in his pocket. But the man, without a second's warning, jumped to his feet and took off like a scared rabbit.

'Bill!' I yelled. 'Come quick!'

He came running, but the man was already in his car and coasting off down the steep grade into the valley, driving without headlights or engine and gaining momentum by leaps and bounds. Bill sprang into the patrol car and took off after him.

'Watch the woman,' he yelled over his shoulder.

I watched the woman, although I didn't think it necessary. She was still sitting with her head buried in her lap, hadn't moved a muscle since Bill dropped her there. I knew she was sloppy drunk, the same as the man, and I was beginning to wonder if she had passed out, when she finally raised her head and managed to focus her eyes on me.

'Where ish he?' she demanded. 'Where ish my hushband?'

I said, 'Don't you know?'

She shook her head.

'He went down the road,' I said. 'The ranger is with him, I hope.'

She began to blubber. 'He's gone. Dishappeared on my wedding day.' Suddenly she stopped, then deliberately raised her hand and pointed an accusing finger directly at me. 'You took him!' she screeched. 'You got my hushband away from me!'

I blinked and shook my head. 'No. I wouldn't want him. I mean, I have a husband of my own.'

'Never satishfied,' she said, ignoring me. 'I had one hushband and wash satishfied. But not you. No. You've got to have two!'

She made a move to get to her feet, and I wondered whether to sit on her or take to my heels. Then she started to rise, and my mouth must have fallen open inch by inch as I stared. There was more woman than I was accustomed to seeing in one package. She came up by degrees, like a folding rule. No wider than a self-respecting rake, she was well over six feet tall; I felt like a Pygmy looking up from a deep hole.

'You—you're mistaken,' I managed, hoping my voice would reach up to her. 'Your husband will be back. Let's go inside. I'll get you some hot coffee, and you can tidy up a bit.'

'No.' She stood weaving dangerously, her big hands clenched into hard fists. 'I want him to shee what he's done to me.' She raised a hand to explore a bruised cheek and probed gently at a blue and green bruise that was slowly closing her left eye. 'He'll be shorry when he shees me layin' here, dead as a mackerel.'

'Oh, come now,' I said quickly. 'You're not going to die.'

'Oh yesh I am,' she said defiantly, and suddenly took off in long loping bounds across the moonlit yard, looking not unlike an ungainly kangaroo. It was so unexpected that for a second I was as inanimate as a clothing-store dummy. Then it dawned on me what she was about to do.

'Good heavens!' I shrieked, and took off after her.

She was vaulting straight across the yard towards the canyon wall above Indian Creek.

'Wait!' I yelled. 'Don't jump. You'll kill yourself!'

But I could see that that was just what she intended to do. With a desperate, last-second diving tackle I seized her around the knees and brought her down almost at the edge of the dark drop-off, where we landed in a swirling mass of churning feet and flying elbows.

'Y-you can't do that,' I panted, hanging on like a bulldog. 'I won't let you.'

'You little whiffet!' she snarled. Then she stood up, jerked me to my feet like a rag doll, and shook me so hard my teeth rattled. 'You ain't big enough to stop me!'

That made me mad. 'All right,' I snapped. 'Go ahead and jump! Go on, and see if I care!'

'Herbie's gone,' she said brokenly. 'He won't come back to me ever again.' She looped her long arms around me and started to bawl. 'Without my hushband I don't want to live! Unnerstand?'

'Well, I want to live!' I yelled. 'Leave me alone.'

She shook her head, stumbling with the effort. 'No.' She was suddenly racked with a crying jag. 'You ain't goin' to get my hushband, either. I'll fix you!' She gave me a quick shove towards the precipice.

'What's going on here?' Suddenly a strange man was standing before me, his fingers gripping my assailant's arm. 'You're drunk,' he said, peering into her face. Then he looked at me.

'I—I'm not,' I stammered. 'I just look that way. She tried to push me over the ledge.'

'Lucky I happened along,' he said. 'I stopped here at the ranger station to report an accident back there at the bottom of the hill.'

My heart stopped beating. 'Bad?' I asked.

'I think so. Other people were there. I didn't stop.'

I thanked him and hurried off as fast as I could to the station to call headquarters. When I turned from the telephone, I found the tall woman sitting in the living-room, wringing her hands and sobbing noisily.

'My poor, dear Herbie,' she wailed. 'He's dead, or hurt an' bleedin' all over the plashe. My duty ish at my hushband's side.' She staggered to her feet and pointed a finger at me. 'You take me to my hushband.'

'No,' I said quickly. 'I'm not taking you anywhere.'

She stopped wobbling and her eyes bored into mine.

'Woman, you're takin' me!'

'No!'

She seized my arm. 'You take me to my hushband or I'll— Unnerstand?' Her fingers tightened, and she dragged me towards the open door. Then she suddenly stopped and stood staring at me as if I weren't there.

'Shay, that couldn't be my Herbie,' she said to herself. 'He washn't drivin' a green car. Ish a black one.' She dropped my arm, and her fingers slowly curled into tight fists. 'No. It washn't Herbie. He got away, you hear? Clean away from me! Killin's too good for the little bum—too good for . . .'

I wasn't hearing what she said; I was reeling under an impact that struck me a sledge-hammer blow. I reached up and seized her by the shoulders.

'Did you say green?' I asked in a hollow voice. 'Was it a green car that was wrecked?'

'Thash what I said. But it washn't Herbie, the little rat.'

'How do you know it was green? Who told you?'

'The man said it wash a green car. Thas' what he said.'

In the distance I could hear the wailing of an ambulance siren, and I suddenly sat down, closing my eyes to shut out the vivid picture of Bill, crushed and unconscious in the wreckage of his green patrol car at the bottom of the grade. Then I closed my eyes tighter and held my breath as I heard a car stopping in front of the station and footsteps hurrying towards me. Someone was coming to prepare me for the news that had to be told, coming to tell me there had been an accident and——

'Marge, you're crying. What's the matter?'

I looked up, doubting my senses. Bill was standing there

grinning down at me, patting my shoulder with one hand while the other retained a firm grip on the coat collar of little Herbie. I jumped to my feet, and so did Herbie's wife, but I pushed her to one side as easily as if she had shrunken to the size of her diminutive husband.

'Oh, Bill!' I gasped, clawing at him. 'I'm so glad. I thought you were dead.'

'Dead?' He looked oddly at me. 'Oh, you heard about the accident. This little man here sideswiped two fellows in a big green Hudson while he was trying to get away. They're taking both of them to the hospital for a check. I found this fellow piled up against a tree without a scratch on him.'

The woman placed herself solidly in front of Herbie and menacingly folded her arms.

'So!' she growled deep inside her. 'You wash runnin' away from me, wash you? You little whipperschnapper!'

'Now, Mamie. Wait!' Herbie pleaded, looking like hara-kiri would be a pleasure. 'I wouldn't run away from you, dearie. You're my own true love. You know that, sweetheart!'

I didn't believe what I saw, but Mamie—all of her—slowly folded over and gathered the little man in her powerful arms and hugged him snugly to her bosom—just as the paddy wagon arrived. She was still fawning over him when Bill led them outside, and they were almost inside the wagon before she suddenly halted.

'Shay!' she barked. 'If he washn't runnin' away from me, where wash he goin' in such a big hurry?' She swung around facing Herbie.

'N-now, Mamie!' Herbie started to beg. 'Mamie, my love! You know I wouldn't . . .'

They were pushed inside, and there were sounds of great activity emanating from the rear end of the paddy wagon as it rolled away to the jail at park headquarters.

In 1937 we were transferred from Yosemite to Boulder Dam National Recreational Area in Nevada. It was quite a change from the big trees, the green mountains, and the waterfalls of Yosemite, but we did enjoy a winter practically free from snow. But

155

somewhere, somehow we must have offended Allah, for we were still stationed there in March during the usual spring flood that lasted for seven days and nights and left the desert a floating quagmire such as had rarely been seen before.

Bill, as usual, took everything in stride. In case the bridge was washed out, you somehow managed to ford the stream; desert patrols could still be maintained in spite of rainstorms, sandstorms, and wheels miring down to the axles. But it was while struggling with a bogged-down car that it happened. Bill got a hernia, and it became worse so rapidly that we were forced to contact the Marine Hospital in San Francisco, where he was ordered to report at once for surgery. After I'd spent an hour on the telephone checking on every possible mode of transportation, I was fit to be tied.

'What on earth can we do?' I asked Bill. 'There are so many washouts the railroad has cancelled all trains. The airport is closed until further notice. The highway department says so many bridges are out there isn't a chance of driving. No through traffic is on the roads at all. What can we do?'

'We'll have to drive,' he said. 'Don't seem to have any choice.'

'But the bridges are gone. The highway department just said——'

He stopped me. 'I know. This has been the wettest season so far on record, but there must be a way out of here, somewhere. We'll make a run for it tomorrow.'

He took the car away to be serviced, and I sat down to indulge in some high-powered worrying. From what I had just been told, there wasn't even the glimmer of a chance of getting to San Francisco, where the government would assume all responsibilities for the operation—or to get to any other place—until some of the washed-out bridges were replaced. It had stopped raining, at last, and the desert was fast becoming dry, but streams of any size would remain raging torrents for days to come.

I knew it was imperative to get Bill to the hospital as soon as possible. He never admits to being ill, although he thinks the first twinge of pain in my little finger is of such grave importance that hospitalization with attending physicians is immediately

156

indicated. But from the look on his face and the grim set of his jaw I knew he was suffering intense pain. When he returned with the car, he sank into his chair for a few moments before speaking.

'Can't go south,' he said slowly. 'I made some inquiries. We'll take a chance and head north.'

That would be almost like starting for Mexico by way of Canada.

'It's the only possible way,' he went on. 'Rains haven't been so heavy up north. There's a chance we can circle back through California to San Francisco. Let's get to bed. Want to get an early start tomorrow.'

At five o'clock the next morning we were ready to leave. The car was waiting out front in the roadway, where he had parked it. We had no garage. I persuaded Bill to lie down in the rear seat, and for once he made no objection. I slid under the wheel and stepped on the starter.

The road was dry, and we made good time until we reached the first stream. The bridge was gone, but I managed to get to the other side as the water wasn't too deep for fording. But at the next stream I was flagged down by a watchman.

'Bridge is closed,' he said. 'Nobody can get across.'

'But I must get across,' I said quickly.

'It ain't safe, lady. Some of the piling has washed away.'

I was getting desperate. 'I'm taking my husband to the hospital. He's there in the back seat. See for yourself. I must get across!'

The flagman took a look at Bill's pale face and said for me to wait. He hurried away and returned in a few minutes with the man in charge. An hour later, and with some temporary supports hastily set in place beneath the swaying bridge, I carefully drove across and headed for Reno.

Since the rain had stopped, the day before, the wind had been gaining velocity by the hour, and there was now a steady gale. Far up ahead I could see what looked like a dark storm cloud that blotted everything from sight. I held on to the wheel, trying to keep the car on the road. Then it happened—the last thing on earth I would have expected. The engine sputtered, coughed

157

once, and died, and almost at the same instant a pounding hail-storm descended on us.

Bill sat up in the rear seat. 'What's the trouble?'

'I don't know.' I shook my head, and my startled gaze travelled across the instrument panel and stopped. 'We're out of gas!'

'I filled it last night,' Bill insisted, shouting over the roar of the hail. 'Every drop it would hold.' He opened the rear door, climbed slowly to the ground, and removed the cap from the gas tank. Then he inserted a measuring stick that we kept in the car for that purpose. 'It's empty,' he called. 'Someone must have stolen it during the night.'

I felt myself getting a little panicky. 'What will we do?'

'Pull over to the side of the road,' he said calmly. 'The battery will take you that far.'

It did, and Bill slid in beside me.

'I'm frightened,' I chattered. 'What's going to happen to you? It's probably miles to a gas station and you might die before help comes!'

'I'm not going to die.' He grinned at me and rummaged in the glove compartment. 'Take it easy, Marge. I'm going to take this flashlight and get out in the middle of the road. I'll flag down the first car that comes along.'

'The first car?' I said suddenly. 'There aren't any cars!'

'Bound to be one some time.' He got out, closing the door behind him.

I was experiencing my first real rain-and-hail storm, and it was unbelievable—the day had turned almost as dark as night. The hurricane wind was driving the pellets before it like a million particles of flying steel; it rattled like shrapnel against the glass. I couldn't see as far as the cap on the radiator. Bill stood braced beside the car, his face a mask of agony, the flashlight ready in his hand. I waited, and prayed, and waited.

An hour passed, a seemingly endless hour, filled with shrieking winds, blasting hail, and a rising surge of panic that warned me I couldn't much longer hold in check the gnawing fear that was mounting inside me. We could easily be waiting for something that wasn't going to happen. Suppose the bridges ahead were washed away and no traffic could get through? Even if the bridges were intact, it would require a pressing emergency to force another car out in a storm like this. But Bill hung on doggedly, flashlight in one hand, the other gripping the door handle for support.

Then the car was upon us, without warning. A pale yellow glow suddenly appeared through the haze, and Bill was waving frantically with his flashlight. The headlights swam nearer, passed by, and the car was gone, leaving a dark void behind. I was so let down I couldn't move. Bill leaned near the window and grinned in at me. One second he was there before me, and the next he was gone, disappearing in the direction taken by the car. I whirled around to look. Nothing was in sight; even Bill was now swallowed in the roaring inferno. Frantically I tried to open the door—the wind held it rigidly fast. I tried the door opposite and it flew open at the first touch. But before I could get out, Bill was back, climbing inside and closing the door behind him.

'The man stopped,' he said quickly. 'Saw my flashlight just in time. I'm going with him.'

'But he can't get through,' I cried. 'They won't let him cross that bridge back there.'

'Told him about that,' Bill said. 'He's going to take the cutoff about a mile back and angle off towards Death Valley. He thinks there's a gas station at Indian Wells.'

'Bill, I'm going with you. I'm afraid to stay out here alone.'

He shook his head. 'You'll have to stay here, honey. This man has an important engagement to keep, but he's willing to drop me off at the gas station if we can find it. I'll have to walk back or catch a ride, if I'm lucky. It might be miles.'

I started to protest that he was in no condition to battle his way through such a storm, but he was gone, and I was alone, and I was frightened. Anything could happen to him out there on that deserted stretch of road; he could be run down by a car; he could suddenly become so ill and weak that he would be unable to continue. In such a storm as this he could die—and these storms often last for hours on end.

159

After I had waited for what seemed countless hours and was preparing to make a frantic search for him, a car drew up alongside and Bill got out, with two large cans of gasoline, which the driver helped him pour into our empty tank before departing. It was the same man, a travelling salesman, who had taken Bill to the gas station and then been kind enough to bring him back. We have always been sorry we didn't learn his name or address so that we could express our true thanks, for which we had every due cause: during the next few hours, as we slowly ground our way through the wind and blinding rain, we met no living person or thing.

Bill insisted on driving, but I wouldn't budge from behind the wheel. He said he felt fine—and even looked it. I have never been able to understand how he can recover so rapidly. He can be so ill you're sure it's already too late to call the doctor, and a few minutes later he will be in the patrol car roaring off on an emergency call. He has been shot through the stomach, the neck, one leg, and a hand. He has been knifed, his hip was once broken, his shoulder smashed, and both wrists broken—twice; there were also a few rattlesnake bites, but after all the other disasters, they seemed of no prominent consequence. Of course, when he's sick, he's as low as anyone else, and our constant bumping over the desert road soon had him once more curled up in the rear seat, bathed in perspiration.

Long before reaching Reno, I decided against the San Francisco hospital; I would get him into the first one I could find. It was after dark when we finally arrived in Reno, and I lost no time in locating a good motel, where I hastily tucked Bill into bed, and went in search of a hospital, any hospital. I found one that would accept him the following morning, and I hurried back to the motel. I heard it the instant I opened the door—that odd little tune about the monkey and the flagpole—but I wouldn't believe I was hearing correctly. Slowly I pushed open the door and peered inside. I didn't believe it, but I had heard right. Bill was standing there before the mirror, shaving, his body swaying to the tune that came bubbling out through the lather, one foot tapping out the rhythm.

'Bill!' I exploded. 'You get right back in bed this instant! In the morning you're going to the hospital. I've been over there, and——'

'You know, Marge,' he interrupted, without losing a stroke, 'I've been thinking. We may never be in Reno again. Tonight we're going to do the town!'

'Have you lost your mind?' I cried. 'You're so sick——'

'Who, me?' He turned to look at me, incredulous. 'Never felt better. Get into your pretties. Reno, here we come!'

We did the town. I knew there was no keeping him down unless he was actually dying. We started with a wonderful dinner in a large hotel and continued breathlessly on through all the glittering casinos, ending the late evening with Bill trying to outstare the one-armed bandits standing menacingly inside each door.

Early next morning we headed cross country for San Francisco. Donner Pass had been buried by new snowslides, but we followed the rotary snowplough and were the first ones through the high pass. Several times on the long drive Bill was again writhing in pain, and each time he was forced to take to the rear seat for what small comfort he could find. By the time we reached San Francisco I was so numb I couldn't remember having crossed Bay Bridge with all the roaring traffic. At the entrance to Marine Hospital I had one final skirmish with Bill. He wanted to postpone the operation, just one more day, which would afford us time to 'do the town' before reporting. Again he was feeling 'fine'.

I manœuvred him up to the incoming desk, and a few minutes later he was safely tucked into bed. I had insisted on a private room for him, but none was available. The forty-man ward, where they took him to the farthest corner bed, was the last place I would have chosen for a quiet recovery. Bill said it was made to order. I waited for the doctor, a lieutenant-commander, in the hallway after he had made the examination.

'I will operate in the morning,' he informed me.

'At what time?'

'I haven't set the time yet.'

'But I want to know,' I persisted. 'May I call you later?'

'It won't be necessary,' he said. 'You can't be present, you know. You can see him the following day.' He turned on his heel, then stopped. 'Better leave your phone number at the desk, though, in case we want you.'

I swallowed hard. 'You mean if—if he——'

'Leave it at the desk,' he repeated, and strode away.

For the first time I felt that I already had lost Bill, and I stood staring at the blank wall, fighting back the tears, until a nurse stepped out from the ward.

'Please,' I said, trying to control my voice. 'My husband's in there.'

She smiled. 'Don't worry. Thirty-nine other fellows are keeping him company.'

'I—I mean I don't want him in there,' I mumbled. 'I want him to get well. Can't you put him in a private room?'

'You're lucky he's in a ward,' she said slowly. 'It's time to start worrying when they take 'em out of there.'

'But——'

'Look,' she said sweetly. 'When they put them in a private room, it's because their luck is running out—fast. Understand?'

'You mean——'

She nodded and tripped off down the corridor.

I stumbled out of the hospital and made my way towards the car. Bill and I had never been separated and already I felt hollow inside, as deserted as if I already had donned widow's weeds. For a long time I sat in the car trying to decide what to do. I just couldn't stand being alone in a motel, and a hotel would be even worse. At last I started the engine and drove blindly off, not knowing or caring where I was headed. I realized where I was when I noticed I was on Market Street. Suddenly I stepped on the accelerator and headed once more back across Bay Bridge, went on through Oakland, and covered another fifteen miles until I reached Hayward, where my brother Paul was living.

At a time like this I was sure I could use all the bolstering my own flesh and blood could offer. Never before had I experienced that all-gone feeling associated with calamity, and to me it was intimately associated with mayhem, butchery, and the gentle art of bloodletting. Everything had changed so swiftly from the moment I left Bill at the hospital and drove away by myself.

I would have been just as contented—or miserable—at a

hotel, for my brother's conversation, logical as it was, only reached me in a hazy sort of way. Nothing seemed to register except the fateful last words that nurse had spoken: 'When they put them in a private room, it's because their luck is running out —fast.' Why did she have to say that? Could it be that they were expecting that to happen? That reminded me of the doctor's request for my telephone number, and I called the hospital at once and gave it to them.

That night I slept fitfully on a couch in the living-room, where the telephone was within reach. By noon of the following day I was beside myself. The telephone hadn't rung once, and my brother said that was good, the hospital would have called if it had been necessary. Of course I knew he was right—unless they had lost, or misplaced, my number. If that had happened it would be impossible to locate me through the directory. I put in a hurried call.

'Ranger Merrill,' the desk reported, 'is doing as well as can be expected.'

I replaced the receiver and tried to feel relieved. I couldn't.

Next morning I was up bright and early. When I started for the hospital, I found myself crowding the speed limit to the last mile, but at Oakland I forced myself to slow down and get a grip on my nerves. There was no reason why I wouldn't have been notified if it had become necessary to contact me, I told myself. And Bill had assured me the operation was not really a serious one. Even the nurse's story about removing dying patients from the ward to private rooms was losing its sting, once I was able to regard it more calmly. A sense of comfort and well-being seemed to flow over me for the first time in days, and I climbed the steps to the hospital with a firm, sure stride, unable to wait for the elevator. And each step upwards seemed to justify the glowing pride I felt in my new-found tranquillity. My deportment, I was sure, would do a lot for Bill. I paused outside the ward door long enough to regain my breath, then, arranging a courageous smile on my lips, I stepped inside.

The bed assigned to Bill was in the far corner of the large room, and I went directly to it. But he was fast asleep, his head burrowed beneath the pillow, as usual. I sat on the edge of the bed, watching his rhythmic breathing, and smiled a little as I recalled the past few days. I really had tortured myself; every disaster that possibly could befall a man had come to pass—in my too-vivid imagination. Countless times I had all but buried him, and here he was, sleeping as soundly as a newborn babe. I felt I had learned a valuable lesson that I wouldn't soon forget. There was a movement under the blankets, and I got to my feet as he stretched and sighed lustily.

'Wake up, sleepyhead,' I whispered. 'You have company.'

He was quiet again, making no move at all, so I reached over and lifted the pillow from his face.

For a second I was too stunned to speak or move. It wasn't Bill at all. The man blinking up at me was a total stranger.

'Oh!' I gasped. 'I'm sorry. I thought you were my husband.'

I turned quickly away to hide my confusion and to get my bearings. How could I be so completely wrong? I would have sworn I could walk straight to Bill's bed, and I was forced to take one more look at the man to be sure he wasn't Bill. Could he be in the opposite corner? He wasn't, and then I began scanning each row, each bed, in dead earnest, while my hard-gained deportment began dissolving around my ears like a paper halo in a rainstorm. When I realized there were no more beds to peer into, I suddenly felt faint, and the ward began a wobbly circuitous movement that somehow propelled me to the door. Just outside I saw a nurse.

'W-where's my husband?' I mumbled. 'Where's Ranger Merrill?'

'They took him away.'

I seized her shoulders for support.

'You—you mean——' I couldn't say it.

The nurse nodded. 'Moved him to a private room yesterday.'

The building started to collapse on me, and I leaned hard against the wall. 'Take me to him,' I begged. 'Please, I must see him!'

She steered me down the long hallway, into a shorter one, and stopped in front of a door that bore no number. I seized the latch and started inside, but the nurse pulled me back and told me to wait. Then she went into the room, closing the door behind her.

Again I leaned against the wall and tried to pray, but she was back almost instantly.

'You can't go in now,' she said. 'You'll have to wait out here.'

Panic descended on me in full force. He was dead, or dying, I was certain. They were preparing me for the shock. My head was spinning, and my eyes refused to focus, but I had to know the truth—now.

'Tell me.' I seized her hands and stared hard into her eyes. 'Tell me what happened. Is he—is he——'

'The doctor will be out directly,' she said, freeing herself. 'Don't go in there. Wait right here.' She hurried away.

I dabbed at my swimming eyes and stood staring at the closed door in front of me. The suspense was stifling, and I found it almost impossible to breathe. If only he was alive! Anything could have happened and I was sure it had, but I would have been so grateful to have him back even if he had lost a leg, or both legs; I would give anything just to have him look up and smile at me once more. But I could tell what had happened from the way they acted—the presence of Death was everywhere.

The door finally opened and a nurse walked out, a covered tray in her hands. The doctor followed a moment later, softly closing the door behind him. While I tried to speak he started off along the corridor, then paused and came back to me.

'You're Mrs. Merrill?'

I nodded dumbly, biting my lips.

He opened the door and stood to one side. 'You may go in now.'

'Me?' I managed to say. 'Alone?'

'I think he would want it that way.'

My legs suddenly turned to rubber. 'I—I can't!' I chattered. 'Won't you . . . Will you please go in with me?'

He took my arm and led me through the doorway.

'Hi, Marge! Say, I had my appendix out, too.'

I stopped in my tracks. I leaned heavily on the doctor. I was overwhelmingly sick with relief.

'Here,' the doctor whispered to me. 'Better sit in this chair.'

'You been sick, honey?' Bill asked anxiously. 'You don't look so good.'

The doctor handed me a glass of water.

'This ranger of yours is quite a patient,' he said, his words barely reaching me. 'Had to move him into a private room here to keep him quiet. He was entertaining the whole ward.'

'Come clean, Doc. . . . You know you wanted to talk guns. . . .' Bill's voice seemed to be undulating, as if it had a loose connection. 'Run down to the car and bring me my thirty-eight, will you, Marge? Want to show it to Doc, here . . .'

I was so stupefied, and so exasperated, and so utterly relieved —I gulped a swallow of water and went and got the gun.

Eleven

A RANGER'S life is one that, judged by the wildest flight of imagination, never approaches the fringe of monotony—something is forever happening. Although Bill seems to have had more than his share of hair-raising adventure, interesting and frequently exciting experiences are the lot of every ranger. If you enjoy meeting people, from important foreign potentates to Sam Spindelshank of Singletree, Iowa, if you are fascinated by deep canyons and towering mountains, by still blue lakes, rushing streams, and tumbling waterfalls, if you like woods, animals, bright sunshine, and unadulterated adventure, if the earthy smells of the cool, green forest cause your blood to run fast—and if you are not averse to the evolutions of exacting labour—then you never will become bored with the life of a ranger.

One thing that always intrigues me is the periodic moving from one related area to another, or even into a different park with which we are not familiar. From the time Bill and I were first married, this experience has been one that we never seem to tire of. Always there are new trees to study, new flowers, strange people, and a host of new animals to explore.

Olympic National Park in northern Washington is a wild retreat for mallard ducks, and their V formations in the sky are a familiar and lovely sight. The icy waters of Lake Crescent harbour the strange Beardsley, a large game fish indigenous to no other known location in the world. There are hordes of raccoons and lesser animals, plus a generous supply of mountain lions and the exclusive tule elk, large-antlered animals which travel in great herds across the mountains. Here you find the Rain Forest with its profusion of ferns and moss-covered trees. This is truly a wilderness, and indeed, Olympic National Park is also known as the Wilderness Park. In this area are found the trees which are used for telephone poles throughout the country and for high masts on ocean-going vessels. These trees reach dizzy heights, nearly 300 feet, and are so dense that the edge of a cutting resembles nothing so much as a field of giant stalks of grain. Sheer granite walls a mile high also add to the magic splendour of Wilderness Park.

The regions surrounding Yosemite are bulging with green-clad mountains, tumbling waterfalls, acres of wild poppies, redbud, and lupine. Hidden in the forest are the deer, the bear, and uncountable smaller animals. The bears once reached such proportions that the government ordered scores of them captured and dispatched to other locations. In 1924, hoof-and-mouth disease struck California, and hunters were hired to kill off the deer. North of Yosemite twenty-two thousand were destroyed, and within five years this area was again a fine hunting ground.

When we were transferred from Boulder City, in 1937, to General Grant National Park in California, which is now a part of Kings Canyon National Park, I really got into my stride. From the very first Bill insisted that I become familiar with our surroundings, wherever we lived, and he has never been too tired to help in every way possible. I attended campfire lectures by park naturalists to learn about the flowers, the birds, and all living, growing things. Discourses at headquarters gradually brought into focus the park's history from the Ice Age down to the present. From a ninety-year-old Indian squaw I learned the art of weaving baskets from raffia and pine needles, and later I was asked to teach weaving and wood carving. When naturalists conducted nature walks along the trails, I was often left behind with a small interested group, to point out the flowers, birds, trees, and animals. Bill always prevailed on me to spend a part of each day in the outdoors, summer and winter, and he never objected or complained if, as a result, our meals were sometimes late or if they completely failed to materialize.

It was during World War II, while our men were busy training with the FBI in sabotage and espionage methods for dealing with fire bombs, that we women were the busiest. Many rangers had joined the fighting forces and could not be replaced. If our coastal cities were bombed, particularly the smaller towns and communities, the population would descend on us for protection, and we women were trained for this emergency. We had classes in sewing, nutrition, canteen work, home nursing, first aid, mechanics, and communications. We were called the Blue-jeans Brigade and learned to extinguish fires and to repair and drive trucks. Bill was highly in favour of all my activities. Also, for the first time, we were allowed to plant vegetable gardens inside the park, and the time allotted for tending them was known as the social hour; it came each evening after dinner. Of course, the deer also worked in our gardens—right after we had gone home —and then the bears took over for the rest of the night. But before World War II, hundreds of victims from the Dust Bowl were moved into General Grant by the ERA. Ragged, under-nourished, grimy beyond description, they were a sorry and pathetic sight. By comparison, the characters in the *Grapes of Wrath* seemed part of a fairy story. Two hundred families were quartered in a tented city near our station, and Bill's troubles began at once. The men were employed in the park constructing trails and roads, and many of them seemed to be suffering from an acute attack of laziness. The women took care of their canvas homes and looked after the children.

Overnight the appearance of the neat camping site changed from a well-taken-care-of area to something resembling the back alley of a disreputable tenement district. Odd pieces of furniture, papers, bottles, and broken parts from old cars were strewn promiscuously over the landscape. Large shiny garbage containers stood in long rows, empty, while refuse from most of the two hundred tables lay on the ground, just outside the tent flaps from where it had been hurled. Front yards were being utilized as bathrooms, while toilet bowls were pressed into service as laundry tubs for the family wash.

The children posed another problem. They came to the school, which was operated solely for their use, hungry, in cast-off clothing that neither covered them nor kept them warm. They were entirely unsanitary, and discipline was something of which they had never heard, no less experienced. Nearly every boy carried a knife in his pocket, or a blackjack—and knew how to use it; the girls fought with teeth and fingernails, and each foot was empowered with the wallop of a Missouri mule. Illiteracy was something most of them had in common, and the teachers, as well as the public-health nurse who called once a week, had their work cut out for them.

To me the most amazing thing of all came to light on the first payday. Cars streamed out of the park in a steady parade until the camp was empty as a desert ghost town. When they returned late that night, most of these people had spent their last sou, were howling drunk, or had made purchases of items for which they would never have any earthly use. Instead of buying quantities of food, which they all needed so desperately, their pockets were emptied primarily for silk shirts, boxes of candy, and cheap costume jewellery. A few days later, when they were once more hungry and destitute, they immediately appealed to Bill, in the mistaken belief that the ranger in charge somehow could supply all their wants. This led to some exciting interludes, to say the least, and at one time all but launched a full-blown riot. They were a strange people who spoke a strange tongue.

Jeff Kites was in no way different from the rest—tall, spare, unshaven, his questioning eyes peering out from beneath a great shock of unruly hair. It required very little imagination to picture him working over a still somewhere back in the hills of Kentucky, his home before he migrated to Oklahoma. It was about nine o'clock one evening when he opened the station door and ambled into Bill's office.

'Howdy,' he said. 'My woman's out yonder. She's a grannyin'.'

Bill looked up from his papers, puzzled.

'She's a-goin' to birth a young'un.'

'Oh. A baby.' Bill lighted his pipe and grinned. 'Congratulations.'

Jeff Kites was a lean statue as he stood propped against the edge of Bill's desk. 'Hit's her first birthin',' he said solemnly. 'She's a-feared. Scairt plumb to death.'

'You let me know,' Bill said, 'in plenty of time. It's sixty five miles from here to the nearest doctor, you know. When do you expect to become a father?'

'Any minnit.'

'What!' Bill shot out of his chair like an explosion. 'Are you sure?'

The man nodded. 'Yes. Any minnit now.'

'Bring her in here—and hurry,' Bill directed. 'I'll call the doctor.'

The doctor was in surgery.

'But I have a woman up here at General Grant who's going to have a baby,' Bill insisted to the office nurse.

'I'll try to get in touch with him,' she promised. 'I'll call you back as soon as I can.'

Bill turned around, swabbing his forehead. The mountaineer was back in the office with his wife. She was a tiny thing in her early teens and looked more like a child than a married woman who was about to give birth to a baby.

'Come along, woman.' Jeff Kites was urging her across the room. 'Get a hold on yourself.'

The woman stopped to lean heavily against her husband. 'I can't go nary nuther step,' she panted. 'Got to blow a minnit till I ketch my wind.'

'Put her in this chair,' Bill said, bringing one forward.

Gratefully she sank down on the cushions and looked up into his eyes.

'Will you holp me?'

'Of course,' Bill assured her. 'The doctor's nurse will call me the second she reaches him. He'll be right up.'

171

'I'm a-feared,' the woman said simply, gripping her husband's hand. 'I'm scairt to death.'

'You can't fault her none,' Jeff said to Bill. 'Hit's her first birthin'.'

Suddenly the girl moaned weakly and doubled up in pain. Beads of perspiration began coursing down her pale face. Bill again seized the telephone.

'You've got to send the doctor,' he said, trying to hold his voice in check. 'This thing is going to happen mighty quick!'

The nurse said, 'Well, in that case, Ranger, it looks like you're going to be the doctor.'

'What!' Bill let go both barrels. 'See here, I'm no doctor. I've never even seen a baby. I mean, a little baby. I don't know——'

The nurse cut in: 'You'll have to deliver the baby, Ranger. Doctor is still tied up in surgery—it was an emergency. He can't possibly get out there in time. Here's what you do.' She gave specific instructions. 'You'll get along fine!'

'Oh no I won't!' Bill snapped. 'But—I'll try.'

As he hung up the receiver the girl was seized by another severe pain, and with one arm Bill swept the top of his desk clear, covered it with a blanket and gently placed her on it.

'Stay with her,' he called to Jeff. 'I'll be right back.'

In the kitchen he put a pot of water on the stove to boil and dropped a pair of scissors into it. Then, snatching a handful of towels from the cupboard, he hurried back into the office. In his first-aid kit he found some sterile rubber gloves and began stripping a pair on his fingers as he watched the girl writhing on the blanket. The pains were now coming at ever-shortening intervals, and she was moaning pitifully, teeth clenched, her face bathed in perspiration. When the telephone rang he answered it at once.

'Hurry, Doc,' he said quickly. 'If you get here right away . . . Oh!'

It was a neighbour calling on the phone.

'Can't talk now,' Bill snapped. 'We're having a baby. I mean . . . Call me later!'

A new sound had reached his ears, a gasping sort of wail that told him the time was at hand. He had just enough time to exchange his gloves for fresh ones when the baby arrived. He prayed for strength and followed the nurse's instructions.

'There, young fellow,' he said, admiring the newborn. 'Now you're on your own.'

An hour later the ambulance arrived to remove the mother and child to the hospital. The park furnished a ranger escort, and the caravan took off in grand style. But the wailing sirens and flashing red lights were to produce unexpected results, as Bill learned on the following day.

To prevent a recurrence of the night before, he checked the entire camp, searching out expectant mothers and informing each and all that headquarters had issued permission for them to be transferred to a location nearer a hospital. But the jobs of their men had to be threatened before they would consent to leave in such common fashion. They indignantly insisted that they were just as good as Jeff Kites' woman, and she had ridden off in a nice shiny 'contrapshun' with rangers, sirens, and pretty red lights.

The next day Jeff Kites ambled back into Bill's office and stood fingering his old hat, embarrassed and ill at ease.

Bill asked, 'What's on your mind, Jeff?'

'Well,' he said, painfully shy, 'you can lend me a helpin' hand, iffen you saw fit.'

'Be glad to,' Bill agreed. 'What is it?'

Jeff Kites grinned happily. 'The woman an' me was a-talkin',' he said earnestly. 'We was a-talkin' of the young'un you helped to birth. Hit would pleasure us a heap to name hit to you!'

And so, for the very first time, and proud as a peacock, Bill became a godfather.

The Yule season in the forest is celebrated in a manner that often seems strange and unreal to the teen-age generation of today but that transports most of their elders back to the glories of a childhood spent revelling in the simple tales of the old McGuffey's *Readers*. We not only love our Christmas customs but often, because of our isolation, find them a necessity. With an axe on his shoulder, Bill always goes out into the snowy woods and chooses a beautiful fir for our Christmas tree. I spend days decorating the house with fir, yellow pine, sequoia and tamarack cones. Many of the tree ornaments we make from the ends of tin cans, cut into different designs and embellished with colourful sequins glued on to the shiny surface. Candied popcorn balls are still with us, as well as long, looping strings of the white kernels, which we drape in sweeping arcs from the ceiling. The mantel is piled high with cedar boughs and mistletoe, while the entire room is bathed in the yellow light from a profusion of flickering candles securely wedged into their pine-cone holders. It is a season we look forward to with great anticipation, and one we always hope to share with some of our friends.

My brother Paul came to spend his vacation with us in 1941, while we were still living at General Grant. He arrived a few days before Christmas, in the middle of the preholiday preparations. At our 6,600-foot elevation there was always plenty of snow during winter months, and Bill parked Paul's car near the roadway below our station in the only area he had been able to keep clear. There was also plenty of ice to be had, and Bill lost no time in appropriating enough to pack the new ice-cream freezer which Paul had brought. For the next hour my brother took charge of the decorations while I baked a cake. Bill was busy turning the freezer crank.

'You know, Marge,' he said, after a good deal of cranking, examining the contents of the freezer, 'this stuff is cold as ice, but it doesn't freeze.'

'Keep turning the crank,' I said over my shoulder. 'It'll be ready by the time my cake is done.'

But it wasn't, and we couldn't understand why. Of course Bill wouldn't admit defeat, and he added more ice and poured on great scoops of salt and continued to crank the thing until he was practically blue in the face and ready to topple from his stool. And he was determined to conquer it without help from us if it took all day—and it just about did. The cream at last hardened to a frosty consistency, but refused to become thoroughly frozen. Bill felt he had at least won a moral victory, as we were able to dispose of the stuff, which we did by drinking the chilly soup to the last drop. Later we learned the cause of his dilemma: the freezer was designed to operate properly only when the crank was turned to the right. Bill is left-handed.

We were invited out that night to a potluck dinner, and the only way to get there was by skis, as the side road where our friends lived hadn't seen the snowplough in more than a week. Paul didn't care for any more snow that day, so just after dark Bill and I took off alone on our three-and-one-half-mile journey. It was a beautiful moonlit night, and Bill was singing lustily as we glided down the snow-packed road towards the valley. Skiing always does something to me. Skimming swiftly over the white snow with a biting wind rushing against your face, the easy rhythm of your body as you swing past the trees, plunging down the steep gullies and up over the rises—these produce an exhilaration that is like nothing so much as a cloud-skipping flight in the midst of an impossible dream.

We each carried ski-poles in our right hand. In his left Bill was carrying a pot of scalloped potatoes, and I was balancing a beautiful three-layer cake, with a towel carefully wrapped around it and knotted on top for a handhold. We had covered a mile or more when Bill stopped to adjust a ski binding—or so I thought— and I drifted on ahead. Intoxicated with the resplendent beauty of the night, I was startled when he suddenly shot past me with a yell that would have sent a wild savage scurrying for his tepee. He was flying like the wind, a cloud of fine snow swirling in his wake, the pot of scalloped potatoes swinging madly in his hand as he disappeared over a slight rise ahead. It was a familiar trick of his, and I should have suspected it sooner. I topped the rise and plunged down the grade after him.

His flying start had carried him far down the road, but I was gaining on him. Then he skidded badly approaching a sharp turn, and I was almost upon him. I had a fleeting glimpse of the lighted window of our friend's cabin down ahead as we rounded a clump of trees, but I was so intent on the race that I wasn't prepared for the sudden turn Bill was making to the left. The next instant I knew why he had done it. Instead of following the road around to the front of the cabin, he was snow-ploughing down a steep short cut into the rear yard. I tried to turn after him and found myself hurtling diagonally out towards a sheer drop-off high above the cabin. Swinging my skis sideways and sending snow flying over my head, I tried desperately to stop. But in a flash I knew I could never make it in time and, with no chance to think what I was doing, I automatically headed for a young sapling, the only tree between me and the cliff. I stopped against it with a sudden thud, but my three-layer cake didn't—it shot out of my grasp and fell with a sickening plop far down at the bottom of the gully, while the towel sailed gracefully on, making a perfect three-point landing on the cabin's side porch.

'Are you hurt?' Bill called as he struggled back up the bank.

I shook my head, gasping to regain my breath.

The cabin door flew open and Bob ran outside.

'What happened?'

'We were racing,' Bill shouted. 'I guess Marge lost her cake.'

'The race, too,' Bob laughed, reaching for the white cloth at his feet. 'Looks like she threw in the towel.'

The next day it started to snow again, and continued for six days and six nights. We already had had a heavy snowfall before this storm struck and gradually, like a rising white tide, the snow climbed up the sides of our cabin, closed in the windows, and eventually drifted entirely across the roof. Bill and brother Paul were busy with shovels keeping the front door free and digging down to open the chimney draught. Luckily, we had plenty of food on hand. It would have been difficult to get more since the snow-plough operator had quit his job, and it was almost impossible to travel over the soft snow on skis.

That night one of the big trees, a dead one, went down under the added weight of the snow. It was several miles away, but our house rocked with the thud of the giant crashing to earth. It snowed and blew and snowed some more. When the surface became packed we got out our skis and went down to the parking lot in search of Paul's car. Of course, it was nowhere in sight, but we finally located it under five feet of snow, by probing beneath the surface with our ski-poles. Paul was anxious about getting back to San Jose, where he was teaching school, so we dug down to his car and opened a passageway to the road. Then Bill, although he had never operated the rotary plough before, managed to get it under way and to open the highway. I was fast asleep that night, long after midnight, when I felt a hand on my shoulder.

'Get up, Marge,' Bill whispered. 'Come on!'

'What's wrong?' I stared up at him. 'Why aren't you in bed?'

'It's wonderful outside,' he said. 'We can't waste such a night sleeping. There's a full moon out there. Get up!'

When we stepped outside it was breath-takingly beautiful—a fairyland pageant bathed in silver lay glittering before us. The mountains and valleys were buried beneath a frosty blanket of diamonds with pools of blue shadows floating beneath each swaying tree. It was a virgin world created especially for us, and we made the most of it.

The various times we were stationed at headquarters in Yosemite Valley we always took full advantage of our location and enjoyed some wonderful experiences. In the early days of the movies, there was usually at least one company present shooting pictures in the park. Laurel and Hardy, William Powell, Gary Cooper, Jean Harlow, Frederic March, Wallace Beery—all of them were there at one time or another. I had great fun figure-skating for sport scenes in the news reels and once doubled for a well-known actress in skating, sledding, and skiing sequences for winter scenes in the picture she was making.

The valley was always beautiful in winter. The large Camp Curry parking area would be flooded and allowed to freeze; then pyramids of blocked ice were placed at intervals around the rim of the skating rink, with animals sculptured from ice mounted on the peaks. Often the ice-blocks had coloured lights frozen inside them, and when they were turned on the entire area was bathed in a wonderful magic light.

Usually I spent every free moment I could find on the ice, and although I was no professional instructor, I enjoyed helping a number of people learn to skate. One was a young girl who came wobbling across the rink one night and anchored on to me just in time to prevent repeating the calamity she had been staging all over the rink.

'Oh! I'm sorry,' she panted. 'I'm having such a dreadful time.'

'Let me help you,' I offered.

That was the way it usually happened, and this girl was no

exception, barring the fact that she probably possessed less natural skating ability and more bulldog determination to learn than did the average person.

'Do you think I'll make it?' she inquired, several hours later. I nodded. 'If perseverance counts for anything, you will.'

'Oh, I just have to,' she said. 'I must.'

'It can't be that important.'

'But it is,' she assured me, and introduced herself. 'In my next picture I have some skating sequences that I must do alone.'

She was Norma Shearer, and she made it.

We were back once again at General Grant during the war year 1941 when we heard the plane coming in one night over the station. It sounded like the wailing of a banshee as it dived down towards us. Bill darted outside and was recovering a parcel, trailing long streamers, from where it had dropped in the snow, when I joined him.

'Sure hope they've found them,' he said, opening the package and spreading out the sheet of folded note paper. 'Poor devils.'

I hoped so, too. Bill had talked of little else since it happened, and already a week had passed. Nineteen P-30s had been flying from March Field to Sacramento Air Base when they ran into a heavy October snowstorm. Five of the planes iced up so heavily they were forced to drop from formation and eventually crashed somewhere in the desolate Back Country. For seven days now other Army planes had been searching with no success.

'Two of them are alive,' Bill said, scanning the note. 'They've been seen from the air.'

'Thank heaven,' I said. 'At least they're safe.'

Bill shook his head. 'I wish they were. This note says their planes crashed on Sugar Loaf Mountain and the pilots seem to have landed somewhere in Dead Man's Canyon. The Army can't fly them out of a place like that.'

'They can't let them die there,' I said. 'What can they do?'

Bill frowned. 'It's my district. I think we'll soon be hearing from the Army.'

We did, a half hour later. It was the colonel calling from Hammer Air Field.

178

'We've spotted them,' he said. 'They're holed up in a cabin on the side of a mountain.'

'Any smoke?' Bill inquired.

'Yes. They have a fire going.'

'You're sure there are two pilots there?'

'Yes, saw them waving from the ground.'

'Good,' Bill said. 'You know if they're injured?'

'Can't tell. We're dropping food and blankets and medical supplies. But they've got to be brought out of there, Ranger, and the Army may not be able to get to them in time. Will you take charge of the rescue? I'll see that you get all the help you need.'

'I'll go in after them,' Bill assured the colonel. 'That's part of my job. Send me a map with the location marked on it. I'll need a crash crew—a good one. It's mighty rough going up there.'

It was late in the afternoon when the crew arrived, two truck-loads of men, with a Major Morley in charge. Bill collected the men and took off at once, equipped with head lamps, ropes, and two portable radios. The one-way road was deserted, as the high-way patrol, at Bill's request, had blocked it off to all sight-seers. It was already dark when the party reached Horse Corral.

'This is the end of the road,' Bill told the major. 'From here on we follow our nose. The men should be fed now and rested. We'll get an early start in the morning, as soon as it's light enough to see.'

'Wait till morning?' Major Morley said shortly. 'Why?'

'Because it's practically impossible to find your way around up there in the dark. And my pack animals won't be here until morning.'

'Why?'

'We don't keep pack animals out here this late in the fall. I've had to order them up from the valley.'

'Do we need pack animals?'

'We sure do,' Bill replied. 'If we find the pilots injured or suffering from exhaustion, it's the only possible way we can get them out.'

'Well,' the major said impatiently, 'I don't agree with you about waiting. If you are forced to wait for your animals, well and

179

good, but we must reach those men as soon as possible. I'll leave Captain Hale with you. I'm going to push on.'

'Very well,' Bill said. 'I'll give you Ranger Bates as a guide. Hope you get there before I do.'

The four pack animals arrived early the following morning, and Bill headed in with a group of eighteen soldiers. From the start the going was rough—straight up, straight down, around and over boulders and fallen trees, and it was bitterly cold every step of the way. It wasn't long before the soldiers began showing signs of dropping by the wayside, and Bill soon learned the reason. The troops he had drawn were composed of volunteers from the engineers and mechanics, together with a few yard birds of all descriptions—new and unseasoned men, none of them accustomed to high elevation. In the emergency they were the first men the colonel could lay hands on, and they had been rushed up to the park. Bill figured they had a good twenty miles to travel, in and out, and with the deep snow, slippery footing, steep climbing, and high altitude, this was equal to a good many additional miles under normal conditions.

By the time the party reached Cattle Camp most of the men were ready to drop in their tracks, especially Captain Hale, who was suffering from a chest cold. Bill had no intention of leaving anyone behind; every man could prove vital before the job was finished. But when he had given them a chance to rest and was ready to move on, one group complained they were simply exhausted and could not continue. Bill was on the spot, for, tired as they all were, he knew that if he allowed one man to remain behind, the entire party would be demoralized.

'I know just how tired all of you are,' he said to the men. 'I'm not exactly enjoying it myself. But we have a job to do that must be done as soon as possible. I doubt if any of you know what it means to be lost up here in this wild country. Those pilots disappeared over a week ago, and they might be injured and starving. If they are, it will take every man of us, working in relay teams, to carry them out on stretchers.'

'I can't make it,' one man spoke up. 'I'm so tired I can hardly breathe.'

'It's the elevation,' Bill assured him.

'No.' The man leaned against a tree, breathing hard. 'I just can't go on.'

When several of the men nodded their agreement, Bill knew he had to act quickly.

'I will not be responsible for any man left behind,' he snapped. 'How you protect yourselves will be strictly up to you.'

'Protect ourselves from what?' one man asked.

'Yeah,' another joined in. 'I ain't seen nothin' up here but squirrels.'

Bill pointed towards the old Cattle Camp cabin close at hand. 'Notice the door and windows,' he said quietly. 'They were barricaded for the winter with planks six inches wide and two inches thick. They've been ripped off like toothpicks and are lying on the ground. Take a good look at them. Chipmunks didn't do that.'

For a moment the men gazed, silent, then a big Negro sergeant sauntered over and picked up a sliver of the shattered wood. He peered at it, then back at Bill.

'What done it, Boss?'

'Bears.'

'How—how come?'

'Hungry,' Bill said. 'Looking for something to eat.'

'You mean . . .' He suddenly dropped the splintered plank and his eyes grew large as he pointed a finger towards the ground. 'Is that . . . Is them——'

'Bear tracks,' Bill said.

Each impression left in the snow was almost the size of a family washtub.

'Lordy!' the soldier gasped. 'I ain't gettin' social with no bear that big!'

Suddenly rejuvenated, the entire party pressed on with a renewed vigour that was astonishing. Of course, the going was still tortuous and got increasingly worse as the hours wore on. The major and Ranger Bates were still somewhere ahead, as was evidenced by the wandering tracks in the snow, which trailed off in ever-widening circles that showed they had often lost their bearings and trudged many unnecessary miles in the blackness of

181

the night. Bill met their party as the major was starting on the journey out.

The two surviving flyers were uninjured, well and hardy. One had parachuted into a tree within sight of a deserted cabin perched on the side of a mountain; the other came down several miles away. They had got together when the second one saw smoke floating up from the chimney of the old cabin where the first one had holed up. Food drops from the air had solved their eating problem. Major Morley and the two pilots mounted horses and soon were on their way back to Hammer Air Field. But as Bill and his party headed out it soon became apparent that Captain Hale's heavy cold, because of the high altitude, was becoming an emergency. On the rugged downgrade he became so completely exhausted that Bill was forced to assign the Negro sergeant to assist him across the mountains. And as the party finally approached Cattle Camp, he staggered and almost fell into the sergeant's arms.

'I'm sorry,' he said weakly. 'I'm done in. Can't make it any farther right now.'

It was plain to see that the captain was through for the day—his putty-grey face told its own story—and Bill led the way into the old cabin. A fire was laid in the grate, and some food and a huge roll of blankets were brought inside. Then Bill hurried out to get a bucket of water from the creek and almost tripped over the big Negro sergeant, on his knees just outside the door, intently examining the enormous tracks in the snow.

'Here,' Bill said, handing over the bucket. 'Know how to make coffee?'

'You bet, Boss,' the sergeant grinned. 'As a first-class cook, I'm a general.'

'Fine,' Bill said. 'Fill the bucket and bring it along.'

'Yes, suh.'

Bill strode back inside. 'I'll leave you here for the night,' he said to Captain Hale. 'By morning you should be ready to make it on out. We'll fix you some hot coffee. The sergeant here will——'

He hesitated as he glanced over his shoulder. The sergeant was standing right behind him, eyes the size of saucers, staring at the heap of chewed-up tin cans littering the floor.

182

'What—w-what done that, Boss?'

'Bears,' Bill said. 'When they find canned goods they always chew them open and drink the juice.' He turned back to the captain. 'You'll be comfortable enough here for the night, sir. I'll be back in the morning with horses.' He unholstered his forty-five and handed it to Captain Hale. 'Just in case you have guests during the night.'

'Where you want this here bucket put, Boss?'

'You're the cook,' Bill said. 'Make some good coffee and whip up a hot meal for the captain. Something else—it gets plenty cold up here, so don't let the fire go out during the night.'

'You—y-you mean . . . But look here, Boss. I ain't goin' to be up here tonight. I's goin' with——'

'You stay here with Captain Hale,' Bill said. 'I'll be back about seven in the morning, with horses.'

'We stay here all night?'

Bill nodded and started for the door.

'Boss! You g-got another them guns? These bears must be powerful hungry . . . An' they're awful big!'

Bill grinned. 'You'll find an axe in the woodshed. See you in the morning.'

Next morning Bill was back at Cattle Camp bright and early. The two men were up and about, he could tell, from the smoke spiralling straight up from the chimney. He had visions of a steaming cup of coffee, but these came to an unexpected end as he pushed through the doorway. Captain Hale and the sergeant were huddled close together on a long bench before the fire, blankets draped around their shoulders. The captain was fondling the forty-five while the sergeant retained a death grip on the axe cradled in his lap. Bill experienced a sudden flood of thankfulness that he had rapped before opening the door.

'Sleep well last night?' he asked, casting a glance at the empty bunks.

Said the captain, 'Too cold to sleep.'

Said the sergeant, 'Let's git out of here!'

Outside, as they were ready to leave, the sergeant once more paused to gaze at the huge tracks in the snow, the axe still clutched in his hands.

'You dead sure them's bear tracks, Boss?'

Bill nodded his head.

'They sure grows 'em big up here.'

'The usual size,' Bill replied. 'Of course, these tracks were much smaller before the sun melted the snow around the edges.'

A wide grin slowly spread over the sergeant's face. Then he got to his feet and tossed the axe back inside the cabin.

'Boss,' he said anxiously, 'just git me back to camp. I's sure got some catchin' up to do on my sleepin'!'

Twelve

WATER and snow surveys in the mountainous Back Country, exploratory trips during the winter to determine the potential water runoff the following spring, are vital and necessary, even though they are often accomplished at no small risk to the men involved. Bill has made these trips for years, on snowshoes or skis, trips that often took days and sometimes weeks. In fact, he made the first survey ever undertaken in Yosemite for the state of California, when there were no well-stocked cabins available for shelter during the below-zero nights and all supplies were carried strapped on his back.

Dark clouds were hanging low over Yosemite the day Bill and Ranger Erling took off on the regular midwinter survey. In spite of the dark skies, the weather report predicted clear cold days ahead, and they lost no time in getting away, as the snow was ideally packed for cross-country skiing. The second day out the sun came through, and the weather was beautiful until they started on the long sweep back from the farthest outpost point on their route. Then ominous storm signals began appearing from every direction.

It's no fun to be caught in a winter storm high in the desolate mountain regions, and both Bill and Ranger Erling were well aware of what might lie ahead. Three long days of travel still remained between them and home, and there was yet one more survey to make—in an outlying territory that had not been checked that winter but that had been included on their agenda. They had got under way long before daylight and were hot and damp with perspiration, for although dark, threatening clouds were beginning to roll up from the horizon, the sun was still shining brightly.

'Soon as we take the reading,' Bill said, 'we'll swing back and head for the next cabin.'

'It's a long way to go,' Ranger Erling reminded him.

'Be dark before we get there,' Bill agreed. 'But there's no other place to get in for the night.'

They were standing at the edge of a small stream where a tree had fallen across the water, and Bill immediately stepped up on the trunk and started across. He had covered about half the distance when his skis suddenly slipped on the snow-covered bark and he found himself standing in the ankle-deep water of the little stream. But he waded across, climbed the far bank, and continued on. Bill knew his feet were wet and that he should change his socks, but he was comfortably warm, and there was no time to lose if they were to reach the cabin for the night. They took the reading and hurried on.

Darkness closed in long before they reached the cabin, and it was with a sense of relief that they closed the door behind them. Ranger Erling quickly built a fire while Bill opened some cans from the food-safe. It was not long before they turned in and were soon sleeping soundly. Two hours later Bill was wide awake, sitting up on the cot massaging his burning feet; they had become frost-bitten from exposure after he had fallen into the little stream.

When Ranger Erling awoke next morning he was so nauseated he barely made it outside the cabin, and Bill joined him almost immediately. It was the canned food they had eaten the night before. It had probably been frozen and thawed out too many times. But the most pressing problem was Bill's frosted feet, which now were swollen and beginning to turn grey. But they had to continue on their way; there was no alternative. Bill managed to struggle into his shoes and they set out.

They were still two days from home and faced with a long, wearisome journey to the next cabin. Their mounting hunger was making them weak, and Bill was suffering so intensely with his feet that they were forced to halt at ever-shortening intervals. Then the storm, which had threatened for so long, struck them with all its fury. It was a raging, howling blizzard that swirled down around them, blotting out the landscape and making it necessary for them to stay close together to avoid becoming permanently separated. It got colder by the minute, and it soon became an effort to breathe as the blizzard constantly lashed the snow into their faces.

Neither spoke of what was foremost in their minds—nothing could be gained by admitting all sense of direction was gone—but in the bitter cold they must for ever move on if they were to survive. Lack of food was beginning to take a heavy toll as their strength gradually ebbed under the gruelling march, and the dogging fear that they were probably travelling in wide circles was something that they tried to banish from their reeling senses.

It was far into the night when the storm suddenly lifted, as quickly as it had begun. A few minutes later a cold moon rode up over the edge of the mountains, showing Mount Hoffman plainly visible in the distance. They got their bearings. The cabin was still an hour's march away, but the vision of warm shelter and steaming food brought some urgency to their dragging steps and they struggled on.

Snow was drifted high around the door when they finally arrived at the cabin, but they managed to get inside. Ranger Erling lost no time getting a fire started, but the chimney, whose cap had blown away, was so packed with snow that the room was soon filled with smoke, and Bill had to hold open the cabin door until the fire melted a draught channel through the clogged chimney. Then, almost simultaneously, they found that two further calamities had befallen them. Ranger Erling discovered that someone, probably a party of thoughtless campers, had consumed the last morsel of food in the place, as the empty cans hurled in a far corner gave mute evidence, and Bill removed his shoes to inspect his frozen feet.

The absence of food, which they so sorely needed, was bad enough, but the condition of Bill's feet was unlike anything they had ever seen. Blood had seeped from the broken blisters into the socks, and he had to place his feet, socks and all, to soak in a pail of water before he could remove them. When he managed to get them off most of the skin from his toes came off with the socks. The toenails were beginning to turn black and loosen. Several times that night he bathed his feet from a bottle of rubbing alcohol that Ranger Erling found in the station's first-aid kit. When morning came he forced his swollen, almost useless feet into his shoes, and once more they started for home, with Ranger Erling in the lead, breaking the trail.

Of course I had no way of knowing what was happening to Bill and Ranger Erling on the trip, but as time for their return drew near I became a little tense, as I usually do. When they failed to appear on the day I expected them, I found myself watching the weather and waiting through most of the night, listening. But the day that followed I was certain would bring them back, and I prepared my dinner in advance and drove to Happy Isles, as far as I could go in the car, and waited for them to appear on the trail.

The snowstorm had passed, but it was followed by a strong wind that was sweeping through the canyons like a hurricane, piling huge drifts of snow ahead of it. Daylight was beginning to fade and I was growing restless when I first caught sight of them. They were following the trail around the side of the mountain, and I couldn't determine what was wrong with the picture they presented. Unhooking the binoculars from the dashboard, I pressed them to my eyes. It appeared that one man was making his way towards me, dragging something behind him, and my heart almost stopped beating.

Men had come back like this before, when one of them had been injured, or worse, and I strained to bring the picture clearly into focus. While I watched, the wind slackened for a moment, and I could see that the first figure was breaking trail while the second, hunched down on his skis, was propelling himself with his hands. I watched for what seemed hours, as they drew nearer, and was so intent that I heard the rumbling without realizing what was about to happen. Then I dropped the glasses and was immediately frozen in my tracks as I stared up above.

The mountain seemed to be moving. It looked like a creeping movement at first, and was so high up that the sound barely reached me, but I saw that the whole side of the mountain was tumbling downward! The dull rumbling suddenly burst into an upheaval that erupted boulders as large as autos and sent them crashing down the mountainside, sweeping trees and tons of snow in their path—and Bill and his partner were directly underneath!

I screamed, and stared, and prayed. It sounded as if the end of the world were at hand. It was horrible! When the roar gradually subsided and the snow dust cleared, I raised the glasses to my eyes, afraid of what I might see. At first I saw nothing. Then I located the spot where I had seen them and there they were, slowly climbing out from beneath the overhanging ledge that had saved their lives.

When they reached the car they were too weak and exhausted to speak. I held the door as Ranger Erling rolled in and practically collapsed on the rear seat, and I fought back the tears as I watched Bill crawl in on his knees. Somehow we got home, after delivering Ranger Erling to his door, and Bill began soaking off his socks while I put in a hurried call for the doctor. Later, Bill asked for a glass of hot milk as I tucked him into his bed. It was quite some time before he was as good as new.

Bill was appointed National Park Service representative to the Chicago Century of Progress World's Fair in 1933, and we spent four months there during the run of the giant pageant. It was quite an experience, exchanging the cool dignity of the forest for the tinselled hurly-burly of the city. It came almost as a shock to us, although city life was not new to me and, of course, Bill had been born in Chicago. But there is something about living in the great outdoors that for ever seems to cheapen man-made things as compared to Nature. Awe-inspiring as a New York skyscraper can be with its architectural perfection, or the eye-stretching spans of a San Francisco Golden Gate suspension bridge, they seem insignificant beside the great forest trees.

Of course we enjoyed the excitement of the big city; there was also a certain thrill to be actually living on the scene of the many happenings that we had been reading about in the newspapers, some not exactly to our liking. Our first night there we were awakened by a shattering explosion as a car loaded with thugs was given the machine-gun treatment at our kerb. The notorious Touey brothers were holed up a half block away, according to the papers, and Bill was forced virtually to stand guard over his uniforms when he sent them to be cleaned, as a trade war was in full acid-throwing swing. And the weather was hot, unbearably hot. How we longed for a gentle breeze from the cool forest as we lay at night in our broiling apartment, straining to capture a stray breath of fresh air. The only saving grace of our stay was provided by Mr. and Mrs. G. O. Schoolcraft, Bill's uncle and aunt, who were living at the Edgewater Beach Hotel, with whom we spent many delightful evenings doing the town.

The last assignment Bill had been given before leaving Yosemite was an attempt to rescue a young man who had disappeared in the regions back of Half Dome. He was recalling the episode one night as we were sitting in our sweltering room.

'You know, Marge,' he said suddenly, 'come to think of it, that young fellow was from Chicago. Though we never reached him or even found a trace of the body, it might be comforting to his parents if I called on them and explained just what happened.'

A few days later he managed to get their address and spent an evening with them. He took along all the photographs he had of the wild terrain surrounding Half Dome and went to some lengths to explain the exact mechanics of a wide-scale rescue mission in that rough country. He assured them that nothing had been left undone. He had even taken with him about twenty Indians, the best trackers obtainable anywhere.

'Indians!' the father gasped incredulously. 'No wonder you never brought my boy out. The Indians got him!'

It was of no avail for Bill to point out that the wilds of the mountains, Indians included, are far safer than any large city.

The weather seemed to get more torrid, day by day, and the huge throngs at the exhibition reached a peak of 375,000 on the Fourth of July. On the way to our apartment that evening we were nearly trampled to death. We struggled along countless city blocks, rode buses until they became stalled in the crowds, took our turns on the elevated lines—actually spent a half hour trying to get across Michigan Avenue—and finally arrived at our sweltering apartment in a taxi Bill was fortunate enough to capture.

When we finally returned to Yosemite, bedraggled, benumbed, and pretty much bewildered, Bill had only seven dollars left in his pocket. But we were happy as a pair of bear cubs to be back once more at our home in the woods.

We get some prize characters in the park, too, and Timmy was one we never will forget. He came in as a seasonal ranger for the summer, and Bill still insists it was the longest summer ever entered on the record books. Not that Timmy was a bad actor—he wasn't, not at all; he was merely the type of person things happen to. Nearly everything about him was the reverse of what you would expect. His family tree had all the branches intact and he had just graduated from a fine Eastern college, but Timmy's appearance insisted he was hatched out on a mountain stump somewhere in Wyoming. The cowlick at the crown of his head always stood erect, fanning in the breeze like a patch of blooming thistles. Although he was a big boy, with feet so outsized his shoes were made on a special last, he had the small, sensitive fingers of an artist. His voice, which in a boy of his stature should have been a resounding bass rumble, came out a piping squeak two notches above high tenor.

Bill assigned him to the cabin next to our station, a small one-room affair with bunk, chairs, and a fireplace. The nights were still cool at our high altitude, and before returning to our quarters that evening, Bill pointed out the stack of wood for the grate. When I happened to glance outside a few minutes later, red flames were spurting up like a blast furnace from the big chimney. Bill ran outside, got the hose, and hurriedly dampened the dry shake roof before stalking into the cabin. Timmy was unfolded in front of the hearth admiring the roaring flames, grinning like a big Cheshire cat.

'You have a chimney-fire. You'll burn the place down!' Bill yelled, hurling a handy bucket of water on the flames. 'The wood you put in there must be full of pitch.'

'Yeah,' Timmy nodded. 'It burns better!'

A few days later when he left his cabin, with another roaring pitch-fire licking up the chimney, the fireguard printed a sign that read BURN ONLY SMALL PIECES OF PITCH IN THIS FIREPLACE, and tacked it to the mantel. That evening Timmy came to our door to inquire why, after Bill's warning about using the pitch-soaked wood, had someone now left a sign directing him to burn nothing but pitch? Whenever anything contained the merest hint of a double meaning, Timmy always pounced on the wrong one.

Things were just lying around waiting to happen to Timmy. Like the time he bought a new shotgun. He came home with it one Saturday night, and most of the day Sunday he spent admiring it where it rested on the pegs above the mantel. Towards evening Bill happened to notice him coming out of the cabin with his gun and motioned me to come to the window and watch. For a moment Timmy stood perfectly still in his tracks, his eyes travelling lovingly over the prize cradled in his arms. Then, like an oversized boy playing cops and robbers, he suddenly spun around and aimed towards some bushes growing at the edge of the woods.

Bill and I grinned as we watched, almost expecting to hear Timmy shout, 'Bang! Bang!' Instead, from somewhere behind the bushes there emerged two men with hands high in the air, pleading for him not to shoot.

Actually they were two escaped convicts who, hiding out until dark, had just happened to be concealed behind the bushes at which Timmy was taking an imaginary potshot.

'Gosh!' was all he could say, as Bill corralled the pair. 'What d'ya know?'

When Bill comes across a rattlesnake warming itself on a rock, he has a way of snatching its tail, whirling around, and bashing its head against a tree, or whatever is handy. This manœuvre intrigued Timmy no end. They were hiking along the trail one day when Bill spied a rattler stretched out on a low retaining wall nearby. He snatched it by the tail, swung around, and rapped its head against the rock wall. Timmy thought the performance was very creditable and said so. A few yards beyond, they came upon another, and Timmy put his hand on Bill's arm.

'Allow me,' he said grandly, 'but I'll go you one better. Watch.'

With a forked stick in one hand he approached the snake and suddenly thrust the spreading end down over the head, pinning it tight to the wall. Then, with the snake unable to strike, he stooped over, seized it just behind the head, and raised it in the air.

'That's the way I've seen it done in the movies,' he grinned expansively. 'You see, this way . . .'

Bill stood watching silently as Timmy's voice faded away in his throat. Slowly his face took on a bilious hue, and his bulging eyes surveyed the long rattler coiled around his bare arm, drawing its coils so tight his fingers were ready to lose their frantic grasp.

'What'll I do, Uncle Bill?'

Bill turned to walk away. 'Kill it,' he said, 'like they do in the movies.'

'I can't let go!' he yelled.

'Hurry up,' Bill said, walking off. 'We have to cover the rest of the trail.'

Timmy got his gun out of the holster, but his hand was trembling so violently he was afraid to shoot lest he hit his hand. He dropped the gun back in its holster and was in the act of snatching a boulder from the ground when he seemed to realize that before he could possibly hurl the rock the snake would strike. Timmy was white as a ghost and trembling violently when he suddenly took off down the trail after Bill, holding the rattler at arm's length.

'Help me!' he panted. 'Help, Uncle Bill!'

Bill slowly turned around and surveyed the scene.

'Why don't you get rid of it?' he asked. 'Try doing it the same way you got it.'

Timmy ran back and grasped the stick, slipped the forked end over the darting head, and pressed it tight against the wall until it fell limp to the ground, where Bill finished it with his forty-five.

Timmy was sent out one night to answer a woman's frantic call that a prowler was in her cabin. The place was in darkness when he arrived, but the woman, trembling in the front yard, assured him there was a burglar inside.

'You see him?' Timmy asked.

'I—I heard him. Just as I was unlocking the f-front door!' Miss Pickett chattered. 'S-sounded like he tripped over a piece of f-furniture.'

Timmy slipped up the front steps and across the porch. Pushing the door open with one hand, he drew his gun with the other and crept silently inside, his heart pounding. This was the first burglar call he had answered. Timmy often got excited and staged some wholly unexpected gymnastics, but he didn't know how to be afraid—he would have seized the Devil by the horns and swished his forked tail across his face had it been an order from Bill.

The living-room he found himself in was dark as a tomb at midnight, but he could make out an archway directly ahead that led into a connecting hall. There was no light on in the hall either, but that side of the house showed a dim light from outside. He was almost at the bedroom door when his toe came in contact with an upended stand lying in his path, and he crashed to the floor, flat on his face. For a minute he sat there rubbing his shins, cursing to himself and listening. Outside, the wind was rattling a loose shutter and sighing mournfully around the eaves, but another sound, much nearer, also reached his ears. Somebody—or something—was moving about inside the old house, the steps silent but plainly evidenced by the occasional creaking of the pine floor.

Quietly Timmy climbed to his feet and switched on his pocket-light. There were two doors leading from the hallway, one at the far end, a swinging door evidently leading to the kitchen, and the one nearby.

'This must be a bedroom,' he said to himself. 'And that's where a burglar would be.'

He snapped off his light and crept to the door; his fingers slowly closed round the brass knob. Turning it silently in his hand, he opened the door a bare crack before stepping to one side, out of gun range, then, inch by inch, forced it wide open. There was a creaking sound of movement from somewhere, and again the eerie silence closed in around him. Straining forward, he peered beyond the edge of the door, his gun levelled, searching the room for a shadow that moved. Then he saw it, was sure what had happened, and strode quickly across to a window that stood slightly ajar.

'That's how he got away,' he muttered. 'Climbed out the window.'

Flinging the window wide open, he thrust a leg over the sill—and suddenly halted as a movement from behind froze him in his tracks. Then came a sharp report, as the bedroom door slammed shut in the strong breeze from the opened window, and he spun around in time to catch the fleeting glimpse of a man across the room (actually his own reflection in the full-length mirror attached to the door) and fired point-blank.

The sound of falling glass filled his ears, followed by a terrific crash exploding from the direction of the kitchen, and Timmy yanked the door open and pounded wildly down the hallway. With no time to lose, he lunged past the swinging door and groped frantically in the darkness for the wall switch. When light flooded the room he stood staring incredulously at the screen door opening on to a rear porch, which was hanging at a rakish angle in a doorframe that had been entirely wrenched from its mooring. But he had no time for reflection; footsteps were flying down the hallway towards him.

'Ranger! Are you hurt? Where are you, Ranger?'

The door burst open, and Timmy clearly saw the woman, the occupant of the place, for the first time. It would add a nice touch right here to say that he found himself face to face with a ravishing blue-eyed blonde whose figure was something straight out of a chorus line—but it just wouldn't be true. Miss Pickett afforded a remarkable likeness to the amorphous fence slat whose name she bore, and her hair could be mistaken for blonde only if seen from a distance and the greying roots didn't show. But her eyes! They were glowing so brightly with eulogistic approval of Timmy's performance that they were almost a fire hazard.

'My wonderful man!' She gushed out the words. 'You saved my life!'

'No, lady,' Timmy sputtered. 'I didn't do——'

'But you did! You protected me with your life!' She took a quick step forward, and Timmy prepared to defend himself. 'You were so brave—so calm——'

'I was excited, lady. I shot the——'

'—the burglar while defending me!'

'Lady. You don't understand.'

'Oh yes, I do understand!' She leaned towards him, her eyes limpid pools of adoration. 'I owe my life to you!'

Timmy tried to step out of range, but he was already backed into a corner of the kitchen, and Miss Pickett was determined to pay her debt to society.

It was just then that Bill, checking on the call, appeared in the shattered doorway and rescued Timmy from his fate. Outside, Bill removed his hat and bowed from the waist.

'My hero!' he grinned.

'Oh, gee, Uncle Bill,' Timmy pleaded, 'I tried to tell her! There wasn't any burglar at all. I shot myself in the mirror, and it scared the pants off a bear that was raiding her icebox. Gosh, I didn't do anything!'

Someone Tossed a Cigarette!

Such a headline would, in itself, be considerably less than world-shaking. But a cigarette dropped in the midst of one of our national parks can touch off a holocaust that costs millions of dollars, does incredible damage, and snuffs out lives like candles in a hurricane—a burnt offering to a careless smoker.

Few people, other than those living in the great forests of North America, have a true conception of a forest fire, recognize the almost superhuman effort required to fight it, or know the terror that grips those trapped in its inferno, in a world engulfed by a leaping, plunging sea of flames. It is something that you see and hear in all its stark reality but can never fully describe.

Bill and I were stationed at Olympic National Park in northern Washington, in the heart of the timber belt, where he was serving as district ranger. We had enjoyed several delightful days of warm sunshine and from all indications were due for more of the same. I was particularly happy about it because Gary, the new temporary ranger, was arriving that day with his wife and baby. They were to occupy the station several miles down the highway from us, and I was preparing to go over and give his wife a hand when the two-way radio in Bill's office, which connected us directly with headquarters in Port Angelus, began calling our station.

One of the lookouts from his tower at the summit of a nearby mountain had spotted a column of smoke. While the fire-dispatcher was relaying the message, Bill already was poring over his maps and charts determining the exact location of the blaze.

'It's near Bear River,' he called to me. 'Probably just outside the park boundary.'

'A small fire?' I asked.

'They're all small when they start,' he snapped. He was already at the door, impatient to leave. 'Marge, you call Gary. Tell him to get over here at once. I'll meet him here at our station when I get back.' The door slammed, and he was gone.

I picked up the phone and called the other ranger station.

'There's a small fire along the park boundary,' I said. 'Bill has gone to look it over. You're to report here at once. He'll be back soon.'

'My wife and baby?' Gary said. 'I can't leave them in the front yard. We're just moving in——'

'Bring them along,' I cut in. 'But get over here fast.'

Gary had just arrived with his family when Bill returned. He hurried into his office and called headquarters.

'It's still a small fire,' he said, 'and it will have to jump the river to get into the park. I'm taking no chances. I'll take the temporary ranger with me and try to put it out.'

'How bad is it?' the fire-dispatcher wanted to know.

Bill told him. 'But it could travel into some heavy brush. If it does, it will be close to that blowdown area, and then we could have a real fire on our hands.'

'Any idea how it started?'

'Wasn't lightning,' Bill stated flatly. 'Probably a hunter or fisherman with a cigarette.'

'Think you can hold it?'

'We should be able to if we don't get any wind.'

'Good luck.'

'One thing more,' Bill said quickly. 'Call the state fire-warden and fill him in on the story. Have him send his nearest crew.'

'Roger.'

Gary had the equipment assembled, and Bill snatched his portable radio from the floor as he turned to me.

'Get on the phone,' he directed, backing towards the door. 'Call all the neighbours—everybody you can reach. Get them over here at the double. See that they get shovels, back pumps, and fire tools from the fire cache. Send them in after us. You know where the fire is.'

I nodded as the door slammed shut.

'Is it going to be a bad one?' Gary's wife asked.

'They always hurry like this,' I assured her. 'The state crew may be miles away, and the park can't wait for help from there. It doesn't pay to fool with any fire.'

Grace was jittery, I could see, as she stood close at my side, clutching her baby to her breast. I called everybody in our area who had a telephone—ten in all. Grace was a frail little thing, and this was her first experience with a fire. I knew just how frightened she must be. But I had no time to console her just then; cars were screeching in from all directions.

'Look, Grace,' I said quickly, 'I have to go out to the fire cache to see that these people find their equipment. I won't be gone longer than I can help. But if the fire-dispatcher calls, or you hear Bill trying to get me on his portable radio, come after me immediately. Understand?'

She nodded.

It took but a few seconds for the neighbours to seize the gear, which is always kept in readiness, and be on their way. Soon they had all disappeared into the darkening forest. I was running back to the station when I first noticed the slight breeze that had sprung up. It was a steady breeze that was moving in one direction. It shouldn't hinder the fire-fighters too much in their work. I knew the men would soon be scraping a wide firebreak in front of the oncoming flames, pushing back the tinder-dry needles and fallen limbs, cutting out brush and small trees, removing everything that would burn from a path wide enough to prevent the fire from jumping across. Others would be ready with back pumps, which are just that—pumps strapped to the back and operated by a hand lever—putting out spot fires caused by flying sparks and burning debris hurled high in the air by terrific heat. Bill called just after I got back to the house.

'State crew has arrived,' he said. 'Fire is almost three acres in size, still outside the park across the river. Think we can hold it if the wind doesn't change. Notify dispatcher.'

'Are you and Gary all right?'

'All right. Call you later.'

I called headquarters and gave them Bill's message. This was necessary as headquarters was too far away to pick up Bill's portable. Neither could Bill receive messages from headquarters; the fire-dispatcher would have to call me, and I would pass his instructions on to Bill.

Night closed in, but there was no thought of sleep. I didn't dare leave the office, and Grace remained across the desk from me, curled up in a chair, wide-eyed with fright—as she had a perfect right to be. Bill called in as often as he could with a report of the progress of the fire, which I relayed to the dispatcher. At midnight they were still holding their ground, and Bill said he thought the fire might burn itself out by morning. By about 3.00 a.m., however, I knew something had gone wrong. The sky, which I could see from the large window behind Grace's chair, was gradually beginning to change in colour. A few minutes later Bill called again.

'Wind is changing,' he panted. 'We are still holding it in check, and the wind may die down. But get word to the fire-chief to stand by.'

'You all right?'

'We're all right. Call headquarters at once.'

I alerted headquarters and sat waiting, praying they could contain the fire while there was yet time, hoping I could prevent Grace's eyes from straying to the reddening window at her back.

'They're all right,' I assured her. 'Bill says everybody is safe.'

'It must be horrible out there.' She closed her eyes and shuddered. 'After the holidays last year I burned our tree. It went pouff! Like gasoline poured on a flame. The forest is full of Christmas trees!'

Then the towering flames leaped the river, and trees inside the park began burning like tinder. The fire was now Bill's responsibility, and he called me at once.

'Fire has jumped river and is in park at east boundary. West wind blowing. Advise state fire-warden. Have dispatcher send fifty men and equipment to set up a fifty-man fire camp. Will need overhead to handle it. Send a hundred lunches, also head lamps for men.'

It was just daylight when I heard the trucks arriving from headquarters. The men were at the station only long enough to get Bill's fire-truck; then they too disappeared into the forest.

With the coming of daylight, the leaping red glare faded from the sky, but a heavy smoke cloud now covered the heavens as far as the eye could see, causing a weird, unreal glow to settle over the landscape, transforming it into a strange scene as if from some unknown world.

'How long will it last?' Grace suddenly asked.

'No one knows—a week—a month—a day.'

'Will it get worse?'

'That depends on many things——'

'Look!' she cut in. 'Ashes are beginning to fall in the yard. The fire's coming this way!'

I took her by the hand. 'I don't think so. Heat from the fire always carries ashes high in the air. They fall for miles around.'

'But how can we be sure? My baby——'

'Look, Grace, we have my car if we have to make a run for it. I must stay here to relay messages back and forth. Bill will warn us in time if it gets too dangerous.'

Bill was on the air again. 'Marge, call dispatcher. Tell him state and Forest Service want every available man to stand by. Fire west of river, has crowned and is heading west. Park fire confined to small acreage but could use twenty-five more men. Anything can happen. Looks bad.'

'Are you and Gary all right?'

'All right.'

I got through to headquarters and had just signed off when I heard the fire-chief calling the dispatcher from the two-way radio in his car.

'I'm at the fire. Wind rising. Fire jumping road in spots. Could be serious. Send Bill twenty-five more men. Call you later.'

My heart suddenly came up into my throat. I had been so busy with my own worries that I had completely forgotten Mary, the ranger's wife living at the far end of the Sol Duc Road, which the fire-chief had mentioned. The camp ground there was usually well filled at this season, and there was just one way out from that area—the road leading past the fire. That they hadn't been asked to leave was sure proof they were so far in no danger, for I knew that the park service would not hesitate to disrupt the vacationers if an emergency arose that called for immediate action. I tried reaching Mary on the telephone, but the wires, supported mostly by trees, were down. The radio began stuttering with interference, so I was unable to read the message, but I was sure it was the voice of the fire-chief talking to headquarters. A second later the radio was clear, and I heard the call go out to Mary.

'Fire is nearing road. Notify all campers. Leave immediately. Get out! Get out at once!'

A long, agonizing hour later we saw the caravan from Sol Duc passing the station, camping equipment piled hurriedly into the cars, heading out of the park. Mary was the last, like a captain quitting her ship.

Again night fell over the forest, and the sky was once more filled with boiling black clouds outlined in angry red from the roaring fires below. I persuaded Grace to get some sleep while I continued my vigil beside the radio. From time to time Bill called to keep headquarters informed. They were backfiring from the road, using tractors and men in an effort to control the swirling conflagration. Behind them the fire-truck was constantly patrolling the road, putting out spot fires as they appeared.

The following day I drew my first long breath. The wind was dying down, and there was a chance that the men might now win their battle. Bill called in and said it looked favourable, and if they were able to hold it he would be home by night. But that evening he decided against leaving the scene, said he might be home later. I continued at the radio. Messages were for ever flowing back and forth. It was early morning when a rap sounded, and I opened the door.

'How is my wife?'

I looked at the strange man standing there, slumped in his tracks. He was a fire-fighter, I was sure; he was dirty beyond words, his clothing burned in spots from falling embers, his pants torn at the knees. Weary, bloodshot eyes gazed out at me from behind a stubble of beard that was singed and curling at the ends.

'I'm afraid I can't reach your wife,' I said. 'The telephone is out and——'

'Telephone?' he said dazedly. 'You mean Grace isn't here?'

It was Gary—so miserably filthy, so beaten, so completely exhausted, that I had failed to recognize him. But he couldn't wait for a hot meal, had to get back. Just came to get more K-rations for the men. Grace ran to make some sandwiches. He couldn't wait for them, either. Stumbling with weariness, he headed back into the woods, where he was soon lost to sight.

About noon came the word I had been dreading to hear. It was the state fire-chief informing headquarters that the fire was practically out of control. A brisk east wind had suddenly turned into a gale, and flames were jumping the fire-lines everywhere, crowning into treetops, flashing across acres of timber like heat lightning. While the park fire was still under control, the conflagration across the river was rapidly getting completely out of hand.

'Looks like it's going to be a big one,' he said.

I knew exactly what this implied. We had been through it before. Too many times. The road would soon be lined with traffic headed for the fire. Private cars bulging with loggers, sailors, merchants, anyone who could wield a shovel, chop a limb, tote a water-bucket, cook a meal over a make-shift fire, and get away before the holocaust reached him. There would be trucks loaded with supplies—food, water, cooking utensils, trucks burdened with crates of shovels, back pumps, sleeping bags. The state fire-warden called headquarters. 'The fire is out of control. Wind fanning it west.'

That evening Bill called in. The radio truck had arrived at the scene and was in touch with headquarters. That meant I was relieved from my siege at the radio, and Grace and I drove down the road towards the fire, drawn by I don't know what, except that our men were in there, somewhere, fighting.

One entire side of the mountain range was blazing, a churning, roaring, wreathing mass of flames around which men were straining, gasping for a breath of air where there was nothing but smoke and flames. Great trees were toppling and crashing down, exploding blasts of sparks and flying embers high into the boiling smoke clouds above. I looked back towards the valleys and homes, where mothers were trying to comfort the little ones, drying their frightened tears. Brave women, who prayed for their husbands and sometimes died with them.

I felt myself burning with anger. Thousands of acres of beautiful, sturdy giants, trees that for scores of years had been growing and expanding to towering heights, suddenly destroyed in a few hellish days, days turned black with boiling smoke that belched from the bowels of the earth, with consuming heat and soaring flames that leaped higher and ever farther until the whole earth seemed to wreathe and crash and roar as if the wrath of hell were turned loose on the land. Somebody dropped a match! Someone flipped a cigarette!

I knew what was happening in there; it had happened before. I could visualize another Tommy, a young lad scarcely out of his teens, in there fighting, straining to preserve his home, his job, the only world he knows. He works mightily to maintain the firebreak he has carved out of the forest—a wide path free of anything that will burn. He is in charge of a sector, as are other men, young and old, along the cleared line. The fire is sweeping down towards him, a roaring, crashing inferno that shakes the ground on which he stands. Trees above are toppling, crashing, dislodging boulders as large as trucks and sending them hurtling down the mountainside.

Flames are roaring nearer, leaping from tree to tree; the heavy carpet of pine needles is a blazing wall behind. Animals are running madly before it, elk and deer with hides burned bare, hoofs melted to stumps, eyes blinded. A rabbit darts unknowingly between Tommy's legs, its fur blazing, spreading fire as it runs across the break into the dry needles on the other side. He rushes after it, flailing with his shovel at the tiny flames as they spring into life. The fire now needs no wind to fan it into fury; it creates its own wind with the tremendous updrift of its terrific heat. It's like standing before a draught furnace now, and a tree, its sap beginning to boil, suddenly explodes, erupting a blinding flash that leaps into the dense upper branches.

It begins to crown, but Tommy is powerless to fight so far above the ground. High in the air it leaps the firebreak, and all his sweat and toil go for nothing. Another will have to be built farther back, if there is time. The roaring mass is upon him now, heat that sears and cracks the flesh, smoke so blinding and heavy that he gags, retches. Leaping flames are everywhere—it happens so suddenly—nowhere is there a place to take cover. He sags to the ground, searching for a breathing space beneath the choking smoke; showers of burning embers falling on his heat-parched shirt ignite it into a blazing bier, and his hair flares into a bright torch as the great holocaust roars down over him.

Back at the station Grace and I sat and waited through the night, nodding in our chairs. The house was ghostly still after the confusion of the past days; even the radio was silent now that the transmitter truck had reached the scene. In the early morning hours Bill called, said for me to stand by in case the radio truck should develop unexpected trouble. It was important for them to maintain a message channel at all times with headquarters.

'If the wind should change and you and Grace should be in trouble, I'll let you know in plenty of time so you can get out.'

He hung up his transmitter, and Grace looked questioningly at me.

'Suppose something happens to him, a broken leg or he gets trapped in the fire?'

'Nothing will happen,' I said, with a good deal more conviction than I felt.

Each day the sky got darker, and the few cars on the highway moved cautiously, their headlights boring into the gloom. It was hard to tell where night left off and dawn began. Then one night we were wakened by traffic rushing by the house, and it continued through the night and until noon the following day, a steady flow of cars and trucks heading east on the highway. From a highway patrolman I learned that one section of the fire had taken off cross country from where it had started near the park and was now bearing down on a small village farther down the highway towards the ocean. Hundreds of men were fighting like demons to check its course, but the town residents were forced to leave their homes behind as they fled to safety. When the traffic disappeared we knew the escape road had been cut off by fire.

It was days later before Bill and Gary finally returned to the station. The fire was still burning fiercely as it swept on through the forest, but the main conflagration inside the park boundaries was at last conquered. Bill kept a watch crew for days constantly patrolling the burned area to guard against new fires bursting forth from charcoal stumps and smouldering roots buried underground. Each night he joined the men, watching from vantage points, listening for the crackling of another small blaze of the fire that was for ever springing into life.

The little town lying in the path of the fire was not entirely consumed, but charred evidence of that hell on earth lay twisted in mute evidence everywhere. It seemed a miracle that any part had been saved, for at one point the fire had travelled thirty miles in six hours. Fifteen hundred men had risked their lives to bring the holocaust under control, and it was not completely extinguished until thirteen months had passed, months of long nights when your head automatically raised from the pillow to listen for the crackling of another fire starting up. Now skeletons of hordes of woods animals lie bleaching in the ashes of the forty thousand acres of virgin forest that were reduced to cinders and rubble by an act for which there can be no possible vindication.

All because someone tossed a cigarette!

Thirteen

ONE balmy spring morning in Yosemite, Sally and I decided to drive over to Wawona ranger station, where Bill was occupied for the day. The warm sunshine was a heartening tonic for me after several feverish weeks spent indoors with an illness that had required the services of Sally, a registered nurse from the city. For a girl who had spent most of her days inside metropolitan hospitals, she had adapted herself remarkably well to our rather rugged life at the station. Every spare moment which presented itself found her at the window peering longingly out into the cathedral-quiet forest surrounding us, and all wood animals simply enchanted her, from an occasional bear or deer wandering across our rear yard to a tiny chipmunk returning her inspection from the window-sill.

Sally was capable of but one consuming hatred—snakes. Little ones, big ones, poisonous or not, they aroused in her a wild urge to kill. And she was not afraid of them, either. In fact, Bill had warned her several times about her activities with a broom or hoe handle. Snakes I can take or leave alone, preferably the latter;

Sally had to exterminate every last one that crossed her path. We were idling along about a mile from Wawona station when she suddenly stepped on the gas and the car shot forward.

'Snake!' she muttered, leaning intently over the wheel.

It was a large rattler, coiled in the centre of the roadway. Sally bore down upon it, aiming the left front tyre at its head. She missed and stopped in a swirl of dust to throw the car in reverse. When we backed to where the snake had been, it was wriggling off through tall grass beside the road.

'For heaven's sake!' I cried, as she scrambled outside the car. 'You can't kill all the snakes in the world. Let it go.'

'Gotta kill it!' she snapped, glancing about for a weapon.

A short slender limb was lying beneath a tree, almost at her feet, and she seized it and advanced boldly on her enemy.

'Please, Sally!' I wailed. 'You're liable to get——'

The snake coiled to strike, and she brought the limb down with a Goliathlike blow on its head that broke the rotting limb into several flying sections.

'Come on,' I begged nervously. 'You've done your deed for the day. Let's go.'

She looked at me, the light of battle still gleaming in her eyes. 'Got him!'

'No,' I said quickly. 'It's only stunned. Sally, get away from it!'

Defiantly she kicked it out on to the road beside the car and held on to the side of the car as she repeatedly brought a sharp heel down on its head. Then she stooped over to examine her kill, I hoped, but I closed my eyes, unwilling to witness what I was afraid might happen.

'Thought I couldn't kill him?' she asked, climbing in and starting the engine. 'Didn't think it was dead, huh?'

I explained what once had happened to Bill when he was patrolling a trail on horseback. Catching a glimpse of a big rattler wriggling up a steep bank just ahead of him, he had leaned over and unsnapped the shovel from his saddle. He was dismounting when the snake suddenly fell off the steep bank, landing right at the horse's feet. His mount snorted and reared, hurling Bill flat on his back alongside the snake. He lunged desperately with the shovel, missed the head, but cut the long, wreathing body into two pieces. Still, before he could leap to safety, the half with the head attached had coiled and struck, sinking its fangs into his wrist, barely missing the vein.

Several things happened simultaneously when we arrived at Wawona station. Sally stopped the car, and we climbed out. Then, just as she leaned back to cut the engine, I heard the rattle for the first time. Bill, who had been ambling across the yard, suddenly sprinted towards us.

'Look out!' he was yelling. 'Jump back!'

But we were so frozen with fear we couldn't move, I, holding on to my side of the car, Sally with one foot on the ground and a buzzing rattlesnake coiled on the running-board almost between her knees.

The next second Sally plopped on the ground ten feet away, where Bill had hurled her, and the report of his forty-five startled me out of my trance.

'How did that snake get on your running-board?' he demanded as I came around the car.

I shook my head, speechless, then looked at Sally.

'I—I put it there,' she chattered. 'I thought it was d-dead. The rattles—I wanted the rattles.'

'Well.' Bill suddenly grinned and turned to the car. 'In that case I'll get them for you.'

'No!' Sally gasped. 'I don't want them—ever!'

When Bill offered to help her to her feet, she said she was very comfortable, right then, just where she was, and preferred to sit for a spell. It was plain to see that Sally's snake-killing urge had come to an end.

In the mountains things seem to reach a climax with a swiftness seldom found elsewhere. Nicholas Roosevelt, *New York Times* correspondent, several years ago asked to accompany Bill on a snow survey he and Ranger Wagner were preparing to make. Of course Bill agreed, happy to have the added company on the long trip through the Back Country. The newsman was outfitted completely, including pack and snowshoes, the same as the rangers.

They took off early one morning and began the first long,

steep climb out of Yosemite Valley. Everything went as expected until they reached Vernal Falls, where everything went wrong with an abruptness that nearly cost them their lives.

The trail they had to follow angled almost straight up along one side of the high waterfall, and the fine spray blowing over the trail had paved it and the adjoining mountainside with a coating of ice. Working their way upward was a long, difficult job, but they made it at last, with Roosevelt, climbing in front of Bill, finally pushing his head over the top. He got slowly to his feet and carefully started across the slippery but almost level expanse of ice towards a guard-rail a few feet away. Then it happened.

Roosevelt began drifting to one side, so slowly and gently his progress was scarcely perceptible—like a slow-motion sequence in a movie—yet he could not control his movement, walking or standing. While Bill stood in his niche, watching carefully but afraid to utter a word, the *Times* correspondent tried making his way up the ever-so-slight grade to the rail and safety, but it was like straining for the final straw in a nightmare as he continued to slide gently, with every step, towards the edge of the precipice.

'Lie down!' Bill called. 'Spread your arms and legs.'

Roosevelt did as directed, and the drag of his body on the ice slowed his movement, but he was still moving, slowly and surely, towards the frightening drop-off that would hurl him to certain death.

Hooking his toes in the chipped-out top step, Bill lay prone on the ice and reached out his hand. Roosevelt waited until the split second when he would be nearest Bill, then reached out his arm and lunged. Their fingertips met, parted. Quickly Bill loosened one foot from the foothold in the niche and stretched again a little farther. Their fingers met, overlapped, and finally locked at the first joint. Then Bill's toe slipped from the icy niche where he was anchored, their grasping fingers came apart, and both men began slowly inching towards the precipice.

Bill struggled, lunging back to regain his toe-hold, but it was gone for ever, and the effort only increased the momentum that was carrying them both to eternity. It was maddening, moving so slowly you could scarcely detect the movement, yet unable to lay hand on any object that could arrest your glide.

'Bill! Above your head!'

Ranger Wagner's shout brought Bill back from the abyss of hopelessness, and he turned his head slightly. The end of a broken guard chain was dangling almost overhead, and he prepared himself for the spring that either would halt his descent or increase his approach to the drop-off, depending on luck.

Gathering his spread arms and legs under him was like releasing a brake and his movement immediately gained momentum. Then his hand shot out and his fingers clamped tight on the last link of the chain. It wasn't much, just enough to stop his descent, with his legs continuing on, in a slow arc, far to one side. He had a glimpse of Roosevelt desperately reaching for his sprawling foot, but he was just out of reach.

Pulling himself up by the chain, Bill was able to grasp it with the other hand and soon had one leg hooked over the guard-rail. And Roosevelt, miraculously, had managed to halt his descent, hanging up on a small protruding rock showing above the icy surface. Quickly Bill untied the rope provided for lashing snowshoes to his pack, attached it to a broken chain, which he unhooked from the guard-rail, and turned to the reporter, still spreadeagled on the ice, his face turned away towards the drop-off.

'Don't move, Nick,' Bill called. 'I'm going to throw you a rope, but don't move a muscle until I tell you.'

Coiling the rope in one hand, he took a grip on the attached chain and threw. The rope snaked out like a lariat and struck the ice—it was short by several feet.

'Don't move,' Bill cautioned. 'Going to try again.'

Ranger Wagner, standing helpless in the top niche, was holding aloft his lashing rope and making motions that he would throw it to Bill, but it was a short length, and the chance of wind blowing it out of Bill's grasp was too great a risk. Quickly Bill reeled in his rope and tossed it to Wagner, who added his length to the end. Then Bill retrieved it and prepared to try once again. Roosevelt was lying still as death, not moving a muscle lest his slight contact with the protruding rock be broken.

'I'm ready to try again,' Bill shouted. 'If I miss you, don't move. If the rope strikes you, grab it quick, for it might spring you loose.'

Carefully coiling the rope, he stood up straight and hurled it across the ice. The rope shot out like a catapult, arched in the air, and dropped—still short of its mark. The tension was more than the journalist could bear—the frozen rock beneath him was giving way—and he started once more slipping slowly towards the precipice, now but a few feet away.

'Grab it!' Bill yelled. 'Behind you!'

For a second the reporter was perfectly still, except for his curled fingers frantically digging at the frozen ice. Then he turned his head, saw the end of the rope slowly fading from his reach, and lunged in desperation. With the exertion, he was beginning to glide down over the last hump at the edge of the drop-off—when his clutching fingers found the end of the rope.

Bill pulled him to safety, and they sat down right there, at the head of Vernal Falls, and waited while Ranger Wagner brewed some hot tea before continuing on. Nicholas Roosevelt had looked forward to an exciting trip; the adventure came more swiftly than any of them had expected.

Leslie Ferrell and Bill have been almost inseparable companions since they first met as young boys on a shakedown cruise while serving in the Coast Guard, and followed this adventure with another by joining the Forest Service. Although Mr. Ferrell later became a prominent Southern California druggist and Bill, as a United States ranger, has spent his life in various parts of the country, nothing has ever separated them for long.

The morning their biggest adventure started, Ranger Ferrell, resplendent in his Forest Service uniform, was patiently urging his mount along the incline of the back road he was patrolling. It was a drowsy sun-filled day that seemed to cast a spell of lassitude over the draught-parched forest stretching farther than the eye could see. He was topping the rise in the highway when he saw two spirals of smoke curling up from either side of the road ahead.

Putting spurs to his horse, he dashed forward, but even before he reached the small fires, he realized what was happening. Two Mexicans, blazing newspapers in hand, were applying the torches to the tinder-dry cedar shrubs in an effort to touch off a conflagration that would require their paid services as members of a fire-crew to extinguish. This sort of thing had been done before, many times.

'Stop!' he yelled, galloping headlong towards them.

But the two young men, taken completely unaware, took off like frightened rabbits. Ranger Ferrell sprang from his horse and drew a forty-five.

'Halt!' he shouted. 'Stop or I'll shoot!'

The fleeing men showed no inclination to stop—they were sprinting down the side of the road as fast as their legs would carry them, and Ferrell took off after them. He didn't want to wound them, and shot once, over their heads, thinking it would check their flying feet. Instead, the fleeing men put on an extra burst of speed, and he was forced to lower his forty-five and squeeze the trigger. Ferrell is an expert shot, and he aimed at the Mexican's sombrero but, because he was off balance from the chase, the bullet struck the man in the shoulder and sent him sprawling on his face into the ditch.

With the second shot the other stopped in his tracks, raising his hands above his head. A few minutes later the fire was extinguished, and the two men were marched away to headquarters.

When the case was presented at court, the judge dealt out six months to each man, plus a stern lecture on the seriousness of their crime, a felony punishable by one year in prison and a fine of one thousand dollars. As they were being led away, Gregorio, his arm still resting in a sling, whirled around and called down on Ranger Ferrell's head a string of blistering maledictions that ended with an eye-flashing promise of annihilation on their next meeting —for which the judge promptly added an extra six months to his sentence.

Late one afternoon the following summer Bill and Ranger Ferrell were preparing for a trip to the mountain town of Big Bear, where Bill had an early appointment for the evening. It was the peak of the fire season and, although both were off duty for the day, the district ranger frowned on their being so far away in case of a fire. But the issue was settled when a ranger friend of Bill's agreed to remain on call at Burnt Hill station until midnight, at which time they expected to return.

They were heading their horses out of the drive when they

noticed a road crew working at one side of the highway, and they had gone but a few yards when one of the workmen suddenly leaped out into their path. It was a deliberate move to stop them, and they reined in sharply. Ferrell leaped to the ground and approached the man, who was launching a flow of profanity at him.

'It's Gregorio,' he muttered under his breath.

'Wait,' Bill snapped. 'He might have a knife——'

Ranger Ferrell didn't wait; he was racing towards the gesticulating workman.

The crew boss stepped between them. 'What's going on here?'

Bill leaped to the ground. 'This workman of yours is the firebug Ranger Ferrell winged in the shoulder last summer.'

The boss looked at Gregorio. 'I remember. You said you'd get Ferrell, goin' to kill him. I don't need you any more—you're fired.'

'No,' Ranger Ferrell said quickly. 'Look, I don't want to be responsible for this man losing his job.'

'I said he's fired.'

'You don't understand. He was cussing me out, and I'll take care of that myself, but the other score is settled. He served his time.'

The road boss shook his head. 'That was your affair the first time. This time it's on me. Gregorio's been a troublemaker from the start. Don't want him in my crew.' He turned to Gregorio. 'You're finished.'

It was just past midnight when the two rangers returned to Burnt Hill station. While Ferrell put away the horses, Bill strolled over towards the station, now dark and silent. It was a moonless night, black as only the night can be in the middle of the forest. Snapping on the porch light, he stood a moment looking about him, waiting for his companion to appear, then casually opened the door, and strode inside.

With the door latch still in his hand, he paused, aware of that indescribable something that warns all is not well. Then, before he could press the light switch, an unseen hand jerked his forty-five from its holster, and he felt the gun quickly jabbed into his back. It flashed into his mind that someone, probably a thief, had slipped into the station in the few minutes intervening between the time the relief ranger had left and their return. But the speculation was cut short by the blast of the gun, and Bill spun around and crashed to the floor. For a reeling moment the person stood over him, repeatedly pulling the trigger, but the gun had jammed. Then the weapon was hurled into Bill's face, and racing footsteps pounded out of the room.

Ranger Ferrell was crossing the rear yard towards the house when the shot rang out in the night, and he took off like a rocket, gun in hand. As he rounded a corner of the station a man was dashing across the lighted porch and fast disappearing into the darkness.

'Halt!' he yelled, and sent a bullet whining over the man's head.

When the man dashed on, Ranger Ferrell lowered his sights, and the gun barked. The figure spun around as two more reports blasted the night. The fleeing man pitched heavily to the ground, a bullet in his groin, another below the heart. Whirling round, Ferrell ran into the station.

'Bill,' he called, snapping on the lights. 'Are you all right?'

Bill had pulled himself up and was sitting in the middle of the floor, his shirt open, exploring with his fingers.

'Got a hole here in front,' he said. 'Don't understand it, either. He had the gun in my back.'

Dropping to his knees Ferrell ripped the shirt up the back. A soft-nosed bullet had smashed into Bill's right hip, passed through the body, barely breaking the skin as it lodged in front just behind his belt buckle. Seizing the first-aid kit Ferrell got some compresses and applied them front and back, encircling them with lengths of gauze bandages, and rushed him off to the hospital.

Six months later Bill was back on the job, good as new, and Ranger Ferrell was cleared by the district attorney—justifiable homicide. Oh yes, the third party proved to be the firebug Gregorio, who couldn't distinguish between the two rangers on a dark night.

Fourteen

THE strange and unexpected, as well as the dramatic and sometimes hilarious, events that come to life in the twenty-eight national parks and eighty-two national monuments of our country are often things that simply could never happen anywhere else. Of all the sight-seeing areas, Yosemite National Park in central California, with its close to one million annual visitors, surely must rank near the top of the list in this respect.

Here you have 1,189 square miles of gorgeous scenery, some of it so primitive and secluded it has seldom been seen by anyone but the rangers and a few hardy hikers. There are nine beautiful waterfalls, with Yosemite Falls plunging down nine times farther than Niagara; solid rock formations, such as Half Dome, which rises 8,850 feet high, and El Capitan, a wedge of glistening perpendicular granite reaching to 7,200 feet; the giant Wawona Tree, with the roadway tunnelled through the centre of it, and other forest giants with a circumference of 90 feet, many of them over 300 feet high. When you have all this, plus visitors who have travelled from every country in the world to marvel at its rich beauty, situations that are at times a bit unusual, if not downright startling, are bound to develop.

One of these incidents, or rather its aftermath, took place before my bewildered eyes during a trip I made to Yosemite Valley as a park visitor before my marriage. I was spending a vacation with my sister, whose husband was then stationed at the park, and she and I were returning one day from a hike up to the dizzy heights of Glacier Point. As we were passing the ranger's club house, Norma suddenly came to a halt, then slowly edged over to one side of the road, motioning me to follow. When I joined her I saw she was watching two young rangers cavorting like a pair of yearling colts out behind the quarters. The only thing unusual about this was that they were taking turns blasting each other with a powerful stream from a water hose, and what made this so intriguing was that they were both fully clothed in their costly dress uniforms.

I asked, 'Why in the world are they doing that?'

'Let's find out,' Norma said with a chuckle, and led the way around to the back yard.

We could hear them shouting and laughing as we skipped across the lawn, but when they caught sight of us approaching, their horseplay came to an end and a look of anxious concern replaced their smiles. One of them took several steps backward before the taller one hesitantly greeted us.

'Better stay where you are,' he added quickly.

'Why, Carl,' Norma said, laughing outright. 'Tell me, what happened?'

'Don't ask me,' he said, 'or I might be tempted to tell you.'

'You're ruining your uniforms,' she gasped. 'Don't you think . . .'

But I wasn't hearing what they said; I had suddenly lost all interest in what might have happened to them. My glance chanced to meet the level gaze of the other ranger, and my knees so completely turned to rubber that I was having a wild battle staying on my feet. And when he grinned at me I grasped my sister's arm for support.

'Please,' I whispered. 'Norma, please introduce me to that handsome ranger!'

She peered closely at me for a moment, probably recognizing the symptoms, then took me by the hand and started leading me across the yard towards him.

'No!' The young ranger threw up his hands, and a look bordering on panic flashed across his face. 'Don't come any nearer, please. Stop! Stay away from me!'

For a moment he nervously stood his ground, then, as we drew nearer, suddenly wheeled around and bolted away into the woods like a scared rabbit.

It was several months later before I learned what had caused my dazzling young ranger to stampede. In fact, I didn't get the entire story until after I had married him. Then Bill told me what had happened.

He and Carl Danner had been on their way back to headquarters from a patrol when Carl suddenly pulled off the road and stopped. 'Look there, Bill,' he called, pointing up into a big fir tree. 'Isn't that Smoky up there?'

Bill squinted into the sun. 'Sure enough. And he looks scared.'

Springing from the car, they ran over to the tree, where a strange dog that had somehow wandered into the park was barking excitedly and making every effort to hurl himself up into the lower branches. Perched precariously near the top of the tall tree was Smoky, a full-grown bear that Bill, while stationed in an outlying district, had raised from a tiny cub. Smoky was a tame bear—that is, as tame as bears ever get; but now he was so frightened by the charging dog that he was thoroughly dangerous. Dogs are not permitted inside the park, so to Smoky this dog was a strange and terrifying experience. They could see he was completely unnerved and was trying to climb even higher into the smaller top branches.

'Wonder if he can get down,' Bill said. 'He's too fat to be up there. Might kill himself if he fell.'

'Why don't you go get him?' Carl grinned. 'He's your baby—I dare you.'

'Call off the dog,' Bill said quickly. 'I'll go up and get him down.'

Shinnying up the rough tree trunk took a bit of doing, but

once he reached the lower limbs Bill easily hauled himself upward. It was a long climb, as California firs grow to unbelievable heights. Carl, after corralling the dog, sprawled comfortably in the cool shade beneath the tree where he could enjoy the action above and indulge in a bit of private kibitzing.

The plan Bill had in mind was to climb above Smoky and then descend on him, forcing the bear down. But just before Bill reached him, there was a splintering crash as the limb Smoky occupied gave way, and a second later he came plunging straight down. A big limb just over Bill's head broke Smoky's fall, and he managed to hold on. Bill, directly beneath him, found himself in the wrong place at the right time, as something had to give when the big bear made so sudden a stop.

For a moment Bill was almost blinded, and he nearly lost his balance as he gasped for breath and frantically swabbed at his drenched face with both coat sleeves. When he had cleared his eyes and taken quick bearings, there began a descent which, Carl swears to this day, has never been approached for wild abandon and sheer speed.

Carl, beneath the tree, had also presented a perfect target for the bear, but had escaped the worst.

'That was the reason,' Bill later told me, 'that Carl and I were showering each other with the water-hose.'

'But why did you run when I wanted to meet you?' I asked.

'I still wasn't in any condition to meet any good-looking girl,' he grinned. 'Especially you!'

On the next occasion Bill and I had to meet each other, we once again almost missed being introduced. It was at a dance in the ranger club during May of 1930, where I'd gone with my sister, Norma, and her husband, Russel, who was then chief clerk at Yosemite. It was a gala night of soft lights and muted music, with handsome uniformed rangers everywhere. Of course Russel knew the rangers by name and presented them to me in an almost continuous procession, as soon as he could pry them free from their dancing partners. I was having a marvellous time dancing with a young temporary ranger engaged by the park for the summer season. When Bill entered with a party of guests, Russel made his way over to him.

'Want you to meet Margaret,' he said. 'Only take a minute.'

'Margaret who?'

'Margaret Becker. My wife's kid sister.'

Bill shook his head. 'Haven't got time, Russ.'

'Take only a second.'

'No. I'm tied up with these Australian guests. The super-intendent asked me to look after them. Some other time.'

Russel was standing at the edge of the dance floor, a few minutes later, when Bill passed by with his entourage. They were about to disappear into the crowd when Bill halted, stared a moment, and turned back to Russel.

'You know that girl over there?' He motioned towards one corner of the room.

Russel looked and nodded.

'Introduce me, will you?'

'Thought you didn't have time to——'

'I haven't time to meet the kid sister, Margaret what's-her-name. But this is different.'

'Different?'

'Good gosh, yes! That girl over there is the one I've been waiting for. I'm going to marry her!'

The young ranger and I were moving out on to the floor for the next dance when I felt Russel's hand on my arm. I turned around and found myself face to face with one of the handsome rangers Norma and I had discovered a few weeks before blasting each other with a water-hose. This was the one I had wanted to meet, the one who took off into the woods before we could get within shouting distance. He didn't seem at all shy now, as he stood smiling down at me.

'This is Ranger Merrill,' Russel was saying. 'He wants to meet you. Bill, I'd like you to know Margaret What's-Her-Name Becker, the kid sister.'

Russel insists it happened exactly that way. I don't remember. All I knew right then was that it was happening to me all over again, as it had the first time I saw him—my knees were turning to rubber, and I was sure I was slowly sinking to the floor. The Australians were taken in tow by another ranger, and Bill and I danced the entire evening, not knowing (or caring) whether the tempo was fast or slow, a waltz or a fox-trot. When the dance was over, we drifted with the rest outside to where Bill had parked his car. I had so completely forgotten the temporary ranger who had been my partner in the early part of the evening that I was startled when he suddenly loomed up in front of us.

'I'm taking Miss Becker home,' he said.

'Oh!' I gasped.

'If you're ready, Miss Becker?'

'Just a minute,' Bill said. 'Miss Becker is my girl. We didn't know we were going to meet here tonight. You understand?'

The summer ranger didn't understand, and said so.

'This girl,' Bill said evenly, 'is the one I am going to marry. Understand now?'

He did.

I didn't.

The next night Bill made it perfectly clear. We were with a group at Indian Caves, singing around a campfire when he leaned close and whispered: 'I wasn't fooling last night. I'm going to marry you.'

'Good heavens!' I exclaimed. 'You scarcely know me.'

'Known you all my life. We just didn't meet,' he said earnestly. 'I've always known the tone of your voice, the way you would smile, the sparkle in your eye. You're not someone I've known just a few short hours; I've been in love with you for years. It's just that you took so long getting here.'

I was too confused for a moment to make a reply.

'I've never been in love,' I finally told him. 'I want to be certain it's you—not the forest. You see, I've always dreamed of living in the forest, the mountains, ever since I was a little girl in pigtails. Now you're offering to make that dream come true. Don't you see? I've got to know.'

'Of course I see. Always knew you'd like it here, always have known that. We'll get married right away and live up at Tuolumne Meadows and——'

Someone was calling Bill's name outside the entrance to the cave. The colonel wanted him to drive with him to San Francisco. They would be leaving at five in the morning.

'That means we'll have to wait a few days,' Bill explained. 'But I'll be back just——'

'I won't be here,' I said. 'I'm leaving for home tomorrow.'

'But we're getting married and going to live here!'

'I've got to have time to think about that. When I'm sure, I'll let you know.'

'But you can't go now!'

'My arrangements were made a week ago,' I said. 'I'll have to go. Tomorrow night I'm stopping over with a girl friend in Berkeley. Dee is expecting to meet me at the train.'

Bill was full of questions—who was Dee, when would I arrive home, how soon would I start back to Yosemite? I felt I didn't want to leave him, to go back to the city, but I had full intentions of being married but once. I had to be sure.

When I left the train next day at Berkeley, the first person I saw was Bill. He had delivered his colonel in San Francisco and driven back to Berkeley, where he located my girl friend. They were waiting there as I stepped to the platform.

So we were to have one more evening together; no one could say Bill did things by halves. But the evening was too crowded to be entirely satisfactory. He had to be back in the bay city at an hour unheard of on a balmy moonlit night, so we drove Dee home and settled ourselves on her porch swing, where we could be alone—except for Grandma. Dee's grandmother was a sort of female Puck, though dried and shrivelled by her eighty-odd years. She could have been Methuselah's older sister but for her flashing eyes, which never strayed from us for a second.

Making herself comfortable in a chair round the corner of the porch, she rattled her newspaper and rocked furiously, but it was a secret little game she was playing all alone, as I realized when I first noticed her impish eye regarding us through the leaves of a potted geranium at her side. Bill was still trying to dissuade me from continuing my trip back to the city, and when I finally said I thought it best that I go and that I would try getting a position next summer in the park so we really could learn to know each other, Grandma shot up out of her rocker, unveiling her anxious face above the geranium, and shook her head vigorously. When the night air became too much for her, she reluctantly made her way inside the house, but not out of hearing distance. From just beyond the open window I could hear her grunted protests at my obstinacy.

It must have been quite a blow to her when we went for a drive, but the hour when Bill would have to leave for San Francisco was drawing near, and he insisted on presenting his argument in private. But it seemed there was no place where we could be alone. Berkeley is a college town, the home of the University of California, and every street we explored was bumper to bumper with student cars of every description. With time fast running out and still no parking space available, I said, as much to divert his mind to other channels as anything else, that I thought it only fair to mention the fact that he hadn't, in so many words, actually proposed to me.

That was a mistake! Bill immediately halted the car, right where we were, and with boisterous cheering erupting from front-yard audiences and pointed exhortations called from students leaning from open windows, I promised—in the middle of Elm Street—to be his bride.

When I entered the house Grandma was waiting up for me.

'Are ye agoin' to marry the ranger lad?'

I nodded.

'Don't be awaitin' too long,' she said softly, then smiled indulgently. 'My goodness! I haven't had so much fun since Old Bess run away with the bobsled!'

Life in the city, I soon learned, had somehow lost its attraction for me. The dusty streets and incessant roar of traffic offered a dim contrast to towering mountains and the cool solitude of the green forest. Bill wrote daily, letters smudged with ashes still bearing the tangy odour of campfires, enclosed in envelopes often crowded with crude hand-drawings and the scrawled names of the rangers through whose hands they had passed.

My staunch resolution to wait finally weakened, and I returned to the place where I belong. Bill and I were married at the little white courthouse in Mariposa and have lived in the woods to this day—and will love it always.

Where I as a young bride once searched out experienced ranger wives to give me the advice I so sorely needed, I now find youngsters coming to me with the same questions. I am aware of a deep sense of humility, and a wee bit of pride, when memory travels back over the years we have spent with Nature. It has been a good life, a full one.

Through the past twenty-five years every desire I've known has been fulfilled. Unlike Mahomet, who repaired to the hills when they refused his bidding, I have had the mountains come to me. Not that I in any manner was as wise as the sagacious old sage, but because the mountains, the forest, all that has made my life complete, came as an added bonus accompanying the man I married—my ranger.